THE CHRISTIAN REALISTS

Reassessing the Contributions of Niebuhr and his Contemporaries

Edited by
Eric Patterson

Foreword by Jean Bethke Elshtain

University Press of America,® Inc.
Lanham · Boulder · New York · Toronto · Oxford

Copyright © 2003 by
University Press of America,® Inc.
4501 Forbes Boulevard
Suite 200
Lanham, Maryland 20706
UPA Acquisitions Department (301) 459-3366

PO Box 317
Oxford
OX2 9RU, UK

All rights reserved
Printed in the United States of America
British Library Cataloging in Publication Information Available

ISBN 0-7618-2620-3 (paperback : alk. ppr.)

∞™ The paper used in this publication meets the minimum
requirements of American National Standard for Information
Sciences—Permanence of Paper for Printed Library Materials,
ANSI Z39.48—1984

Contents

Foreword by Jean Bethke Elshtain — v

Preface — ix

Chapter 1 **Niebuhr and His Contemporaries: Introduction to Christian Realism** 1
Eric Patterson

Chapter 2 **Niebuhr and His Critics: Realistic Optimism in World Politics** 25
Eric Patterson

Chapter 3 **The Prophetic Realism of John Foster Dulles, 1937-1945** 53
Mark G. Toulouse

Chapter 4 **Herbert Butterfield and the Limits of Christian Realism** 81
Malcolm R. Thorp

Chapter 5 **Martin Wight: Politics in the Era of Leviathan** 103
Daniel Young

Chapter 6	**John Coleman Bennett in Contemporary Context** David McCreary	137
Chapter 7	**Cups Half Full: John Courtney Murray's Skirmishes with Christian Realism** Leon Hooper, S.J.	159
Chapter 8	**Christian Realism in a Pluralistic Society: Interactions between Niebuhr and Morgenthau, Kennan, and Schlesinger** Roger L. Shinn	177
Chapter 9	**The Ironies of Christian Realism: The End of an Augustinian Tradition in International Politics** Roger Epp	199
Select Bibliography		233
About the Contributors		237

Foreword

Jean Bethke Elshtain

If ever there was a time for that complex mode of thought called Christian realism, that time is now. In my recent book, *Just War Against Terror: The Burden of American Power in a Violent World*, I lament the loss of the Niebuhrian tradition, with its unblinkered approach to politics and power (The reference point is, of course, to Reinhold Niebuhr, although his theologian brother, H. Richard Niebuhr, is also an essential figure in American religion.). Our capacity to read correctly the signs of the times seems to be collapsing all around us, beginning with a widespread inability to make essential distinctions. From the pulpit as well as the podium comes a great deal of loose talk that cannot distinguish a soldier from a terrorist, justice from revenge, or a legitimate war from random violence. Many of the arguments Niebuhr confronted, and rejected, as he parted company with the Fellowship of Reconciliation and other pacifist-oriented groups, we confront once again. One characteristic of this pseudo-pacifism—by that I mean the view that the United States can never use its power in justifiable ways, so this country can never fight a just war—is the inability of those who embrace it to look the facts in the face.

Niebuhr, were he living, would find much that is being argued in the public arena drearily familiar. Just as the claim was that we could negotiate with Adolph Hitler, so we hear that we must try to understand and attempt to ameliorate the anger of radical Islamist fundamentalists, a group that must be distinguished from the vast majority of ordinary followers of Islam. One wants to say: "What about the following don't you understand: 'every Muslim who believes in Allah and wishes to be rewarded [should] comply with Allah's order to kill the Americans and plunder their money wherever and whenever they find it...?'" The words are, of course, from one of Osama bin Laden's *fatwas* against the American "infidels" and their allies, that "freak entity" Israel. If one ponders what there is to negotiate about if someone seeks your total destruction, the response is likely going to be the suggestion that, somehow, Osama bin Laden really cannot mean it. Deep down, he must be a reasonable man.

One appreciates ever more Niebuhr's frustration with these sorts of arguments when he confronted them in the 1930s. What he, and other Christian realists treated in this volume taught us, is that there is no substitute for getting as full and accurate a picture of what is really going on as is humanly possible. This is not fact-fetishism. It is, instead, a deep appreciation of the fact that our descriptions of the world and our moral evaluations of that same world are embedded with one another. The complex phenomenon we know as Christian realism involves a cluster of interrelated parts, including an epistemology, a way of knowing the world; a moral philosophy; an ontology; a theology. What this realism does not offer is a comprehensive political ideology of the sort Marxism and other ultimately destructive ideologies offered. It is, instead, a rich, nuanced way of looking at the world that offers few 'knock-down' arguments about what a policy should be. There are often several possible approaches or policies compatible with the Christian realist's assessment of a situation.

Should we tighten up sanctions, increase the number of flights over a no-flight zone, beef up our forces in the region as a back up to other measures? Or should we make one final attempt and then commit to coercive disarmament—war—in order to remove a dangerous threat? Are there possibilities we have not considered? What might these be? What would not be possible would be to assume no serious threat exists when it does; no danger is present when it is; no crimes and violations are taking place when they are. What Christian realism will not permit is the substitution of illusion and wishful thinking for a rigorous assessment of the play of forces. Christian realism reminds us that no human activity can ever be thoroughly sanitized of power and interest. If, as St. Augustine argued, politics is the attempt to "reconcile competing human wills," then it is, by definition, an activity that will always be fractious and one in which, this side of the eschaton, it is dangerous folly to assume that all human wills can be brought into permanent harmony.

Christian realism is frequently taxed with being a gloomy assessment of reality. This charge of pessimism is false. Niebuhr and his colleagues within the tradition of Christian realism, indebted as they are to the great Augustine, embrace the theological virtue of *hope*. Hope is not the same thing as optimism. Often enough, when Christian realists are criticized, the contrast to their alleged 'pessimism' is a wholly unwarranted optimism. Optimism is the conviction that everything will turn out all right. Optimism insists on looking only at the 'best case' scenario in each and every situation. Unsurprisingly, many optimists eventually wind up cynics because the world never works out the way optimists believe it *should*. Hope, by contrast, is lodged in a theological anthropology that sees human beings as created in the *imago dei*. Each person is, therefore, a pearl of great price. Each is capable of loving neighbor and serving community. Each, alas, is also fallen, hence enters the world with a heritage of "original sins" that means our lives can never attain a standard of perfection. But we can, nonetheless, follow Augustine's two cardinal rules, or try to: to do no harm and to help whenever we can.

Harm often comes when good persons fail to act. The ethnic cleansings and genocides of the recent past tell us that—if it had not occurred to us before. The German anti-Nazi theologian, Dietrich Bonhoeffer, in the dark days of World War II, joined a conspiracy to assassinate Hitler. For his complicity in this conspiracy, he was hanged by the Gestapo in the waning days of the war. During his time in a Gestapo prison, Bonhoeffer wrote many letters and essays. In one of them he criticized those who retreat into purity in times of great danger; who put their own virtuousness ahead of the "contamination that arises from responsible action." Christian realists understand the dilemma of dirty hands. So did Bonhoeffer. That is why he—and they—insist that the question always to be put before us turns on our concrete responsibility to, and for, the world. We are bidden to ask *not* "How can I do the morally pure thing?" but, instead, in Bonhoeffer's words, "What is to come?" Taking a good, hard look, what is to come? All of the thinkers taken up in this wonderfully written and edited volume help us to better respond to that daunting question.

Preface

One thing that should not surprise scholars of history, politics, or philosophy is that most "new ideas" have probably been thoroughly considered, argued, and perhaps discarded at some time in the past: "there is nothing new under the sun." Thus, we should not be surprised that contemporary Christian activism, associated with both the political Right and the political Left, is rooted in the thoughts and deeds of earlier generations. The Christian realists are part of this heritage. Debates about just war, international law, reconciliation, human rights, political order, justice, and the like which have been center stage in the American religious scene as of late were all considered with great eloquence and depth of insight in the mid-twentieth century by Reinhold Niebuhr and his contemporaries. This book does not suggest that these individuals had the final say on any subject, but rather that we err in forgetting that great minds dealt with problems that are relevant today.

In my own study of Niebuhr, I was fascinated by allusions to his colleagues and collaborators: the Christian realists. Unfortunately, there is very little biographical writing on most of these figures. Indeed, the dearth of scholarship on the Christian realist thought of important figures such as John C. Bennett, John Foster Dulles, Martin Wight, and Herbert Butterfield is astounding. This volume seeks to remedy the situation by providing the reader with a side-by-side comparison of Niebuhr and his contemporaries. The individuals whom you will meet in the pages that follow are high Church and low church, American and British, Protestant and Catholic, and from various points of the political spectrum. These individuals shared a concern for approaching policy from an ethical and pragmatic perspective rooted in the Western Christian tradition. Preparing this volume has helped me understand the nuances of agreement and disagreement among the Christian realists and their critics—I hope the book provides a similar service to future readers.

This project would not be possible without the contributions of others. First, I am honored to collaborate with the scholars who co-authored this work. Second, I thank Bruce Bimber and Daniel Philpott for encouraging me to pursue this endeavor and for serving as intellectual role models at a formative time in my career. I appreciate University of America Press for publishing works on religion and public life; although religion influences political phenomena worldwide, the topic seems to be out of vogue in the American academy. Finally, I am especially grateful to my wife, Mary, for her encouragement and support. My work on this volume is dedicated to my maternal grandmother, Agnes Marcelle Smithson. She is a person of faith who models Christian service, excellence, and thoughtfulness.

Eric Patterson
Costa Mesa, California

Chapter 1

Niebuhr and His Contemporaries: Introduction to Christian Realism

Eric Patterson

It is often said that the enormity of issues that confront us in domestic and international affairs at the beginning of the new millennium is unique in history. This perspective argues that the end of the Cold War resulted in a totally new international system dominated by a single superpower and threatened by dangers inconceivable in the past: environmental degradation, ethnic nationalism, religious fundamentalism, states imploding due to civil war, and the proliferation of nuclear, biological, and chemical weapons. However, this view forgets that just a half-century ago many feared for the very survival of Western civilization. Consider the perils of the mid-twentieth century: the economic catastrophe of the 1930s and the subsequent rise of militant nationalism and fascism, the Holocaust and similar atrocities in the Japanese empire and the Soviet Union, the advent of atomic and nuclear weapons, and the Cold War rivalry between East and West that daily threatened to escalate into a war that would have obliterated mankind.

To many thinkers at that time, it seemed that the prevailing Western ideology of liberal idealism lacked the pragmatism and the creativity for dealing with this complex of issues. Those who disavowed the idealism of the era called themselves "realists." This book focuses on a group of realists who were distinguished by their commitment to Christian, generally Protestant, faith and looks at their views on the political dilemmas of their day.

The purpose of this book is two-fold. First, the volume is an introduction to the idea of Christian realism—the idea that one can have a normative position based in the Christian tradition and yet be "realistic" in approaching social and political phenomena. In historical terms the Christian realist "school" was a collection of theologians, laymen, academics, and policy experts that were influential in Anglo-American political debates for about thirty years. From the mid-1930s until the 1960s Christian realists such as Reinhold Niebuhr, Herbert Butterfield, and John C. Bennett argued that Christianity provided a foundation for understanding the root causes of political problems.

The second purpose of this volume is to record some of the political debates that Christian realists engaged in and detail their policy prescriptions. This is important not only to demonstrate how Christian realists thought, but because many of the issues these individuals considered are perennial dilemmas that speak to us today: can the moral person fight in a war? Does democracy have a moral justification? How should society balance order and justice? The contemporary reader will find that the positions of the Christian realists on these and other social issues often seem fresh and relevant to today's uncertain world.

The vast majority of the existing literature on Christian realism focuses on the thought of a single individual: Reinhold Niebuhr. This is due in large part to his strident prose and compelling oratory manifested in a blizzard of written works and his superhuman calendar of speaking engagements over a twenty-year period. Thus, most volumes on Christian realism neglect the thinking of other major Christian realists. The approach of this volume is to acquaint the reader with various Christian realists and let those thinkers "have their say." In addition to a chapter on Niebuhr there are chapters on Christian realists such as John Foster Dulles, Martin Wight, and Herbert Butterfield. Furthermore, a discussion of secular "Niebuhrians" (Morgenthau, Kennan, Schlesinger) and a chapter on the Catholic thinker John Courtney Murray are included in order to compare how individuals from other traditions viewed politics "realistically" during this period.

The rest of this chapter is designed to introduce the reader to features of Christian realist thought as well as to twentieth century debates over liberalism, pacifism, democratic theory, and morality in international politics. The Christian realists were not a school in the sense of a defined ideology or statement of purpose; rather, Christian realism was a movement that viewed politics ethically and pragmatically. This chapter will demonstrate that although individual Christian realists did not agree on every issue, there are general similarities in their works. Mid-twentieth century Christian realists owed much of their political theology to Augustine's *The City of God* and reacted against the failed promises of interwar liberalism. More specifically, this introduction looks at how Christian realists critiqued two strands of liberalism in the 1930s and 1940s: the political idealism associated with Woodrow Wilson and religious idealism in the form of pacifism and the Social Gospel. The chapter concludes by discussing whether Christian realism was revolutionary or reactionary in Anglo-American political scholarship.

The Advent of Christian Realism

Many identify the advent of Christian realism with Reinhold Niebuhr's *Moral Man and Immoral Society* (1932). Niebuhr was a pastor, theologian, social activist, and writer. Over the following decade Niebuhr published several books as well as hundreds of scholarly and journalistic pieces while keeping a demanding speaking and lecturing schedule. One of his primary themes was the failure of liberalism to comprehend the political dilemmas of the day. In *Moral Man and Immoral Society* Niebuhr argued, "a sharp distinction must be drawn between the moral behavior of individuals and of social groups, national, racial, and economic."[1] Although individuals may be guided by ethical guidelines, the behavior of groups rarely was. Instead, groups usually behaved in terms of self-interest, although they cloaked such egoism in moralistic slogans. Moreover, because liberals fail to recognize that collectives act out of interest they fail to see that social relations often rely on force and coercion for change: "society is a perpetual state of war."[2]

The book was a powerful critique of the prevailing liberalism in government, academe, and religion in his day. Niebuhr agreed with liberals that justice was the quintessential goal of domestic and international life but argued that existing attempts to foster the objective were shortsighted. More specifically, Niebuhr criticized the two predominant liberalisms of his day: Enlightenment rationalism and liberal Protestantism. Niebuhr argued that although reason and religion could point out injustices as well as suggest solutions to social dilemmas, nonetheless neither had fulfilled its promise to initiate change. The theories of rationalists like John Dewey and the pronouncements of churches did little to alter the socio-economic status quo. Rather, the lesson of history was that knowledge and religion promised to liberate the oppressed but instead became tools used by the powerful to justify and maintain their privileged status. Consequently, individuals and groups must look at reforming inequalities of power in order to achieve social justice: "the disproportion of power in society is the real root of social injustice."[3]

Two years later, in *Reflections on the End of an Era* (1934), Niebuhr excoriated the failings of the American capitalist system, but rejected liberal social schemes as "fatuous." Again Niebuhr was arguing that justice was impossible without changing the disparities of power in society. In *An Interpretation of Christian Ethics* (1935) Niebuhr articulated the tension between ethical absolutes and practical attempts at justice in society. Niebuhr argued that we must work toward the ideal "law of love" embodied in the Golden Rule while recognizing that our efforts and motives are under the judgment of the ideal. In short, Niebuhr articulated a call to practical social and political action based on ethical imperatives while realizing that such programs required the mundane details of administration and compromise.

Niebuhr continued to be the primary spokesman for Christian realism, venturing more and more into domestic and international politics. In *The Children of Light and the Children of Darkness* (1944) he attempted to "vindicate" democracy based on realism: "democracy has a more compelling justification and requires a more realistic vindication than is given it by the liberal culture with which it has been associated in modern history." Niebuhr castigated the liberal optimistic view of democracy as the zenith of political and social relations. He countered that democracy is necessary because of human evil: "man's capacity for justice makes democracy possible; man's inclination to injustice makes democracy necessary."[4] By separating powers, checks and balances, and pluralism democracy places a check on the ambitions of individuals and groups.

During the 1940s and the years to come Niebuhr was to write about the war in Europe, the barbarism of Nazism, the need for international organizations such as the United Nations, the Communist threat, containment, nuclear deterrence, civil rights, the Korean conflict, the Vietnam War, and the policies of various presidential administrations. Until the end of his life his thinking was marked by the tensions between power politics and normative concerns. However, although Niebuhr was unique in his voluminous literary output, he was not alone in trumpeting a Christian realist position. His colleague at Union

Theological Seminary, John C. Bennett, published books such as *Christian Realism* (1952) and *Christians and the State* (1958), as well as numerous articles in the 1940s and 1950s that advocated a Christian and ethical stance toward domestic and international dilemmas. Bennett and Niebuhr influenced an entire generation of seminarians at Union and throughout the United States by their Christian realism and its application to politics. Among the best known other American Christian realists were Hans Morgenthau's protégé and long-time University of Virginia professor Kenneth W. Thompson, Ernest Lefever of the American University's School of International Service, and John Hallowell at Duke University.

On the others side of the Atlantic during the 1940s and 1950s, Herbert Butterfield and Martin Wight were the most obvious proponents of positions analogous to Niebuhr's.[5] Cambridge historian Butterfield was a consistent champion of an ethical approach to war and foreign policy but also felt that statesmen must take a "realistic" approach to power in international politics. Like Niebuhr, Butterfield was a prolific writer, including *Christianity and History* (1950), *Christianity, Diplomacy and War* (1953), and *International Conflict in the Twentieth Century: A Christian View* (1960), as well as many journal articles and opinion pieces. Butterfield was a member of the editorial board of *Christianity and Crisis* along with Niebuhr and Bennett, and chaired the Rockefeller Foundation-funded British Committee on International Theory. His close friend and Committee member, Martin Wight, taught international political theory at the London School of Economics and is best known for his posthumous *Power Politics* (1978) and *International Relations Theory: The Three Traditions* (1992).

The issues that Niebuhr and his associates considered in this period were so grave that many church leaders also felt compelled to move away from idealistic-liberal positions to more "realistic" and nuanced viewpoints. Perhaps most important was the 1937 Oxford Conference on Church, Community, and State with over four hundred delegates from Protestant denominations around the world including Niebuhr, Bennett, Paul Tillich, John Foster Dulles, and others. The Conference focused on a Christian response to the gathering war clouds in Europe, and according to many participants Niebuhr's emphasis on individual sin set the tone for the entire event.[6] At this and other conferences and commissions, such as the Federal Council of Church's Commission on a Just and Durable Peace (largely influenced by John Foster Dulles) and the 1948 (Amsterdam) and 1954 (Evanston) World Council of Churches conferences, Christian realists displaced the traditional liberalism of Anglo-American Protestantism with more realistic and "Augustinian" analyses.[7]

The views of Christian realists and prominent religious leaders were published in a variety of forums. Most famous was *Christianity and Crisis*, but Christian realists also were regularly featured in *The Christian Century, Worldview*, and various scholarly journals such as *International Affairs, Survival, American Political Science Review, World Politics*, and *Review of Politics*. Perhaps more importantly, at least in terms of molding public opinion, Christian realists published articles, letters, and editorials in the mainstream press, such as *The Times, The New York Times, The Spectator*, and *Nation*. Moreover, in academe the Christian realists, particularly Niebuhr, were to influence a whole generation of academics and policy experts including E.H. Carr, Michael Howard, Hedley Bull, Charles Marshall, Arthur Schlesinger, Jr., George Kennan, John Herz, Raymond Aron, and others.

What is Christian Realism?

What is Christian realism? According to Roger L. Shinn, "both words in that phrase are important." Shinn writes,

> The ethic was Christian in its serious appropriation of Biblical motifs and classical doctrines: the uniqueness of Biblical revelation, the sinfulness of man and society, the judging and redeeming activity of God, the faith in justification by a divine grace that produces works worthy of repentance, the distinctive quality of Christian love. It was realistic in its criticism of naive idealism or utopianism and its confrontation with the brute facts and power struggles of the contemporary world. This Christian realism, at least at its best, was not an artificial combination of two unrelated motifs. It was realistic in its appropriation of Christian faith, and it was Christian—often recovering orthodox traditions neglected in the modern church—in its realism. It was alert both to the Word of God and to the latest news from European and Asiatic battlefronts, and it constantly sought the relation between the good news of the gospel and the daily news of the world."[8]

In short, Christian realism was a perspective committed to understanding and involvement in politics based on a realistic standpoint. What made the Christian realists feel that their perspective on human nature and political phenomena was "realistic" was not pragmatism but faith in the Biblical doctrines of sin and the Fall.

The Augustinian Theology of Christian Realism

Roger Epp has called the rise of mid-twentieth century Christian realism the "Augustinian Moment" in international politics.[9] By "Augustinian" Epp is specifically referring to the doctrinal foundation of Christian realism that emanates from Augustine's political treatise *The City of God*. Certainly, many Christian realists expressed their intellectual debt to Augustine. For instance, Niebuhr wrote, "[Augustine]...proves himself a more reliable guide than any known thinker. A generation which finds its communities imperiled and in decay ... might well take counsel of Augustine in solving its perplexities."[10] Likewise Butterfield, reflecting on the deepening of the Cold War and the atomic age, stated, "we in this part of the world find ourselves...in the midst of the very kind of catastrophic history that Augustine viewed when writing his seminal *The City of God* in the fifth century."[11] Even secular Niebuhrians agreed that Augustine was valuable. As Arthur Schlesinger, Jr. quipped, "Whatever you say about Augustine, at least he would not have been much surprised by the outcome of the Russian Revolution."[12]

Epp argues that Niebuhr and other Christian realists "reclaimed" Augustine's understanding of political life in four ways. First, the Christian realists parallel Augustine's view of human nature. Augustine saw humankind as God's penultimate creation—made in God's very image with tremendous creative potential but marred by Adam's sin. Because Christian realists tended to emphasize sin and evil in stark contrast to the religious and secular liberals of their day, they were often stereotyped as cynics or pessimists. Second, like Augustine Christian realists saw history as meaningful, linear, and moving toward an ultimate fulfillment. As Herbert Butterfield wrote, "the ultimate faith is the belief that all things will have a final reconciliation—a final share in the redemptive purpose of Christ."[13] A third Augustinian theme is the Christian realist emphasis on order in political life. Augustine's conception of "concord" and his application of it to Rome in the context of barbarian attacks on the empire provided the essential justification for law and government. Rome provided the benefits of commerce, education, and communication despite also being responsible for evil such as slavery and war. Augustine did not apologize for Rome's wrongs, but made it clear that they were lesser evils when the alternative was social disorder and political chaos. Finally, Christian realists appropriate from Augustine the notion of *caritas*, "the love of God and Neighbors as the proper motivation of the will transformed by grace."[14] This "law of love" is the ultimate standard for individual conduct.

Applying the City of God to the Earthly City

Christian realism begins by rejecting the modernist idea that Biblical revelation and judgment is inappropriate for contemporary society. Instead, the Christian realists realized in the New Testament a call for action in dealing with contemporary social and political situations. Most Christian realists were political liberals and sympathetic to the Social Gospel's call for social justice. Nevertheless, Christian realists tended to be critical of idealism that was unwilling to deal with the realities of political power and face the judgmental portions of Christ's message.

Christian realists emphasized the universality of sin: no individual and no collective is free from the guilt of pride and sin. Unlike idealists who could not differentiate between temporal political projects because they all fell short of the law of love, Christian realists argued that distinctions can be made between lesser and greater evils. This was the position of various Christian realists toward Nazi aggression in the 1940s. Germany was not evil incarnate nor was America perfect, but the tyranny of National Socialism was certainly more evil than the foibles of the Western powers and therefore demanded a forceful response.[15]

Thus, one finds in the writings of Christian realists frequent allusions to the tension between individual responsibility and the law of love. On the one hand, Christians are citizens of the world and therefore must use the tools of the world (e.g. politics, force) to act, to participate, and to fight against injustice. On the other hand, Christians must humbly recognize that every behavior falls short of the ideal of the law of love and is therefore censured by the ideal. The individual Christian should act while not neglecting repentance for his or her own pride and evil.

In general, Christian realism relied heavily on Augustine's distinction between the City of God and the City of Earth and was unsparing in its attacks on those, such as pacifists and Social Gospel liberals, who confused the realities of the temporal political order and its justice with the eternal city and its ideals. The City of God was founded on the law of love and was an ideal that cannot be realized in this world. In contrast, we live in the earthly city and must work within its limitations to achieve "approximate" conditions of order and justice. In sum,

Christian realists enjoined everyone to keep in mind the ideals of Christ's eternal kingdom but to work within the constraints of the present imperfect world.

Christian realists recognized the tension in collective life between the need for order and the law of love. Augustine discussed the tension between the demands of the law of love and the behavior of representatives of the state, who, acting on the state's behalf, might violate the law of love. For example, the solider serving in Rome's legions would have to kill at times to protect political order. Augustine condoned such behavior on behalf of the state, arguing that there could be no ultimate resolution of the tension between social order and ultimate moral ideals in the earthly city and that the state and its representatives were obligated to act to preserver the political order. Niebuhr agreed: "order precedes justice in the strategy of government."[16]

The Christian realists had another concern about morality and social life: although individual behavior may be guided at times by ethical concerns, this is generally not the case for collectives. Indeed, groups generally behave based on self-interest and Niebuhr argued that groups amplify the self-interest of their members. Consequently, one finds in the writings of Niebuhr and Bennett criticisms of the moralistic rhetoric of foreign policies that claims ethical purposes but actually obfuscates self-interested motives.[17] Moreover, Christian realists such as Butterfield were especially chary of marrying religion or ideology to nationalism, both because it made political concessions impossible and because it bordered on idolatry.[18]

Finally, Christian realists were strident in their calls for political action to resist tyranny abroad and promote justice everywhere. Niebuhr and his contemporaries argued for the value of democracy, proposed an international body such as the United Nations, warned of complaisance toward the Nazis and later the Communists, advocated containment, argued over nuclear deterrence, and urged the United States to assume a global leadership role. Nevertheless, they did not find in ethical systems, religious tradition, or in the Scripture concrete policy proposals. Indeed, individuals such as Bennett and Butterfield routinely claimed that the insights of the social sciences were both useful and necessary to dealing with the problems of politics and economics.[19] In short, Christian realism had no delimited policy platform or any specific political formula. Instead, Christian realism called for individuals to work from an ethical worldview in a spirit of humility, recognizing that one's efforts might be wrong or in vain, but that one has a responsibility tot try.

In sum, Christian realism was a practical, flexible, and ethical response to the liberal idealism of the day. Christian realists tended to prioritize a language of "power" and "order" in their discussions of political phenomena. In a time of upheaval and uncertainty characterized by the rise of fascism and communism, the second World War, atomic weapons, and the Cold War, the prophetic voice of Christian realism was heeded not only by those in positions of power but also by many in the mass public. As Michael Howard wrote,

> The Christian eschatology, long disdained by liberal humanists even within the Church itself, once again became terrifyingly relevant to human affairs...And the teachers who best provided an adequate framework for understanding were the philosophers and the theologians Niebuhr, Bonhoeffer, Karl Barth, Tillich, who accepted uncomplainingly the remoteness, the inscrutability of God, who saw the focus of Christianity as the Passion rather than the Sermon on the Mount, men for whom the march of humanitarian, utilitarian liberalism, including its change of gear into Marxian socialism, had simply been a long excursion into the desert in search of a mirage.[20]

The Critique of Liberalism

The Christian realists savagely attacked the idealism of the 1920s and 1930s, disparaging it as utopian, sentimental, hyper-moralistic, and even mawkish. The idealism that they were rejecting combined optimism in human progress through reason and technological advancement with a political commitment to the restraint of force in favor of law, negotiation, and arbitration. Moreover, in America and to a lesser extent in Britain, these liberal values were part of a larger idealistic expectation in the church and society that mankind could overcome the dilemmas of its past and build a civilization based on social equality, understanding, and a harmony of interests across communities. The Christian realists attacked this vision as utopian because it failed to take into account the sinful nature of individuals and their communities. Because the Christian realists tended to critique idealism both in the church and in government, this section will look at three liberalisms critiqued by Christian realists: Wilsonian foreign policy, pacifism, and the Social Gospel.

Niebuhr recognized that there were multiple variants of liberalism, such as Joseph Schumpeter's free trade liberalism, Woodrow Wilson's vision of self-determination and transparent diplomacy, John Dewey's rationalism and focus on education, the Social Gospel, and the like. Niebuhr argued that various liberalisms shared a credo:

a. That injustice is caused by ignorance and will yield to education and greater intelligence.
b. That civilization is becoming gradually more moral and that it is a sin to challenge either the inevitability or the efficacy of gradualness.
c. That the character of individuals rather than social systems and arrangements is the guarantee of justice in society.
d. That appeals to love, justice, good-will, and brotherhood are bound to be efficacious in the end. If they have not been so to date we must have more appeals to love, justice, good-will, and brotherhood.
e. That goodness makes for happiness and that the increasing knowledge of this fact will overcome human selfishness and greed.
f. That wars are stupid and can therefore only be caused by people who are more stupid than those who recognize the stupidity of war.[21]

Niebuhr concluded that "liberalism is in short a kind of blindness...It is a blindness which does not see the perennial difference between human actions and aspirations, the perennial source of conflict between life and life...the torturous character of human history."[22]

Christian Realism and Political Idealism

In international politics liberalism, or political idealism, was most identified with Woodrow Wilson's legacy and the faith in international law (Washington Conference System, Kellogg-Briand Pact) and organizations (League of Nations, Geneva Disarmament Conference, World Court) to banish war from international life.[23] Perhaps the most notorious example of this faith in negotiation and accommodation was Neville Chamberlain's short-lived diplomatic "success" at Munich.

The gist of Wilsonian idealism is that conflict in international life is not caused by human sin manifesting itself through individuals and groups as competitiveness, egoism, or greed. Instead, idealists felt that war was caused by a poorly managed international system that allowed imperialist exploitation, exacerbated misunderstanding through secret diplomacy and poor information flows, aggravated competition through trade barriers and arms races, flouted international law, and was unresponsive to domestic public opinion.

When interwar liberals considered the causes of the Great War, they thus saw international anarchy as the root cause. First, economic rivalry, exemplified by tariffs at home and colonial competition abroad, led to intensifying economic and political competition, especially between Germany and the Western powers. Second, the competition and arms races associated with imperialism and nationalism, when combined with the patchwork of military alliances, pushed the European powers into a security dilemma that became increasingly hazardous. Moreover, Wilson looked at the effects of domestic political institutions on the likelihood of war: many of the Central Powers were not truly representative governments: had they been, Wilson charged, their citizens would never have agreed to go to war.

The failure of domestic and international mechanisms to check World War I led to a variety of liberal policy prescriptions. Wilson, modeling Kant, Locke, and Bentham, argued for collective security based on international law and organizations to manage the peace.[24] Wilson's famous "fourteen points" called for "open covenants...openly arrived at" (no secret diplomacy), freedom of the seas and free trade, massive disarmament, national sovereignty and "the freest opportunity to autonomous development" (self-determination), and "a general association of nations...affording mutual guarantees of political independence and territorial integrity" for all states.[25] In short, Wilsonian liberals put a great deal of trust in international law and treaties to commit states to peace and hoped that commerce and democratic institutions would make war unlikely.

Realists charged that this halcyon liberal international order was based on flawed assumptions about human nature and power politics. They argued that Wilson's liberalism proceeded from the illusion that human nature was essentially rational and good. Thus, liberals believed that "enlightened" mass publics and their elected officials would realize that it was morally wrong to go to war. Realists countered that not only were individuals egoistic, but that their collectives, motivated by nationalism, prejudice, and competition, operated primarily on the basis of self-interest. Furthermore, because realists did not agree with liberal optimism that enlightened self-interest would lead nations to eschew war, they were certain that the liberal international order of law and organizations was powerless to stand against the determined behavior of a predatory state. With the rise of fascism in the 1930s and Communism in the late 1940s, Christian realists argued that liberal idealism made the West unprepared to fight against tyranny.

Realism and Religious Idealism: Pacifism and the Social Gospel

Because many of the Christian realists were clergy (Niebuhr), theologians (Bennett, Alan Booth), or active lay people (Dulles, Butterfield, Wight) it should be noted that they faced specifically Christian forms of idealism in Anglo-American churches and ecumenical forums. Two such perspectives were pacifism and the Social Gospel. The former emphasized personal holiness and abstaining from violence, the latter called for social action in order to infuse society with the New Testament ideals of love and service. Niebuhr, and other Christian realists, recognized that both approaches were essentially idealistic. Consequently, Niebuhr's clarion for a Christian realism was a call away from the interwar "theology of idealism" to a "theology of responsibility" when confronting domestic and international crises.[26]

Pacifism as Christian Idealism. In the first three decades of the twentieth century there was a strong pacifist strain in American churches. Notwithstanding traditional American isolationism and neutrality, there were multiple religious sources for the pacifist impulse including the "end times" eschatology of the burgeoning holiness and Pentecostal movements (especially in the South and Midwest), the social perfectionism that undergirded social movements (abolition, temperance, women's rights), and political alliances between some mainline churches and church organizations with social actors such as organized labor. Most importantly, many leaders in traditional and sectarian congregations seriously considered the Scriptural admonitions to peace: "Do good to them that hate you;" "Resist not evil;" "Turn the other cheek;" "My kingdom is not of this world, if my kingdom were of this world, then my servants would fight;" "Avenge not yourselves."

It should be noted that a decade earlier pacifism was attractive to individuals like the Christian realists who took morality and politics seriously. Indeed, for much of the 1920s and 1930s some of these individuals were pacifists: Niebuhr was an avowed pacifist until the mid-1930s, Herbert Butterfield called himself "almost a pacifist," and Martin Wight apparently remained a conscientious objector throughout World War II. One of the things that led Niebuhr to disavow pacifism was the realization, influenced by Marxism, that the underprivileged might never see opportunities open for them if they only resorted to non-violent measures. In addition, Niebuhr was never satisfied with the distinction between "violent" and "non-violent" political action. Niebuhr noted that Gandhi's boycott of English cotton harmed the welfare of English children—although it was "non-violent" it was a harmful technique of coercion.[27]

In addition, the failures of the liberal international order to halt aggression mobilized the Christian realists to call for forceful responses to fascism. More specifically, when Italy invaded Ethiopia Niebuhr and others called for the enforcement of sanctions in support of the international order. Niebuhr later wrote, "a responsible relationship to the political order, therefore, makes an unqualified disavowal of violence impossible."[28] Niebuhr continued to argue that the West must be ready to respond, even with force, to the fascist threat, although up to 1940 he opposed President Roosevelt's rearmament policy.[29]

Realists such as Niebuhr tended to separate peace advocates into two camps. The first were "vocational" or "religious" pacifists (e.g. Quakers, Mennonites, Brethren) who absolutely rejected not only military service, but also any actions that supported the war effort, such as working in the civil service or for the Red Cross. Thus, religious pacifism was ascetic, perfectionistic, and absolute. Such pacifists were willing to live their principles, even if the consequences meant imprisonment or death at the hands of foreign invaders. Most Christian realists tended to respect the position of religious pacifists for its witness to the ideal "law of love."

It was the position of "political" pacifists that drew the ire of Christian realists. Unlike the vocational pacifists who modeled Christ's life of self-abnegation, political pacifists refused to make moral judgments about political categories. For example, many political pacifists argued that there was no such thing as "war guilt" and took the position that the lesson of the first world war was that the material and human costs of war made it the ultimate evil. Moreover, many prominent American Christians argued that going to war in Europe in 1939-1940 was immoral because both sides, the British Empire and the Third Reich, were equally evil. By the 1940s Niebuhr and his associates castigated this "neutrality" as conceited, irresponsible, and naive because liberal pacifists failed to realize that power struggles in human relations could not be overcome by renunciation.[30]

The Social Gospel as Christian Idealism. The Social Gospel was a set of ideas in the late nineteenth and twentieth century that blended Christ's Sermon on the Mount with modern optimism about progress, reason, and scientific advancement. Social Gospel leaders, such as Walter Rauschenbusch, advocated practicing Christ's example of caring for the poor and oppressed, and this then conflated with existing progressive movements such as temperance, civil rights, workplace reform, and women's rights. The Social Gospel was clearly an example of religious and political idealism because its leaders felt that social change could establish the Kingdom of God on earth.

A look at the policy positions and life history of many Christian realists might naturally lead one to conclude that many of these individuals were Social Gospel activists. Niebuhr, Bennett, and other Christian realists were involved in various charitable groups, political committees, and social action organizations on behalf of minorities, labor, the underprivileged, and the poor in foreign countries. Indeed, one of Niebuhr's biographers has called him "a true son of the Social Gospel movement."[31] So as practitioners of the "social gospel" as well as often political allies to Social Gospel advocates, why did Christian realists inveigh against the Social Gospel?

Certainly Niebuhr and other Christian realists were supportive of social programs and political activism to mitigate inequalities. However, Christian realists disagreed with some of the fundamental presuppositions of the Social Gospel as a philosophy. Niebuhr felt that the Social Gospel was too optimistic about individual perfectibility and failed to take into account the reality of individual evil. The Social Gospel was helpful in that it contributed the notion to religious discourse that social and institutional "evils" did exist, but the Social Gospel failed to recognize the cause of the evils: self-interest.

> Whenever modern idealists are confronted with the divisive and corrosive effects of man's self love, they look for some immediate cause of this perennial tendency, usually in some specific form of social organization. One school holds that men would be good if only political institutions would not corrupt them, another believes that they would be good if the prior evil of a faulty economic organization could be eliminated. Or another school thinks of this evil as no more than ignorance, and therefore waits for a more perfect educational process to redeem man from his partial and particular loyalties. But no school asks how it is that an essentially good man could have produced corrupting and tyrannical political organizations or exploiting economic organizations or fanatical and superstitious religious organizations.[32]

To Niebuhr the obvious prescription for dealing with social evils was not a hope that education and a warm meal would solve society's ills but rather countervailing force.

In sum, Niebuhr called Social Gospel liberals "blind" to the realities of social relations. Niebuhr argued that the liberal faith in human nature refused to recognize the negative aspects of the human soul—

instead of seeing human beings as sinful the Social Gospel viewed poverty and ignorance as evil. In doing so, this idealistic position overestimated its capability for substantive change while underestimating the potential for human pride and greed to undermine worthy social projects. Moreover, Niebuhr and his associates attacked the Social Gospel as an example of a larger utopian liberalism that had come to permeate American society—the belief in progress and the efficacy of good intentions—which refused to recognize individual sin as contributing to society's ills and lacked the willingness to tackle difficult policy initiatives to alter existing domestic and international structures of power.[33]

The Christian Realist "Revolution:" Reaction or Transformation?

Christian realism never coalesced into a distinct political platform: it had no policy blueprint, no ideological statement, and no allegiance to a political party; indeed, individual Christian realists voted for and supported diverse parties and candidates. Nor did Christian realism ever amalgamate into a codified philosophical worldview. As one author suggests, "Such an ethic [Christian realism]... could not be static...Christian realism might maintain a poise in motion; it could not settle down to a fixed position."[34] What unified the Christian realists of the 1940s-1950s was a shared outlook that viewed socio-political issues from a "Christian" (usually Protestant) and "realistic" (contra-idealistic) perspective. Accordingly, the flexibility of position possible within these loose boundaries on any given policy was quite large. Of course, with the rise of first the Nazi and later the Communist threats, it seemed at the time that the Christian realist "school" spoke with one voice on major matters of international policy. Indeed, there was a high level of cohesion among these individuals at the time, but this was not due so much to an allegiance to any political model but rather to the magnitude of the threat posed to Western civilization by Hitler and Stalin.

After the "simple" issues of World War II and the early Cold War were addressed, the diversity of domestic and international dilemmas (e.g. Cuba, decolonization, containment, civil rights) was mirrored by a diversity of policy recommendations flowing from the pens of individual Christian realists. As Roger Epp shows in the final chapter of this volume, two such divisive issues were nuclear deterrence and the war in Vietnam. Some, like Herbert Butterfield, felt that nuclear weapons were an abomination and advocated nuclear renunciation while others such as Niebuhr and Bennett argued for the utility of nuclear deterrence. Similarly, by the late 1960s many Christian realists were openly hostile to the war in Vietnam whereas others, notably Kenneth Thompson, were not.

Was Christian realism a revolution in mid-twentieth century political thought? If by revolution one means a transformation or the creation of a new paradigm in the sense of Copernicus or Marx, the answer is "no." The Christian realists left no manifesto and no school of rigidly trained disciples to perpetuate their program. Indeed, over the years the Christian realist tradition has been claimed by conservatives such as Michael Novak and Robert Bease, by some on the political Left such as Robert McAfee Brown, and even by advocates of Liberation Theology.[35]

However, a secondary view of "revolution" includes "rebellion," "renovation," and "reaction" among its definitions. In this sense, Christian realism was a revolution. The Christian realists reacted against the glib utopianism of the Social Gospel and Anglo-American foreign policies. The Christian realists were not "reactionaries" in a conservative sense, indeed, many of them flirted seriously with Marxism in the 1920s and 1930s and remained both classical and political liberals into the 1960s. Instead, they were the loyal opposition, rebelling within the religious and political establishments against the self-deluding truisms of Western political and religious idealism that had produced what E.H. Carr called the "twenty years crisis."[36] In this sense Christian realism is a way of looking at the world, not a structured philosophical paradigm. As Richard Fox writes, "Niebuhr's Christian realism was in one sense a more negative than positive perspective. It did not ordain specific positions on political issues. It demanded only that its adherents follow a middle path between the twin pitfalls of utopianism and resignation, sentimentality and cynicism."[37] The primary critique made by Christian realists like Niebuhr, Bennett, and Wight was that Western policies lacked both creativity and pragmatism in considering power politics. They felt that their faith had something to say both *to* power and *about* power. Their call was for an ethical and practical approach to domestic and international life, and although they often transformed the nature of specific policy debates, the legacy of Christian realism was not a revolutionary or revolutionized model for domestic or international politics.

Overview of the Work

At one time volumes were written about Reinhold Niebuhr by friends and foes alike. In his chapter on Niebuhr Eric Patterson observes the paucity of recent scholarship on Niebuhr and suggests that Niebuhr is no longer studied in political science due to his Christian/moral Realist credentials and because he is associated with political pessimism. The thesis of this essay challenges the latter assumption by studying Niebuhr's work in five areas: anthropology, community, justice, power, and history. Patterson shows that Niebuhr's alleged pessimism stems from the Christian doctrine of sin. This chapter demonstrates that Niebuhr's view of human nature was not predicated on human depravity, but on moral and creative freedom. Patterson calls Niebuhr a "realistic optimist" based on his pragmatic yet hopeful interest in issues of social and economic justice, international order, and political morality. In explicating Niebuhr's views, Patterson provides not only a comprehensive portrait of Christian realism but defends the relevance of studying the Christian realists today.

John Foster Dulles is a complex figure in American Cold War history and it is often forgotten that for a time his work and ethics paralleled that of Niebuhr and Bennett. Mark Toulouse's chapter on Dulles discusses Dulles' "Protestant prophetic realism" from 1937-1945. During this period Dulles was an important voice at ecumenical councils, most notably the 1937 Oxford conference and the 1940 Federal Council of Churches convention that resulted in the Dulles Commission's "Statement for a Just and Durable Peace." During this period, Dulles argued that there was a universal moral law applicable to international politics but Dulles also recognized that politicians are compelled to work for the national interest. He hoped that mass publics would pressure their leaders to behave ethically in pursuit of an "enlightened self-interest." Toulouse's chapter concludes with a discussion of how the Cold War, specifically the Communist threat, changed Dulles. By the 1950s Dulles' faith in a moral universe had evolved into a belief in the moral virtues of American democracy.

In Malcolm Thorp's chapter on Herbert Butterfield we find a discussion of one of Britain's leading Christian realists. Butterfield, a Cambridge historian as well as Methodist lay preacher, is clearly a Christian realist in his concern over human egotism, his advocacy of a "scientific" rather than a "moralistic" approach to international politics, and his emphasis on balance of power and political order. Nevertheless, Thorp shows Butterfield's concern for morality in international affairs. Although Butterfield, like many Christian realists, claimed to "almost be a pacifist," it was the barbarity of Japan and Nazi Germany that led Butterfield to support the Allied war effort. However, Butterfield parted ways with many realists when it came to the Cold War and nuclear weapons. Butterfield was critical of the ideologically driven foreign policies of the US and the Soviet Union because they made compromise and accommodation virtually impossible. Moreover, Butterfield's concern over the ethical conduct of war, based firmly in the Just War and Grotian traditions, led him by the 1960s to become a nuclear pacifist.

Daniel Young's contribution discusses the intellectual development and impact of Herbert Butterfield's friend and colleague, Martin Wight. Young dissociates Wight from the pure power politics approach of realists like Morgenthau, instead locating Wight more in the Whig (Rationalist/Groatian) tradition. Young defines the Whig tradition as emphasizing a realistic, constitutional view of politics associated with Aristotle, Aquinas, and Locke as well as a concern for international law and society. The chapter is excellent in discussing Wight's early pacifism and how he, like many Christian realists, changed his views over time to acknowledge the necessity of some wars. Young argues that Wight was a realist who emphasized the importance of law and morality in international life.

John Coleman Bennett was a systematic theologian and close friend and colleague of Reinhold Niebuhr at Union Theological Seminary. Bennett outlived most Christian realists by two decades and therefore continued to write and speak on political and social issues through the late 1980s. David McCreary's chapter on Bennett is particularly helpful in locating the Christian realism associated with Niebuhr and Bennett in the 1940s and 1950s within contemporary trends in Christianity, including liberal Protestantism, neo-orthodoxy, and process theology. Bennett had much in common with political and religious liberals in identifying social ills that needed to be addressed and the potential for social justice. However, Bennett, like Niebuhr, harshly criticized liberalism for failing to recognize the evil inherent in human nature as a root cause of society's problems and for being optimistic to the point of determinism about progress in human history. McCreary's chapter demonstrates the depth of Bennett's ethical thought applied to politics and considers how Bennett's creative and flexible view toward political dilemmas allowed him to contextualize his approach to any specific problem.

We tend to associate Christian realism with Protestant thought in the US and Britain but certainly there were Catholics thinking "realistically" about politics during the same period, most notably Jacques Maritain and John Courtney Murray. Leon Hooper's chapter on the Jesuit priest Murray provides a discussion of his political insights and a comparison of Murray with his sometime antagonist Reinhold Niebuhr. Murray criticized Christian realists for viewing politics as "morally ambiguous" and faulted them for their "simplistic" view of power politics. Instead, Murray called for a more complex and sophisticated view of social and political life that did not dichotomize between private and public spheres and did not privilege a shallow conception of self-interest. The chapter reports Murray's frequent dialogues with Niebuhr over natural law theory and Murray's debates with Christian realists, socialists, Communists, and even atheists. Moreover, Hooper records Murray's controversial discussion with Rome over his views of civic religious freedom.

Roger L. Shinn considers the interaction between Christian and secular thinkers in his chapter "Christian Realism in a Pluralistic Society." Shinn recognizes that the pronouncements of theologians and avowed Christians on political issues are often greeted with skepticism in an increasingly secular world. Shinn's chapter focuses specifically on Reinhold Niebuhr's relationship with other realists who did not share his conviction that faith should illumine considerations of policy. The author demonstrates Niebuhr's influence on his contemporaries by considering in depth the testimony and writings of Hans Morgenthau, George Kennan, and Arthur Schlesinger Jr. Shinn concludes with a discussion of contributions that Christian realism can make in today's hyper-pluralistic society.

Roger Epp's chapter seeks to answer the question "whither Christian realism?" Epp suggests that the influence of Christian realists in the 1940s and 1950s was due to a revival of interest in religious themes in British and American public life as well as the ability of Christian realists, like Niebuhr, to engage multiple sectors of the lay public in reflection and debate on political topics. Epp argues, however, that the professionalization and specialization of American "political science" in universities and think tanks marginalized the Christian realists. More specifically, Epp shows how the emphasis on "scientific" theorizing and the disregard of normative themes sidelined many Christian realists, who were trained as theologians, from scholarly debates on foreign policy and international affairs. Epp also demonstrates that by the 1960s specific policies, notably nuclear deterrence and the war in

Vietnam, became so divisive that many self-labeled Christian realists could simply not agree with one another. Thus, by the early 1970s Niebuhr had died, his legacy had been appropriated by the Right and the Left, and John C. Bennett called for ending the use of the label "Christian realist."

Notes

[1] Reinhold Niebuhr *Moral Man and Immoral Society* (New York: Charles Scribner's Sons, 1932): xi.
[2] Ibid, 19.
[3] Ibid, 163.
[4] Reinhold Niebuhr, *The Children of Light and the Children of Darkness* (New York: Charles Scribner's Sons, 1944): 6-7.
[5] See Roger Epp, "The 'Augustinian Moment' in International Politics: Niebuhr, Butterfield, Wight and the Reclaiming of a Tradition" International Politics Research Paper, No. 10 (Department of International Politics, University College of Wales, Aberystwyth, 1991).
[6] See Richard Fox, *Reinhold Niebuhr: A Biography* (New York: Pantheon, 1985): 178-180.
[7] Roger Epp, "Power Politics and the *civitas terrena*: The Augustinian Sources of Anglo-American Thought in International Relations," (PhD dissertation, Queen's University, 1990): 252-254.
[8] Roger L. Shinn "Theological Ethics: Retrospect and Prospect" in *Theology and Church in Times of Change: Essays in Honor of John Coleman Bennett*, Edward LeRoy Long, Jr. and Robert T. Handy, eds. (Philadelphia: Westminster, 1982).
[9] See Epp "The 'Augustinian Moment' in International Politics: Niebuhr, Butterfield, Wight and the Reclaiming of a Tradition."
[10] Reinhold Niebuhr, *Christian Realism and Political Problems* (New York, Charles Scribner's Sons, 1953): 143. Niebuhr later said, "I am, however, surprised to note in retrospect how late I was in studying the thought of Augustine carefully. The matter is surprising because the thought of this theologian was to answer so many of my unanswered questions and to emancipate me finally from the notion that the Christian faith was in some way identical with the moral idealism of the past century." "Intellectual Autobiography of Reinhold Niebuhr," in *Reinhold Niebuhr: His Religious, Social, and Political Thought*, Charles W. Kegley and Robert W. Bretall, eds. (New York: Macmillan, 1956): 9.
[11] Herbert Butterfield, *Christianity and History* (London: Bell, 1949): 3
[12] Arthur Schlesinger "Niebuhr's Vision of Our Time," book review of *Discerning the Signs of the Times* in *New Republic* 162 (22 June 1946): 754
[13] Butterfield Papers, Box 92, "Christianity," typescript for Christmas number of Methodist Recorder, 3.
[14] Epp, 5.

[15] See for example Reinhold Niebuhr's "Europe's Catastrophe and the Christian Faith" (London: Nisbet and Co., 1940); "To Prevent the Triumph of an Intolerable Tyranny," *The Christian Century* (18 December 1940): 1578-1580; "Our Responsibilities in 1942," *Christianity and Crisis* 2: 2 (12 January 1942): 1-2. Also see John C. Bennett's "The Churches and the War," *Christianity and Crisis* 2: 15 (2 November 1942): 29-31; "American Christians and the War," *The Student World* 36: 1 (1943): 81-89.

[16] Epp, 123.

[17] For example, see Reinhold Niebuhr, *The Irony of American History* (New York: Charles Scribner's Sons, 1952); John C. Bennett, "The Self-Defeating Attitudes of America's Reactionaries," *Christianity and Crisis* 10: 14 (15 May 1950): 109-112; "American Policy from Asia," *British Weekly* 79: 3360 (5 April 1951).

[18] Butterfield's concern about ideologically-driven policy can be seen in *International Conflict in the Twentieth Century: A Christian View* (London: Routledge and Kegan Paul, 1960). Also see Reinhold Niebuhr, "The Anatomy of American Nationalism," *The New Republic* (28 February 1955): 16-17.

[19] John C. Bennett, *Christian Ethics and Social Policy* (New York: Charles Scribner's Sons, 1946).

[20] Michael Howard, "Temperamenta Belli: Can War be Controlled?" in *Restraints on War*, Michael Howard, ed. (Oxford: Oxford University Press, 1979): 14.

[21] Niebuhr, "The Blindness of Liberalism," *Radical Religion* 1 (Autumn, 1936): 4.

[22] Ibid, 4-5.

[23] Of course, in the US and Britain the idealism of academics and policy-makers was buttressed by strong anti-war sentiment in the mass public. In Britain, the terrible costs of World War I made future wars unthinkable. On the other side of the Atlantic, most Americans felt that it was not in America's interests to be involved in European conflicts, particularly in light of the domestic economic crisis of the 1930s and the 1934 Nye Report that concluded that the First World War was caused by munitions makers. Thus, in both Britain and the US, even had policy makers wanted to be more aggressive in preparing for war with Germany, they were constrained by public opinion to focus on the home front.

[24] For an excellent discussion of the liberal tradition that includes Immanuel Kant's *Perpetual Peace* and Jeremy Bentham's work by the same name, see Michael W. Doyle, *Ways of War and Peace* (New York: W.W. Norton, 1997): chps. 6-8.

[25] For a comprehensive discussion of Wilson's Fourteen Points speech, see Thomas J. Knock, *To End All Wars: Woodrow Wilson and the Quest for a New International Order* (Princeton: Princeton University Press, 1995).

[26] For more on this distinction between theologies of "idealism" and "responsibility" see Kenneth W. Thompson "Theology and International

Relations" in *Theology and Church in Times of Change* (Philadelphia: Westminster Press, 1982): 177-192.
[27] For an excellent discussion on this topic see Richard Harries, "Reinhold Niebuhr's Critique of Pacifism and his Pacifist Critics" in *Reinhold Niebuhr and the Issues of Our Time*, Richard Harries, ed. (Grand Rapids: Eerdmans, 1986): 105-121.
[28] Reinhold Niebuhr, *An Interpretation of Christian Ethics* (New York: Meridian Books, 1960): 170.
[29] Ronald H. Stone, *Reinhold Niebuhr: Prophet to Politicians* (Washington, D.C.: Abingdon Press, 1981): 75.
[30] See Niebuhr's "An Open Letter to Richard Roberts," *Christianity and Society* 5 (Summer 1940).
[31] Stone, 222.
[32] Niebuhr, *The Children of Light and the Children of Darkness*, 17.
[33] See also John C. Bennett, *Social Salvation: A Religious Approach to the Problems of Social Change* (New York: Charles Scribner's Sons, 1935).
[34] Roger Shinn, "Theological Ethics: Retrospect and Prospect," 126.
[35] For more about the legacy of Christian realism, see the final two chapters of this work by Roger Shinn and Roger Epp.
[36] E.H. Carr, *The Twenty Years Crisis* (London: Macmillan and Co., 1940).
[37] Fox, 277.

Chapter 2

Niebuhr and His Critics: Realistic Optimism in World Politics

Eric Patterson

Realism has been the heart of modern studies of politics. Generally associated with a pessimistic account of the individual and human relations, the events of the twentieth century appear as corroborative illustrations: two destructive world wars, the rise of fascism and communism, the Holocaust and similar genocide in the Soviet Union and more recently in Africa and the Balkans, the macabre Cold War threat of nuclear annihilation, and ubiquitous poverty and strife. The cynical legacy of realism claims an impressive genealogy, calling upon the Greek Thucydides, who noted the omnipresence of conflict and the disjuncture of morality and politics. Thucydides in turn sired Machiavelli, who banished morality to the status of a mere political tool of the state and became the herald of the national interest. In turn, Hobbes and Rousseau emerged from this lineage. Hobbes advocated strong government to counter domestic anarchy and evil human nature, picturing international politics as a similarly dangerous state-of-war. Rousseau bemoaned the loss of human innocence and feared the eternal conflict of apparent (selfish) interests. From these roots, the modern reaction to failed inter-war idealism germinated political realism.[1]

However the realist camp can actually be divided into two companies: true pessimists (Machiavellians or Hobbesians) and "utopian realists."[2] The latter differs from its darker sibling by holding a far more optimistic view toward future solutions for today's political dilemmas.

One author calls it an approach "based upon normative ('utopian') and empirical ('realistic') theories. The normative element is made up of an universal appeal, based on reason...the empirical element seeks to make the world of politics more intelligible by seeking to go beyond realism."[3] Pessimistic realism includes scholars such as Arnold Wolfers and Henry Morgenthau, while utopian realism describes thinkers like E.H. Carr and Reinhold Niebuhr.

Certainly among the most influential realists was Niebuhr. A brilliant orator, stunning writer, and tireless traveler, he has been called "without question the most profound thinker of the modern realist school."[4] Academics such as Morgenthau, Arthur Schlesinger, Jr., John C. Bennett, and Paul Ramsey, and politicians such as John Foster Dulles, Henry Kissinger, and Jimmy Carter acknowledged his impact. E.H. Carr noted a special "indebtedness" to Niebuhr's views of morality.[5] George Kennan perhaps put it best, "Niebuhr is the father of us all."[6] However in contemporary international relations courses Niebuhr is rarely studied and has been often quarantined to a mere footnote regarding 'pessimistic realism'. The average undergraduate probably does not even recognize the name, perhaps being too busy studying the latest statistical methods. In light of Kennan's acknowledgement of Niebuhr, one must wonder for what crimes against the discipline has Niebuhr been banished?

Two outstanding charges have been lodged by the academic community. The first is that Niebuhr was a Christian/philosophical Realist. The second was that he was the ultimate nightmare pessimistic realist. Were Niebuhr still alive, he would boast "Guilty!" of the former, but plead "Innocent" to the latter. A simple study of Niebuhr's life without any reading of his work whatsoever would assure Niebuhr's hopefulness; in fact, on many occasions he has been called 'liberal', 'utopian' and 'progressive'. It is to the second accusation which this paper turns. Niebuhr is charged with pessimism in four broad areas: (1) his is a depraved view of the individual and the community (2) therefore politics is an eternal cycle of (3) power struggles in which (4) morality plays very little role. In order to provide for the discipline a much more balanced representation of Niebuhr's thought, this essay will review the charges of critics who call Niebuhr a pessimist, and allow Niebuhr to defend himself on five topics: anthropology, community, justice, power, and history. It will soon be apparent that Niebuhr, rather than being a cynic or a pessimist, would best be described as a realistic optimist.

The Individual and the *Imago Dei*

Any discussion of Reinhold Niebuhr in the fields of ethics, morality, religion, politics, or economics must primarily grapple with his sophisticated anthropology. Unfortunately Niebuhr has been redundantly typecast as a gloomy Cassandra chanting the "depravity of man."[7] Kenneth Waltz wrote, "The whole man, his mind and his body, are according to them [Niebuhr, Augustine, and Morgenthau], defective."[8] Likewise, Howard Williams expresses his dissatisfaction with Niebuhr's "pessimistic view of human nature."[9] Testimony such as the above from a broad range of respected thinkers in international relations is almost certainly convicting. Nevertheless, Michael Smith rightly argues that Niebuhr's conception of human nature and sin is the "most misunderstood part of his work."[10] In order to make any judgments on Niebuhr's political thought, one first must establish what he truly said about the individual, and the relationship between the individual and the collective.[11]

Niebuhr's approach to human nature and its influence on political life was based on his years as a pastor in industrial Detroit, his time in religious higher education, and his keen observation of historical texts and contemporary events. It should be recognized at the outset that it is fundamentally impossible to divorce Niebuhr's practical experience and Christian worldview from his ethics and politics. This immediately contrasts his anthropology and politics from the Machiavellians. He declared in 1940, "In Christian thought sinful self-love is never regarded as an essential character of human nature. Man is in essence a child of God."[12] Like any offspring, God's children (all of humanity) reflect His nature—man created in the 'image and likeness of God'. This is the orthodox doctrine of the *imago dei*, that human beings have certain supra-animal attributes that are characteristic of God, notably freedom, creativity, and potential. Niebuhr believed that God granted mankind moral freedom, and the ability to know and choose right or wrong, as embodied in the myth of Adam and Eve. Furthermore, humanity has creative capability. Although individuals cannot create *ex nihilo* as God can, human intellect is nevertheless capable and designed for creative output—*creatio continuo*. This freedom of moral choice and creative opportunity are the basis for Niebuhr's belief in mankind's 'limitless potential' to transcend itself and forge a uniquely improving world.

Certainly the above is a far cry from the sinister pessimism of realists such as Hobbes and Morgenthau. Because human beings are made in

God's image, they move and exist to a degree above and outside of Nature. Yet because the individual is ultimately a created being, he "is a creature of time and place, whose perspectives and insights are invariably conditioned by his immediate circumstances. But man is not merely a prisoner of time and place. He touches the fringes of the eternal."[13] Niebuhr calls this duality of 'in and beyond' the natural a "vertical dialectic;" man is at once physical and spiritual. Nonetheless, the vertical dialect of creature/creator is not a Manichean dualism or an Oriental binary but rather an organic whole. As Aristotelian substance is indivisibly matter and essence, likewise Niebuhr's man is a unified whole, caught in the tension of limited self and unlimited potential. It is this juncture of finitude and freedom which prompts Niebuhr's often misunderstood view of sin.

Because man is an intelligent creature banished from the protection of the Garden, he recognizes his ultimate vulnerability and desperately desires to survive. Here is the primary departure into Niebuhr's conception of sin: the individual in distress does not turn to God for protection, but turns to self for security. The ascendance of self to central prominence is idolatry and the sin of pride: "Man is mortal. That is his fate. Man pretends not to be mortal. That is his sin."[14]

Pride is self-centered in that it places self at the center of the universe, and exploits opportunities to make itself secure by its own efforts. The sin then is total reliance on freedom without submission to God.[15] Nevertheless, Niebuhr warns against a theology with "an exclusive emphasis upon the ultimate religious fact of the sinfulness of man...[as being] rightly suspected of imperiling relative moral achievements in history."[16] However, Niebuhr believes "all have sinned and come short of the glory of God," and the subtle irony is that human freedom is the seat of sin. Just as free will is the spring from which potential and improvement may flow forth, so too it is the source of human sin. Without moral freedom both human transcendence and human degradation are impossible and man remains solely animal. Nevertheless, lest sin be regarded as the fundamental of the human condition in Niebuhr's anthropology, he counters that Christianity "believes rather that men are egoists in contradiction to their essential natures."[17] Humanity's essential nature lies in the *imago dei*, but as Augustine asserted "all choose to sin." As Michael Smith notes, "an interesting consequence of Niebuhr's dual man is that it allows him an escape hatch from the totally pessimistic view that man is unremittingly sinful."[18]

Thus far Niebuhr has posited man created in God's image with unlimited potential and moral freedom, hamstrung by his recurrent choice of sin. This has an important implication for practical politics: all are created as moral equals before God, and again all are sinners. The first does not allow for intolerance and injustice. The second guards against any Calvinistic attempt to distinguish socially between the elect and the cursed, for in concert with Herbert Butterfield Niebuhr writes, "all historic struggles are between sinful men and not between righteous and sinners."[19] This moral equality of individuals would flesh itself out in Niebuhr's ideas of justice in democracy and in his practical concerns for the working classes and minorities.

In a created world of intelligent persons and rampant sin, Niebuhr observed a universal moral system based on the example of Christ's life and death. Hence self-sacrificial love is the ethic for human relationships and the ideal for humility and forgiveness. The Golden Rule is the foundation of the community, as individuals seek and return amity in a spirit of community. Service and love make up the 'law of love', a statute contradicting the egoism humans often exhibit in their vulnerability.[20] For Niebuhr this scenario points out several interlocking truths. The cornerstone is that community relationships are critical to individual fulfillment, for only through giving may the self attain realization. Christ was glorified upon sacrificing his life at Calvary, likewise individuals transcend the mire of self-centeredness through giving of self. From this account Niebuhr not only provides a basis for collective life and a broadside on selfishness but also foreshadows his strong belief in man's corporate desire.

In evaluating the law of love, one is again brought back to earth by Niebuhr himself. Recognizing human potential and human weakness, he agrees with Marx that there are no disinterested human decisions. Because of human intelligence and the strength of pride with its roots in mankind's fundamental freedom, motives are generally mixed in responding to the law of love. Herein Niebuhr exhibits his typical sparkle of irony by recognizing the opposing forces in the human essence. Furthermore, the individual's lack of objectivity is highlighted in Niebuhr's discussion of the communal sphere, for collective decisions are by their nature compromises.

Niebuhr's own testimony is far from cynical: he neither argues for ultimate human degradation nor ubiquitous evil. In fact he consistently attacks the pessimistic theology of Lutheranism, and ultimately his intellectual mentor Augustine, who focused solely on the depravity of human nature. Niebuhr saw people as essentially children of God. It is only by focusing on the creative and active potential of human beings that makes his calls for cooperation and social justice possible. At the same time Niebuhr derides the liberal-Renaissance "illusion" of the constant goodness of humanity as "naive" and "dangerous." Niebuhr's testimony opts for a more balanced view of choice making, which takes into account knowledge of both the law of love and carnal desire. Consequently, Niebuhr sees the inherent likeness of God in mankind as corrupted by sin, but maintaining its essential freedom and potential for good, and posits these traits as characteristic of communities as well.

Collective Man and the Law of Love

As Niebuhr's anthropology has been warped by some commentators into sheer morbidity, so too has been his view of collective life. Knutsen charges that Niebuhr's view of community affairs "shares the pessimistic anthropology of the conservative tradition."[21] Robert Jervis has filtered his view of politics down to "man wants to dominate others."[22] Williams claims that Niebuhr "derives his stark view of interstate relations, governed as he sees them, by the sin of pride..."[23] Drawing from his understanding of the individual, Niebuhr, like many classical political thinkers (i.e. Hobbes, Rousseau, and Kant), moves fluidly from specifications of the individual to analyses of group life. Though some contest reductionism in such an approach, nevertheless such singular/plural comparisons are still common in international political theory. But for Niebuhr the collective was more than merely the sum of its parts—in his frequent barrages on liberalism he makes the case for man's collective personality. The liberal tradition, anchored in the Renaissance focus on the individual, was the creed of pioneer America. Democratic institutions further sacralized the holiness of the singular in 'citizenship', even as modernity effectively isolated the individual in industrial America. Niebuhr riposted to individualists that man is fundamentally a communal being. His view again is balance, in later years revolting against the Marxism he had placed great hope on as a young man, for Communism became the entire negation of the individual. He asserted that the free individual only truly developed in society. The basis for such a view is again his idea of brotherhood and the law of love—only in association and giving of oneself can the self be realized. This is not only Christian orthodoxy, but also the witness of familial ties, abiding friendships, and community spirit:

There are no limits to be set in history for the achievement of more universal brotherhood, for the development of more perfect and more inclusive mutual relations. All the characteristic hopes and aspirations of the Renaissance and Enlightenment, of both secular and Christian liberalism are right at least in his, that they understand that side of the Christian doctrine which regards the agape of the Kingdom of God as a resource of infinite development towards a more perfect brotherhood in history...The freedom of man makes it impossible to set any limits of race, sex, or social condition upon the brotherhood which may be achieved in history.[24]

So people exist in communities, and the nature of the individual echoes in the nature of collective man. Although a contractarian would conclude that the individual voluntarily enters into a social contract, Niebuhr was unsatisfied with this approach for man has never lived outside of a social setting and has no choice in the political environment into which he is born. Niebuhr instead sees in the group both partial fulfillment of humanity's relational desire and fundamental contradictions to the law of love. The human desire for relationships is satisfied in the practical interactions of people—community life. The application of the law of love herein is three-fold: the primary level is mere obligation—individuals rely on one another for mutual support. A deeper level is the move from simple relationships to more complex interaction over time. Finally, a sense of group identity emerges, as the individuals define obligations in terms of the communal versus the personal.

This is the watershed of Niebuhr's dialectic: pride/selfishness can create a chasm between the potential and creativity of imperfect humanity on one hand, and the ideals of improving institutions apprehending a better social justice on the other. Niebuhr divides pride into three general categories, which recur time and again in his critiques of political units. The first is pride of power—the previously discussed vanity of the individual, recognizing his potential to transcend Nature and his blasphemous solo attempt to become the end of his own existence (will-to-power). This criticism applies strongly to the state that seeks to maximize its interests at the expense of others. The second type of pride is intellectual—a charge with which he largely rakes Communism. This is the elevation of any philosophical or ethical system to a transcendent level, boasting that 'we have all of the answers to Life and History'. Marxism was particularly good at exposing the interest-tainted ideologies of the ages, but turned a blind eye to its own fundamental biases. The final specie is moral pride, the self-righteousness which accompanies intellectual pride and which attempts to justify the morally fetid actions of power. These three strands of pride are plaited into a strong cord of sin, and are the flagrant pretensions and weaknesses of individuals and their nations.

The potential for breaches against the law of love are multiple: foremost is the geometric growth of the will-to-power within the community, which is far stronger proportionately than an individual's will-to-power: "the selfishness of human communities must be seen as an inevitability."[25] The state makes unique demands on the individual, trading a guarantee of security for the minimal insecurity of enhanced government authority, and demanding resources and allegiance from the individual. Furthermore, the state not only requires obedience, but is idolatrous in declaring itself the end of human aspirations, as "cultures and civilizations pretend a finality for them which they do not have."[26] The national myth builds a cult of patriotism which stipulates the ultimate duty of the citizen—self-sacrifice of life. This is both the historic evolution of political life and ultimate institutional pride, for here the state actively manifest the pride of power, intellectual pride in asserting that it is the end of history, and moral pride in turning a blind eye to its actions, or worse, patently justifying immoral policies on its own authority. Niebuhr is one of many realists who observe that at the national level, groups and governments act in ways contrary to individual conscience.

Unsatisfied with the reality of domestic and international affairs, Niebuhr again returns to the ideal: the law of love. Rejecting sacrificial love by the state at the international level as impractical, he prescribes mutual love as the appropriate norm between communities. As the individual is realized in self-giving and relationships which cement community, so collective man domestically and internationally can approximate ideal love by mutual love. He notes, "the fact that various conceptions of a just solution of a common problem can be finally synthesized into a common solution disproves the idea that the approach of each individual or group is consistently egoistic."[27] Mutuality is the norm for collective interaction. Niebuhr objects to a self-sacrificial political ethic, such as appeasement, for it plays into the hands of an even less moral system, such as expansionist fascism or communism. Consequently he recognized that mutual love is the highest form of love possible in politics, and it fleshes out as justice. True justice is the institutionalized approximation of mutual love, the attempt to politically and practically pursue the ideal of self-less love. Niebuhr concludes,

An adequate political morality must...include a political policy which will reduce coercive power to the minimum and bring the most effective social check upon conflicting egoistic impulses in society, it must generate moral idealism which will make for a moral and rational adjustment of life to life, and exploit every available resource of altruistic impulse and reason to extend life from selfish to social ends; and it must encourage a religious world-view which will do justice to the ideals of the spirit which reach beyond the possibilities of historic achievement.[28]

In concluding Niebuhr's evaluation of man and collective man, it is foundational to note Niebuhr's reliance on the *imago dei* as the essence of man in an arena of human imperfection. In humankind's expression of the divine lay Niebuhr's faith in the potential for improving relationships and institutions based on the law of love. Likewise Niebuhr's understanding of sin not only points out inconsistencies in the human condition, but aids in explaining the nature and actions of collective man. Unlike those who stress total individualism, Niebuhr emphasizes people's relationships with others and individual transcendence through self-giving. Though not a classic idealist, Niebuhr's theory is definitely creative and hopeful. Likewise, his analysis of collective life is based on a human need for relationships and ethical constructs of social justice against the national pride and self-interest that often taint and pervert positive international ends, but history reminds us of prophets like Niebuhr exposing the consequences of pride and selfishness. Niebuhr's critique of individual and collective man is not the whole of his work, but merely the background one must have in order to understand his calls for the political body to approximate the ideal of love through order and social justice.

Justice and Mutual Love

One would expect that an alleged pessimist like Niebuhr would theorize about the inability of government to overcome perennial problems such as war and the security dilemma. Waltz witnesses that "the basic assumptions of Augustine and Niebuhr...are useful in descrying the limits of possible political accomplishment."[29] Another reviewer of Niebuhr criticizes that such realism "takes its starting point from the divorce of the actual and the desirable."[30] A student of politics might imagine Niebuhr advising government officials on power and national interests. However, as foreshadowed earlier, Niebuhr was somewhat of a radical as a young man: interested in Marxism, carrying membership with the Socialist party, and even visiting Russia for six weeks in the early 1930s. He supported the candidacy of Norman Thomas in 1932 and 1936 for president (Socialist Party), and even ran himself for Congress as a Socialist in 1932 (he was defeated). In 1940 and 1944 he voted for Roosevelt, who was not only the Democratic candidate, but also the American Labor Party candidate in Niebuhr's New York. Throughout his enduring career his maxim was "equal justice is the most rational ultimate object of society."[31] He championed the cause of the oppressed—in 1932 he condemned segregation of American Negroes, he continuously advocated women's true enfranchisement, and was consistently concerned with the lot of the working class. A tireless campaigner for justice, he wrote, "there are times and seasons when a tolerable justice, hallowed by tradition and supplemented by personal discipline and goodness, gives society long periods of social stability."[32] In fact, it is perhaps both amusing and astounding that some members of the academic political science tradition would call such a visionary and seeming idealist a cynic. He found his socio-ethical system in the Scripture, and propounded it at the domestic and international levels, based on the law of love.

As noted above, Niebuhr felt that the law of love manifested sacrificially was nearly impossible in politics. However, he did provide a three-tier model with which to evaluate the depth of accordance with the law of love generated by a political program or system. Influenced by Augustine and later influencing authors such as Hedley Bull and Michael Howard, Niebuhr proposed political order as the lowest approximation of political love, for although order falls short of the ideal, it nevertheless provides the primary security and stability necessary for fundamental harmonies between citizens and states to develop. A higher plane than order is justice, for justice is impossible without preceding order, though the opposite is not true. Of course the ideal of love is the highest level, and the yardstick by which to measure the other two. Furthermore justice eclipses the minimal gains of order over chaos in providing for balance and fairness. Although he did not use the word, the contemporary idea of empowerment best describes Niebuhr's concept of justice, for it is only when the lowly have sufficient power that political justice is possible in the long-term: "It may be regarded as an axiom of political justice that disproportions of power increase the hazard to justice."[33] Mutual love is institutionalized in justice and is philosophically founded in Niebuhr's understanding of moral equality among men—the practical application of the law of love:

One contribution which Christianity certainly ought to make to the problem of political justice is to set all propositions of justice under the law of love, resolving the fruitless debate between pragmatists and legalists and creating the freedom and maneuverability necessary to achieve a tolerable accord between men and nations...[34]

Order and justice are never the full realization of the ultimate law of love, but are rather potentially improving approximations of that ideal. Hence Niebuhr urges that the ultimate purpose of politics is to devise ways of achieving socio-ethical objectives. In his exploration of such political methods, he regularly harangued leaders for unjust or domineering tactics. He was ever the prophet chastising America and the world community for imperialism, exploitation, and oppression. His concern for international social justice was founded in suspicion of anarchy and tyranny. The former he did not recognize as a benign society of states but rather as a dangerous world in which the will-to-power nakedly manifests itself. Ultimately anarchy is the faulty expression of human freedom at the political level, as collective man desires unchecked liberty from restraint and seeks to improve security unilaterally. On the other hand, Niebuhr equally feared tyranny, the ubiquitous embodiment of order. Tyranny is the imposition of martial order without accompanying freedom or justice. He saw the fascism of the 1930s and 1940s and the communism of the 1950s and 1960s, both flourishing in the loose soil of international anarchy, as proof of his analysis. To balance freedom and order in the cause of justice, Niebuhr called for a central organizing principle.

With chaotic anarchy at one pole representing freedom, and rigid tyranny at the opposite extreme representing base order, Niebuhr balanced the two domestically and internationally upon what he calls a central organizing principle, or a structure for institutional justice. True justice personifies both order and freedom, for it provides safe conditions necessary for realized empowerment. Domestically, Niebuhr saw justice as manifested best in democracy. This provides both a great measure of individual freedom and mechanisms inhibiting predominant power, for "man's capacity for justice makes democracy possible; but man's inclination to injustice makes democracy necessary."[35] In the American checks and balances system Niebuhr found the best historical example, albeit an imperfect one, of social justice via the principle of balanced interests. At the international level, Niebuhr called for similar constitutional checks for and on all states to equilibrate power and foster justice. The concept of justice as it relates practically to power and institutions will be returned to below.

Niebuhr agreed with fatalists that systems of justice are imperfect, but he also contended that justice can be improved. Niebuhr's optimism is founded in a Christian understanding of linear history and human ability for creativity. Justice is the goal of political relationships, and structures of justice can be endlessly altered in order to better approximate the law of love. Niebuhr did not believe society can attain the halcyon of pure justice, for God alone is the executor of history and the only impartial judge. Nonetheless collective man can work toward better expression of empowerment and is required to by his inherent knowledge of the law of love. It is not surprising that Niebuhr the social reformer was seen during his lifetime by many not as a defender of the powerful but as a champion of the meek.

Power as the Means to Justice

Justice as a topic of consideration is only one side of the coin in Niebuhr's thought—the evaluation of power permeates his writing. Perhaps Niebuhr's fascination with power began as pastor of a church in Detroit, where he witnessed and became involved in the violent growing pains of the American industrial labor movement in the 1920s and 1930s. During his pastoral years he served on the Mayor's Inter-Racial Committee, the Detroit Council of Churches Industrial Relations Committee, the Fellowship of Reconciliation, and worked with other similar groups. He openly opposed local mogul Henry Ford and racist groups like the Ku Klux Klan. His criticism of established interest and its accompanying justificatory rhetoric became a study of American life and institutions. Likewise in *The Irony of American History* (1952) he presented a vivid contrast of Stalinist communism with American democracy, similar to comparisons he made a decade earlier between the relative features of fascism and democracy.[36]

However, a large component of the conventional misconceptions regarding Niebuhr's views of the individual stems from misunderstandings of his view of power. Niebuhr did write voluminously about power, but a survey of his work does not leave one with the Machiavellian impression it did for Knutsen: "a minimalist capsule of Niebuhr's view of human nature: that the drive to live, to propagate, and to dominate are common to all men. Second, they accept that conflict is endemic in the human condition..."[37] Similarly, Taylor argues that for Niebuhr, states spend their time on power politics and leave little time for anything else.[38] In contrast, Niebuhr sees power as interwoven with justice: "injustice is the inevitable fruit of irresponsible and disproportionate power."[39] The concept of empowerment was used above to denote justice—active justice capable of action and influence. Niebuhr consistently defines justice in terms of power: economic justice means equitable distribution of wealth, political justice is equated with legal rights and opportunity, and social justice is defined in terms of brotherhood, means, and fairness. For example, writing on the women's movement he observes, "it was not until they could avail themselves of the weapons of economic power and independence that they were able to gain a complete victory."[40] Power is the bedrock of Niebuhr's understanding of justice and the realities of a political being in a political world.

Power is thus a two-fold concept in Niebuhr's philosophy—it is relevant as both ends and means. Adam and Eve represented all of humanity in their jealous desire to be like God, that is, empowered with wisdom equal to God's. Likewise, society's desire is for more than sufficient power in terms of security. A political body desires to be self-provident and self-sufficient, as does an individual. Such is power. This end is achieved by supplementing power. The will-to-power goes a step beyond mere desire, for Niebuhr always noticed the present relative power of the powerful and their desire to consolidate more of it. Consequently power becomes the quixotic means to an ephemeral end—self-realization via ultimate power.

In such a discussion of power it is easy to become jaded with the emphasis on the will-to-power. However, Niebuhr does not condemn power or the temptation for more as evil. Had he, then God would be the chief of sinners. The seat of power is found in the same place as the roots of human creativity and freedom. The Creator granted humans power in order to 'take dominion of the Earth'. Man's creative character is powerful in that he can improvise new social strategies and better the world. Likewise, human freedom is power: dictators from Nero to Stalin have found that the libertine human spirit is the greatest challenge to autocratic rule. Power is inherent in the human process, and should be recognized in Niebuhr's work as both a gift of God and as a responsibility for service.

Unlike Morgenthau and other realists, Niebuhr's starting-point in a discussion of power is far from cynical—power is the ends and means to self-sufficiency and improvement of society, while also being the path to sin. Niebuhr's view can best be understood as ironical, for both great opportunity and potential for wickedness lay in the freedom of humanity. Without human freedom, it is impossible to develop a non-mechanistic formula for the betterment of civilization, for cause and effect are relegated to contrived systemic sterility. Furthermore, the irony of freedom and potential sin through the will-to-power are magnified again at the corporate level, for the state has both far greater freedom and far less resistance to the will-to-power than does the individual. In society, the individual is educated and constrained by the moderating restraints of education, religion, and law. The state in anarchy has no such constraints, the very existence of the state presupposes selfishness: "international peace, political and economic justice, and every form of social achievement represent precarious constructs in which the egoism of man is checked and yet taken for granted."[41] It is the perennial uncertainty caused by vulnerability which justifies the government.

How should power be dealt with? Niebuhr saw in modern democracy the best system to date of justice, for democracy as a system primarily recognizes a competition of interests and seeks to ameliorate the clash of wills, for "some balance of power is the basis for whatever justice is achieved in human relations."[42] Democracy allows for great measures of freedom and openness, unlike tyranny, making possible better decisions based on consensus and fairness. Also, democracy is similarly antithetical to anarchy, for as a political system it puts a high premium on order so as to make greater justice possible. The efficacy of democracy lies in the balancing of power—different factions are juxtaposed in order to build compromise and to dilute power. This method of "matching power with power" is realistic in comprehending the contingent nature of power in politics. Democracy is also idealistic in its egalitarian emphasis on social justice. Niebuhr writes, "democracy is a perennial necessity because justice will always require that the power of government be checked as democracy checks it, and peace requires that social conflict be arbitrated by the non-violent technique of democratic process."[43]

American democracy was illustrative of Niebuhr's arguments, although he was continually advocating that social improvements were necessary in American life. He found in the constitutional checks-and-balances system a central organizing principle for order and proximate justice. Moreover, he found such a balance of power to be an important fulcrum for equilibrium between competing power interests (rival parties and their supporters). Beyond the actual democratic mechanism of government, he also recognized social forces spawned by the Constitution at work furthering balance on the American scene. The two-party system of America has been profoundly stable, moderating radicalism. Other stabilizing factors such as investure of power at various local, state, and federal levels, along with empowerment of non-government agencies (e.g. labor and the press), result in an aggregate of fluid interests. "In a democracy, despite its imperfections, there is such a constant shift in the oligarchy, both in the political and economic spheres from pressure from below, that the oligarchy is kept fluid. It is kept so fluid in fact, that the concept of elite does not really apply."[44] Democracy distributes political and economic power, preventing centralization.

Niebuhr turned his focus then to the international arena, drawing parallels based on the balance of power he observed in domestic democracy. The first important parallel is the need to bring power under social and moral review. This can only be accomplished by a participating citizenry combined with freedom to dissent and freedom of religion and the press. The second lesson for the international is to establish 'religious and moral' checks on the domestic principles of power.[45] After World War II he frequently called for checks on the abilities of the Great Powers in order to match power for power—in fact his diagnosis of the international situation prior to the Second World War and his prognosis for change foreshadowed the UN format. Nonetheless, Niebuhr was not a traditional balance-of-power proponent but rather desired increased interdependence and various constitutional and practical checks on state authority in order to prevent another Great War. He also strongly recommended constitutional governments for all countries, believing like Kant in the ability of popular sovereignty to quell militarism. Obviously such constitutional structures do not simply save states from aggression, but also make domestic justice that much more possible. In proposing international constitutional checks and domestic constitutions around the globe, Niebuhr was combating flagrant oligarchic abuse of power and promoting justice. By supporting international checks he hoped to moderate the anarchy which made the rise of Hitler's Third Reich possible. He believed that the destructive nature of tyranny arose from anarchy and could be thwarted by domestic democracies.

The key to both domestic and international balance-of-power is the central organizing principle, a far different regime than a structuralist balance-of-power or a classical realist portrait of benign anarchy. Niebuhr saw the world system as full of competing power interests, and the way to assuage conflict is to temper figurative balance (or natural imbalance) with practical and constitutional structures. Consequently,

Niebuhr's balance-of-power differs from his realist brethren by acknowledging the importance of institutionalized checks on power beyond traditional power politics, to the point of abridging sovereignty. Some of his ideas for such change in the state system are quite liberal and are mentioned below. However this is not the thorough liberal idealism of Wilson and Zimmern based on faith in human goodness. Rather Niebuhr recognizes human creative potential to develop structures that would moderate human destructive potential.

Power can only be balanced by power. "The principle of balance of power is implied in the idea of constitutional justice."[46] Such a doctrine speaks significantly to the ultimate contest of political wills: the use of force. He wrote, "Society must strive for justice even if it is forced to use means, such as self-assertion, resistance, coercion... which cannot gain the moral sanction of the most sensitive moral spirit."[47] Niebuhr deals with war, force, and coercion throughout his writings, during a turbulent era of world conflagration, revolution, and the arms race. Though a pacifist early in his career, Niebuhr recognized that submission to tyranny was neither just nor loving, further predicting the difficulty of such an ideology at the state level. The horrors of World War I, the fiasco of the Spanish Civil War, the bombastic expansion of Italy into North Africa, and the rise of the Nazi war machine induced Niebuhr to call a nation to arms. Denouncing American non-involvement as far from virtuous but rather self-interested and deriding pacifism as a large-scale abdication of responsibility, he saw in World War II the ultimate failure of the international community to meet power with power. The possession of power obligates a certain responsibility to the bearer in the task of social justice. The West failed to respond by matching Hitler's emerging power, and subsequently war was the result.

Niebuhr's hope was to "save society from being involved in endless cycles of future conflict not by an effort to abolish coercion in the collective man, but by reducing it to a minimum by counseling the use of such types of coercion as are most compatible with the moral and rational factors in human society, and by discriminating between the purposes and ends for which coercion is used."[48] Therefore there is both a domestic and international scope for the use of force. Human relations can and may result in injustice, and it is the duty of the authorities to enforce the strictures of society. Consequently law enforcement and crime deterrence provide for greater justice and are tolerable in domestic life. Likewise in the international realm, the state has the responsibility to combat injustice. This logically may result in military response to a belligerent foe, self-defense, or security stratagems, such as containment. It is *apropos* to note Niebuhr's ambivalence toward armed intervention: he was initially coolly supportive of US policy in Vietnam, but quickly became one of the harshest critics of the enterprise. The state may use force, but only in fulfilling its responsibility to justice.

When should a state resort to violence? The lens through which to evaluate the need for forcible action is that of justice. As illustrated above, Niebuhr's apology for coercion was reactive in nature—responding to violations of the law of love and the laws of civilization which hazard justice. Hitler was a tyrant seeking global domination—he had to be stopped in the cause of justice, and the only method possible in the end was by meeting power with power. The communist colossus could be stunted only by containing power with power. Force is the ultimate balancer of power.

Yet the ethical dilemma was not hidden by Niebuhr when considering war. "We cannot purge ourselves of the sin and guilt in which we are involved by the moral ambiguities of politics without also disavowing responsibility for the creative possibilities for justice."[49] Force is a form of injustice for it transgresses human freedom, and even in the cause of justice coercion dirties one's hands. War is the extinguishing of human life and breaking the law of love, even in self-defense. Niebuhr recognized the moral tension of such power confrontations, and did not try to hide the ethical ambiguity therein. Such tension is further compounded by the duplicity or multiplicity of motivations involved in coercion. Building on his conception of the mixed rationale for any collective action, Niebuhr illumines the prejudicial nature of power action: "Communities must be built by men and nations sufficiently mature and robust to understand that political justice is achieved, not by merely destroying, but also by deflecting, beguiling, and harnessing residual self-interest and by finding the greatest possible concurrence between self-interest and the general welfare."[50]

American foreign policy is replete with examples of actions based in an admixture of goals and ideals. For example, David Lumsdaine and Kathryn Sikkink have shown how US foreign policy has used foreign aid programs and human rights institutions for both moral and political ends.[51] Motives of gain, fear, and glory do not soil the moral goals or the success of an operation, but do contradict moral illusions of virtual disinterestedness and unselfishness. In considering power, interests are never simple and philanthropic—the reality of human intelligence and freedom is the capacity for comprehensive deliberation. Furthermore, at the state and international level, collective interests and the need for compromise play broad roles in the vacuum of sacrificial love.[52]

Niebuhr recognized the realities of power as being both a historic opportunity and frequently in moral tension. Underlying his entire dialogue of power is the principle of responsibility. The individual is empowered by God with creativity and freedom, and therefore is responsible to act. Niebuhr cites Jesus' parable of three men who were given 'talents' by the king to use for gain. The first two doubled their sums by investment, but the third hid his money, lest he lose it. Upon calling the three to court, the king rewarded the diligent servants and punished the latter for forsaking action. Niebuhr draws a parallel between this parable and political life: a unit with political power has a duty to use it responsibly. Proper utilization might include bettering the socio-economic environment of the country, education, welfare, etc. Internationally this would include pressuring tyrannies to change, supporting constitutionalism, working for international order, and the like. Niebuhr saw in post-war Great Britain a model of mature responsibility: a modest democratic state intent on improving the welfare of its citizenry, tending a then relatively benign Commonwealth which it was preparing for independence. Certainly anti-imperialist Niebuhr was not justifying the largesse of empire, but rather using the United Kingdom in the 1940s and 1950s as a standard by which to measure "naive" and "adolescent" America. Niebuhr's challenge was for America to shake off the stupor of past isolationism and act responsibly, as superpower status entailed. Such international leadership as at the UN, in rebuilding Europe, in encouraging democracy, and in containing the Soviet Union were important duties of responsible power.

The evidence shows that power in Niebuhr's thought occupies central prominence as the means to justice in politics. His conception of power is not that of shallow power-as-sin, but rather a recognition of the competitive and necessary potential of power. In his own day he was called a 'liberal' and a 'progressive.'[53] In democracy and abridged sovereignty at the international level he saw opportunities for approximations of justice, through the equilibrating of power around a central organizing principle such as a constitutional agreement. Furthermore he recognized the tragic necessity of coercion in political life and was unashamed to critically examine both the responsibility and the guilt of using power. Rather than pessimism, Niebuhr's concepts of power, empowerment, and responsibility are the avenues to historic advancement.

Meaning in History and The Future

Because so much of Niebuhr's writing was chronologically specific, for example concerning Nazism, Communism, and Vietnam, some may not realize that much of his ethical and political work speaks to outstanding questions of existence. Critics allege that he was a 'defender of conservative power politics' and therefore has little relevance for consideration after the Cold War. R.B.J. Walker bears witness to this position: Niebuhr is "timebound" and "offers little guidance for the future."[54] Ferguson and Mansbach agree that he has little creative to say to the future, "Reinhold Niebuhr's politics are immutable."[55] Ken Booth concurs, "international relations specialists [such as Niebuhr] did not believe in the future."[56] Niebuhr has again been falsely accused. Whether as a young socialist or as an older social ethicist, Niebuhr argued for ideas untypical of popular political realism, believing that history is meaningful, mutable, and linear.

Niebuhr believed in the future—indeed, his historical faith was certainly millennial, for he saw the end of history as the fulfillment of the law of love. He wrote, "The world community toward which all historical forces seem to be driving us, is mankind's final possibility and impossibility. The task of achieving it must be interpreted from the standpoint of a faith which understands the fragmentary and broken character of all historic achievements and yet has confidence in their meaning because it knows their completion to be in the hands of a divine power."[57] Man knows the ideal law of love through Scripture, conscience, and revelation but exists in a reality tainted by sin. The Fall is symbolic of the historic disjunction of the real and the ideal. However the ideal is known and the purpose of history is pursuit of the ideal, comparing present efforts to the law of love.

Niebuhr's politics reveal graphic meaning in history. The end of history is the individual realizing himself in the eternal, and the measure of temporal politics becomes practice of the law of love among people. History's foundation is in the creation of mankind as free moral agents, both capable of and required to act. Moreover, inaction is sin. Man can find political meaning by engaging in the brotherhood of community life.

This fidelity to purposive history does not make Niebuhr a mere eschaton with no words for the present. Furthermore, his view on history is significantly different from Catholic mysticism, Lutheran dualism, or humanistic idealism. Drawing on the Old Testament example of the covenant and the New Testament teaching of St. Paul,

Niebuhr holds a this-worldly philosophy, like Herbert Butterfield and Jacques Maritain. Such pragmatism calls for a realistic appraisal of affairs and concerted action *now* based on Niebuhr's doctrine of the responsibility of the powerful. Niebuhr sees politics as an affair between people, all of whom are sinners, so there is neither room for religious segregation nor self-righteous pretensions: the business of politics is for everyone. Therefore, one way the meaning in history may be apprehended is by political activity and social justice.

Niebuhr trumpets a this-worldly realism in order to combat the errors he perceived in idealistic liberalism.[58] He and others such as D.C. Mackintosh and Karl Barth supported pragmatic social action but spurned the inter-war liberal faith which heralded the Kingdom of God being fulfilled via the (American) Social Gospel.[59] His call was for a pragmatic approach to actual problems, which realistically addressed the context of a world in distress. Consequently, he urged that a 'prophetic minority' rise within the state and exert moral realism by addressing issues of morality and justice while vocally and actively exemplifying the law of love. Although the Church[60] may play a role in such action, Niebuhr's prophetic minority is not coeval with the Church, for he often criticized the short-sidedness of historic Christendom. The prophetic minority consists simply of moral people in the social world who call the state to awareness and accountability.

Thus Niebuhr believed in a meaningful history and in the responsibility of citizens and leaders to attack existing socio-political problems. He preached and predicted change in world politics and assumed the mutability of institutions: "the ultimate purpose of this task is to find political methods which will offer the most promise of achieving an ethical goal for society."[61] Unlike idealistic proponents of the League of Nations and the United Nations who believed the organizations to herald the end of history, he did not believe in the ultimate transcendence of any present institution, and could not philosophically argue for the immutability of any historical structure (i.e. a government, party, organization, etc.). Instead he realized the constant censure of any organization or group by the law of love. Because systems and institutions are not fixed, there is a historic opportunity and a moral responsibility for involvement, reflection, and improvement of the political engines of power and justice.

Hope for improvement and disdain of pretensions by institutions as 'eternal' are founded in Niebuhr's consideration of human freedom. The creative potential of mankind makes better justice possible. The known ideal of the law of love makes such improvement mandatory. An example of the development of government can be found in Niebuhr's evolving criticism of the Soviet Union and the United States. Enamored by the potential of the early Marxist experiment, he later became disappointed by the authoritarianism and the expansionism of Stalin and his successors. Conversely, critical of the inter-war US he became more and more commendatory of the American constitution and the civil rights efforts of the late 1950s and 1960s.

Again, Niebuhr never said the ideal was attainable. Rather improvement is possible and commanded. Still Niebuhr's insight into mixed motives, human errancy, and the perennial guilt of wielding inordinate power temper any historical utopianism. In practice Niebuhr's teleology demanded practical suggestions for advancement, which he readily provided. For example, such a plan is found in his catalogue of changes for a more stable and secure post-war Europe. In 1940 he wrote, "the defeat of Germany, difficult as it now seems, is however only the negative condition of a new Europe. The task will then still remain to create a new Europe, to develop a new system of national interdependence, to abridge national sovereignty sufficiently to accomplish this purpose, to eliminate national barriers to trade, and to achieve a higher degree of justice within each nation."[62] Traditional institutions as well as past political alliances and enmities are mutable in history.

The disjuncture of real and ideal and a this-worldly responsibility to the law of love and justice presuppose a linear view of history. Christian thought relates a genesis and an apocalypse, culminating in the eternal Kingdom of God. Beyond the eschatological language of his writing there is a practical linear dimension. Greek and Oriental religion was cyclic: from the Olympian myths of the seasons to Socrates' doctrine of rebirth (reincarnation), pagan thought was circular regarding history. Such temporal redundancy not only enthused many Medieval scholastics, but has been embraced by many modern historians and political thinkers as well. Both classical realists and Neo-realists generally agree that history is cyclic and unchanging—this is the argument of Thucydides, Machiavelli, Gilpin, Waltz, and others. Some readers of Niebuhr mistakenly categorize him as a cyclical historian, puzzled by his refrain about "perennial forces" operating in history. Niebuhr does note that time and again that certain historic perennial forces recur in politics. At first glance there appears to be a serious contradiction between institutional mutability, proximate justice, and historic improvement on the one hand, and perennial forces on the other. Is there a contradiction?

Niebuhr's discussion of perennial forces relates textually to the necessity for democracy and to weaknesses in the human condition. Such testimony is not that institutions, systems, or historical epochs are truly recurrent in history—hence his measured faith in the potential for progress collectively. Improvement is characteristic of human creativity and dependent on the will. The perennial forces in history are those of man himself—the ever-present tension between finitude and the divine. Until the end of history, humans will always be confronted with choices between good and evil, justice and injustice, responsibility and profligacy. The law of love will only be fully realized beyond natural history, the present organizing structures can only aim at approximating it. But the birth and maintenance of such improving order relies on human ingenuity, which can either subvert justice or uplift it. Hence, individuals can act for good or evil, and their freedom to follow either path is the perennial dilemma of history. However, better institutions which realistically view the human condition and balance power can approximate justice, moderate power, and continue improving until 'the end of the age'.

Because humans are rational, they can study history and not only learn from the accomplishments and foibles of past civilizations but also derive a certain philosophical satisfaction for the deep meanings found in the past. Historical and political constructs created by people are neither immutable nor absolute, for they are both images and mere approximations of the law of love. Moreover, Niebuhr saw the future as an "unlimited horizon" for progress, as humans develop strategies for dealing with the perennial challenges presented by human character. History and the law of love are both a spur and an indictment—a rod of justice and a goad to improve institutions and benefit fellow men based on collective mutual love. Consequently history has meaning for man as his composition and the expression of his creative potential, and points as a reminder to the divine end to which he may choose to endeavor.

Conclusion

Niebuhr's work is by no means a simple read. His complex thought, interesting language, and recognition of omnipresent tensions and ironies in history and reality make him a tantalizing encounter. However there can be no doubt that by his own testimony Niebuhr is hardly a pessimist. His is the "ultimate optimism which has entertained all of the facts which lead to pessimism."[63] Instead of calling the individual depraved, he acknowledged creativity and potential for both good and evil, and saw similar opportunities for the collective. Unlike Machiavelli and his followers, Niebuhr asserted the primacy of ethics and justice and worked practically toward that end as a lecturer, mediator, and advocate for the oppressed. Rather than gloomy predictions of power politics, Niebuhr pointed to love and justice as the ends, and equilibrated power balanced among competitors as a means. Similarly, his prescriptive commentary on current events, such as rebuilding post-war Europe and civil rights, are the words of a creative liberal (and former socialist), not a sterile conservative. In addition, his faith in the meaning for and within history and possibilities for historic improvement are visionary. Because of his views on the law of love, he was not bound to the negativity of non-Christian realists who saw the individual as fallen, but lacked a belief in spiritual redemption. In any event, he must be exonerated from the charge of pessimism.

One wonders what then accounts for the misrepresentation of Niebuhr's work? I suggest that it is most likely that Niebuhr is discredited due to his transparent personal faith, which many scholars feel uncomfortable with in this era of 'cultural wars' within the social sciences. It is encouraging to note that the discipline of social ethics is seeing a revival of scholarship on Niebuhr's writing. However, it is discouraging to note that in the fields of political science and American history a thinker who had such an influence during his lifetime is now relegated to caustic footnotes about "Christian pessimism." Indeed, a comprehensive study of the politics of the interwar years, World War II, and the early Cold War must note Niebuhr's influence both on the leaders and the public of his day. Furthermore, a fresh look at Niebuhr not only provides a major link in the intellectual development of twentieth century American political thinking, but we may also find a foreshadowing of the methods of political activism of moral conservatives and Christians from both the political Right and Left over the past twenty years.

It is little wonder that in the past, Niebuhr's profound analyses at both the theoretical and practical levels have been appropriated by both realists and idealists, pessimists and liberals alike, for he argued for a balanced view which took into account the truths of both positions. Niebuhr's hope for the individual bordered on utopianism, his belief in social justice was clearly progressive, and his prescriptions for power and politics were decidedly liberal. Niebuhr himself eschewed all labels, calling for a 'realistic optimism' in assessing politics: "the qualified optimism of an adequate religion will... nerve men to exhaust their resources in building a better world, in overcoming human strife, in mitigating the fury of man's injustice to man, and in establishing a society in which some minimal security for all will be achieved."[64] Perhaps this is the best title for him, the 'realistic optimist'. Today, many of the fundamental political issues he addressed remain concerning social justice, empowerment, improving institutions, and human potential. As the discipline of international relations looks ahead to the challenges of the next century, it is time to reflect more on the creative and yet sensible themes of Niebuhr, and be both inspired by his faith in the possibility of progress and aided by his suggestions for apprehending solutions to the dilemmas of domestic and international politics.

Notes

*An earlier version of this chapter was published as "Niebuhr and His Critics: Realistic Optimism in World Politics" *International Relations* 15: 5 (August 1999).

[1] Political realism, or being politically "realistic," is differentiated from moral or philosophical Realism (the belief in non-tangible categories of reality) in this work. Niebuhr was both.

[2] Ken Booth says that utopian realism differs from traditional security thinking by its "holistic character and non-statist approach" and its "unease with traditional concepts of security which privilege the state and military power." "Security and Emancipation" in *Review of International Studies* 17 (Summer 1991): 317.

[3] Ken Booth, "Security in Anarchy: Utopian Realism in Theory and Practice." *E.H. Carr Inaugural Lecture*, 7. Also in *International Affairs* 67 (Autumn 1991).

[4] Michael J. Smith, *Realist Thought from Weber to Kissinger* (Baton Rouge: Louisiana State University Press, 1986): 101.

[5] I appreciate Tim Dunne pointing out Carr's reliance on Niebuhr's views on the morality of "common man" and groups. Carr acknowledges Niebuhr's influence in the preface of *The Twenty Years Crisis* (London: Macmillan and Co., 1940): x.

[6] Qtd. in Richard Fox, "Reinhold Niebuhr and the Emergence of the Liberal Realist Faith, 1930-1945" in *Review of Politics* 38 (July 1976): 250.

[7] John Herz, *Political Realism and Political Idealism* (Princeton: Princeton University Press, 1951): 14.

[8] Kenneth Waltz, *Man the State, and War* (New York: Columbia University Press, 1959): 24.

[9] Howard Williams, *International Relations in Political Theory* (Buckingham: Open University Press, 1991): 133.

[10] Smith, 103.
[11] Niebuhr used the gender-specific 'man' in discussing the individuals in politics. The author recognizes that political language has changed since Niebuhr's day. However, for the sake of continuity of expression, this paper will follow Niebuhr's style.
[12] Reinhold Niebuhr, *Christianity and Power Politics* (New York: Charles Scribner's Sons, 1953): 50.
[13] Reinhold Niebuhr, *Beyond Tragedy* (New York: Ayer, 1977): 84.
[14] Ibid, 84.
[15] Reinhold Niebuhr, *The Children of Light and the Children of Darkness* (New York: Charles Scribner's Sons, 1942): 17.
[16] Qtd. in Smith, 101.
[17] *Christianity and Power Politics*, 38.
[18] Smith, 110.
[19] *Christianity and Power Politics*, 35.
[20] *The Children of Light and the Children of Darkness*, 17.
[21] T.L. Knutsen, *A History of International Relations Theory* (Manchester: Manchester University Press, 1992): 223.
[22] Qtd. in Richard Little and Michael Smith, *Perspectives on World Politics*, second edition (London: Routledge, 1991): 93.
[23] Williams, 24.
[24] Reinhold Niebuhr, *The Nature and Destiny of Man II* (New York: Charles Scribner's Sons, 1964): 85.
[25] Reinhold Niebuhr, *Moral Man and Immoral Society* (New York: Charles Scribner's Sons, 1932): 271.
[26] *Beyond Tragedy*, 83.
[27] *The Nature and Destiny of Man II*, 249.
[28] *Moral Man and Immoral Society*, 233-234.
[29] Waltz, 27.
[30] Williams, 27.
[31] *Moral Man and Immoral Society*, 261.
[32] Qtd. in Ronald M. Brown, ed. *The Essential Reinhold Niebuhr* (New Haven: Yale University Press, 1986): 42.
[33] Ibid, 44.
[34] Qtd. in Brown, 96.
[35] *The Children of Light and the Children of Darkness*, 6-7.
[36] See *The Irony of American History*, chap. 6.
[37] Knutsen, 242.
[38] Trevor Taylor, ed. *Approaches and Theory in International Relations* (London: Longman, 1978): 130.
[39] *Christianity and Power Politics*, 144.
[40] *Moral Man and Immoral Society*, 46.
[41] *Christianity and Power Politics*, 38-39.

[42] Niebuhr, *Christian Realism and Political Problems* (New York: Charles Scribner's Sons, 1953): 120.
[43] *Christianity and Power Politics*, 85.
[44] *The Children of Light and the Children of Darkness*, 117.
[45] *The Irony of American History*, 116.
[46] *The Nature and Destiny of Man II*, 284-285.
[47] *Moral Man and Immoral Society*, 257.
[48] Ibid, 259.
[49] *The Nature and Destiny of Man*, 272.
[50] Charles Kegley and Randal Bretall, eds. *Reinhold Niebuhr: His Religious, Social and Political Thought* (New York: Macmillan, 1961): 197.
[51] David Lumsdaine's *Moral Vision in International Politics* (Princeton, N.J.: Princeton University Press, 1993) demonstrates that foreign aid programs cannot be explained merely as a tool for gaining political leverage, but rather have strong moral bases. Kathryn Sikkink's article discusses the increasing awareness and potency of human rights norms in international politics. See her "The Power of Pricipled Ideas: Human Rights Politics in the United States and Western Europe" in *Ideas and Foreign Policy: Beliefs, Institutions, and Political Change*, Judith Goldstein and Robert O. Keohane, eds. (Ithaca : Cornell·University Press, 1993).
[52] Niebuhr wrote, "the fact that power cannot be wielded without guilt, since it never transcends our interest, even when it tries to subject itself to universal standards." *The Irony of American History*, 32.
[53] Niebuhr wanted a "realistic liberalism." See Niebuhr's "Liberalism: Illusions and Realities" in *The New Republic* 133 (July 4, 1955).
[54] R.B.J. Walker, *Inside/Outside: International Relations as Political Theory* (Cambridge: Cambridge University Press, 1993): 124.
[55] Yale H. Ferguson and Richard W. Mansbach, *The Elusive Quest* (Columbia, SC: University of South Carolina Press, 1988): 40.
[56] Ken Booth and Steve Smith, eds. *International Relations Theory Today* (Cambridge: Polity Press, 1995): 332.
[57] *The Children of Light and the Children of Darkness*, 190.
[58] Daniel F. Rice provides an excellent discussion of how Niebuhr targeted the quintessential humanist of his day, John Dewey, as the symbol of amoral, "ineffectual liberalism." See Rice's *Reinhold Niebuhr and John Dewey: An American Odyssey* (Albany, NY: State University of New York Press, 1993).
[59] Robin W. Lovin, *Reinhold Niebuhr and Christian Realism* (Cambridge: Cambridge University Press, 1995): 18.
[60] Niebuhr uses the term "Church" in a variety of ways, but generally means all active believers.
[61] *Moral Man and Immoral Society*, 25.
[62] *Christianity and Power Politics*, 138-139.
[63] Ibid, 182.

[64] Qtd. in Brown, 16.

Chapter 3

The Prophetic Realism of John Foster Dulles, 1937-1945

Mark G. Toulouse

The remnants of both the religious and diplomatic influences exerted by John Foster Dulles's early familial surroundings are unmistakably present in his later life. From the Presbyterian manse of his parents, he inherited moral commitments coupled with a Calvinistic sense of duty, both of which profoundly contributed to the shaping of his worldview.[1] From his grandfather, John W. Foster, and his uncle, Robert Lansing, who both served as secretaries of state for the United States, he learned that he had an individual responsibility to put that sense of duty to work by attempting to transform his moral commitments into practical realities.[2] Though these influences are evidenced in nearly all of his involvements in the international arena, historical contingencies and personal experiences of later years were to bring significant change to the way he understood and utilized them.

Beginning in 1937, Dulles found himself called upon to translate both his prophetic Protestantism and his international political realism into practical service performed on behalf of the Church. At least before late 1945, when events began to harden Dulles's attitude toward the Soviets, he accurately represented the thinking of Protestant realists like Reinhold Niebuhr and John C. Bennett, two well-known Protestant theologians working with the Federal Council of Churches of Christ in America.[3] For various reasons, events and circumstances after 1945 caused Dulles to transform his position from a Protestant prophetic realism stressing the interdependence of nations to a more private notion of religion linked to the democratic ideology of the Free World.[4] But, during the period from 1937 to 1945, John Foster Dulles worked among the churches as one of the most prestigious, prophetic, and realistic voices dealing with international affairs.

Dulles and the Federal Council of Churches

The 1937 Oxford ecumenical conference demonstrated a conception of the church as a community that transcended the boundaries of any particular nation. Largely due to the influence of his father's socially progressive outlook, Dulles grew up believing that the church should always strive to project that conception of itself to the world. However, shortly before Oxford, Dulles had begun to feel that the church was altogether too lax in its attempt to fulfill this responsibility. In his address to the conference, entitled "The Problem of Peace in a Dynamic World, " Dulles—true to his belief in the necessity of adhering to what Paul Tillich has called the "Protestant principle"[5]—asserted that the main obstacles to peace were created by pride and selfishness. These traits could only be offset

> by replacing them [with) some sentiment more dominant and gripping and which would contain in it the elements of universality as against particularity.... What of the democratic nations? What of the so-called Christian nations? They boast of high ideals, but have they the spiritual fire with which to drive out petty instincts which bind them to a system which spells their doom[?][6]

Dulles's experience of the Oxford Conference[7] obviously brought him to a renewed appreciation of his past, and this caused him to reevaluate his perspective in international affairs. As the theologian Bennett expressed it, after Oxford Dulles "went back to his heritage to a certain extent, and there was a certain continuity."[8] Oxford taught Dulles the importance of trying to transform his inherited spiritual values into practical contributions in the political sphere.

The churches, Dulles later wrote, could see the broad picture because "in the eyes of God, all men are equal, and their welfare is of equal moment." "Only through an approach of such universality" can there be "any promise of a solution." Thus Dulles dedicated himself, for a time, to work with the churches so "that the spirit of Oxford should not lie down but be projected through the membership—particularly the lay membership" of all the churches.⁹

As a direct outgrowth of his increasing participation within ecumenical church circles, Dulles quickly earned the respect of Protestant church leaders. On the evening of October 4, 1940, Dr. Walter W. Van Kirk, the secretary of the Department of International Justice and Goodwill, hosted a dinner meeting. Dulles was asked by those present to draft a statement that would serve both to emphasize and to preserve the essential unity of the churches in the face of divisive issues. An earlier attempt in June to draft a common statement to embody the views of both pacifists and just-war advocates, as well as American Christians and Christians of other countries, failed to win support due largely to the criticism of Dulles.

The rejected statement, entitled "A Statement on the Present Opportunity and Duty of Christians," was drafted principally by Van Kirk and Dr. William Adams Brown of Union Theological Seminary for submission to the Federal Council's Executive Committee. In the main, Dulles's criticism of the document centered around his view that the statement presented the Allies uncritically, as if they represented the completely moral side of the conflict, and described the Axis powers as evil personified. He elaborated this view in a personal letter to Van Kirk.

> I am struck by the fact that history shows that in every so-called "Christian" country, in time of war or international stress, the church has uniformally [sic] become the hand-maiden of national politics. The church leaders then see the moral issue as identical with the national issue and call upon church members as a matter of religious duty to support its [sic] own national leaders as being "right." I think one of the great weaknesses of the church is that Christians are thus split by their national interests into opposing and hostile groups, hating each other, and that this is destructive of unity and power in the church. I greatly hoped that in the present crisis the Christian church in this country could avoid concentrating upon the admitted evils elsewhere, slurring over the admitted evils at home and thereby becoming, in my judgment, hypocritical and unChristian.¹⁰

Two weeks to the day after Dulles was asked to draft the proposed unity statement, on 18 October, he circulated for comment and criticism a draft that came to be entitled "The American Churches and the International Situation."¹¹ The statement urged Christians to rise above the hatreds of war in order to maintain fellowship with one another on a worldwide basis. Chief among the thoughts presented in the statement was the plea that Christians recognize the need for repentance, humility, avoidance of hatred and hypocrisy, and the spiritual supremacy of God rather than the state.[12] Dulles presented the statement to the 600 delegates of the biennial meeting of the Federal Council held at the Hotel Dennis on 10-13 December in Atlantic City.

Dulles's role in Atlantic City was particularly influential. In addition to his work on the statement, Dulles led discussion as the chair of the major seminar dealing with the churches and international affairs. The biennial meeting officially adopted Dulles's statement, "characterized by many church leaders...as one of the most significant pronouncements of recent years."[13]

One of the most important actions to emerge from Atlantic City was one of the least heralded at the time. The Executive Committee decided to appoint a commission to be known as the Commission to Study the Bases of a Just and Durable Peace.[14] As described in the minutes of the committee, this commission was to be broadly representative of the communions holding membership in the Federal Council.[15] The directives of the commission were outlined as follows:

> First, to clarify the mind of our churches regarding the moral, political and economic foundations of an enduring peace; second, to prepare the people of our churches and of our nation for assuming their appropriate responsibility for the establishment of such a peace; third, to maintain contacts with the Study Department of the World Council of Churches (now in process of formation); fourth, to consider the feasibility of assembling as soon as practicable after the armistice has been declared in any of the wars now being waged, for the purpose of mobilizing the support of all lands in the making of a peace consonant with Christian principles.[16]

Dulles became the natural choice to chair the commission because, by this time, he was the principle layperson associated with the Federal Council.[17] His impressive work had gained support among leaders of both the interventionist and noninterventionist factions of the church. Therefore, his leadership could provide the council with the unified front it needed in order to make a significant contribution to the attainment of a just and durable peace.

Dulles' work as chair of the commission has been described by those who worked with him as "masterly" and "effective," one of "tremendous zeal and concern."[18] On several occasions, he hid out with four or five members of the commission at his home on Long Island and spent the entire day discussing issues that he or someone else formulated. The commission's membership included Reinhold Niebuhr, John C. Bennett, William E. Hocking, John McNeill, Charles Clayton Morrison, John R. Mott, and Harry Emerson Fosdick, among others.[19]

One of the major documents to emerge from the Dulles Commission was initiated by a resolution from the Greater New York Federation of Churches dated 28 March 1941. Submitted to the Federal Council's Executive Committee, the resolution requested that a study be made by "the ablest possible individuals" that would set forth the "basic principles which the consensus of Christendom would feel should be the foundation of any peace emerging from this war."[20] Formulating principles of this kind meant answering several prerequisite theological questions: "What are the implications of what Jesus said for finding the meaning of history?" "Does God control history?" "How and when does God intervene?"

Dulles felt very strongly that there was something definitive in the life and teaching of Christ to be applied to the practical affairs of human beings. On this basis, he felt driven to make the transcendence of God and the moral law relevant to society as a whole. For Dulles, the only good theology was one that, through practical application, made a difference in the quality of life for human beings. He wanted the commission to make sense of belief in God and in God's moral law so that its pertinence to peace questions could be clearly understood by all. Dulles and the rest of the commission set themselves to the completion of this task. The final product is a good example of Dulles's personal public theology.[21]

The "Statement of Guiding Principles," issued in late February of 1942, was adopted by the Cleveland biennial meeting of the Federal Council in December.[22] The preamble to the "Guiding Principles" explains the logic behind their formulation.

> From [their] faith Christians derive the ethical principles upon which world order must be based. These principles, however, seem to us to be among those which men of goodwill everywhere may be expected to recognize as part of the moral law. In this we rejoice.[23]

The guiding principles themselves were summarized in the Federal Council Bulletin. They clearly express the beliefs of the Reformed theological tradition.

> Moral law undergirds our world; disregard of the moral law brings affliction; revenge and retaliation bring no relief, we must find a way to bring into ordered harmony the interdependent life of the nations; this

requires that economic resources be looked upon as a trust to promote the general welfare; also, because the world is living, and, therefore, changing, there must be ways of effecting peaceful change; colonial governments too, must be administered in the interests of the colonial peoples; military establishments should be internationally controlled; there must be personal freedoms and liberties, without discrimination against nation, race or class; the power of the United States carries with it a special responsibility which we have neglected; a supreme responsibility rests upon the church of Christ; Christians should, as citizens, seek to translate their beliefs into realities; they must seek that the Kingdom of the world become the Kingdom of Christ.[24]

In the Executive Committee meeting of the Federal Council of 23 January 1943, Dulles stated that guiding principles four through nine should be given a new form, "changed from a 'credo' to policies which people can support."[25] Before the next Executive Committee meeting, Dulles formulated what was originally titled "A Just and Durable Peace: Statement of Political Propositions." The title that became famous along with the statement was "The Six Pillars of Peace."

On 16 March, the Executive Committee gave "hearty approval" to the six pillars and adopted the statement on behalf of the Federal Council.[26] The primary objective of the statement was "to provide thinking and action along realistic lines" by "outlining six areas within which national interdependence is demonstrated, and where, accordingly, international collaboration needs to be organized."[27] The substance of the six pillars called for (1) continuing Allied collaboration after the war, collaboration which was to include as soon as possible the neutral and enemy nations; (2) provision for international economic agreements; (3) treaty structures that would be adaptable to changing conditions; (4) assurances of autonomy for subject peoples; (5) control of military establishments; and (6) recognition "in principle" of the right to religious and intellectual liberty for peoples everywhere.[28]

Dulles's hoped these six principles would force recognition that, in at least these six areas, the world had become factually interdependent and had demonstrated the need for political mechanisms that would insure cooperative action. In the cover letter accompanying the first mailing of the statement to all commission members, Dulles wrote that the "nation has now entered upon the critical period where public opinion must be crystallized in favor of organized international collaboration."[29] He feared that the United States would once again walk to the trough of international cooperation but, at the last minute, refuse to drink.

The real contribution of the document, and the reason it was described by Niebuhr as one of those "increasingly realistic" statements made by the commission, lay in its ability to provide a middle road for divergent viewpoints.[30] In an editorial published in Christianity and Crisis, Henry P. Van Dusen explained how this aspect of the statement was valuable.

> But its greater importance lies in the fact that, in our judgment, it furnishes the briefest, clearest and soundest agenda for post-war order which has yet been forthcoming from any source, within or outside the churches.... Thus it stakes a middle course between the two main schools of thought on the organization of peace—those who espouse a single over-all instrument of world order and those who favor a policy of "muddling through" by piecemeal solutions of separate problems.... The Commission's political propositions offer median ground with some hope of winning adherences from both parties.[31]

Besides working on the educational front through printed materials, the commission also sponsored three study conferences centering upon particular aspects of the proposed peace. Of these, two were held for national church leaders and one was convened for international church leaders.[32] The third of these conferences, held in Cleveland during January 1945, addressed both the Dumbarton Oaks proposals and the Bretton Woods agreement. The United States government, probably through Secretary of State Edward Stettinius (a fellow Presbyterian and friend of Dulles), officially requested Dulles's commission to deal with these proposals.[33]

Dulles's work at Cleveland was an important contribution in that it helped to steer the thought of the Protestant church leaders in a more realistic direction. The conference, under his leadership, focused its attention on the relation between Christian purposes and practical politics. As the Federal Council Bulletin reported after the conference, "The churches must constantly seek to maintain a careful balance between prophecy on the one hand and the support of practical achievable results on the other."[34] The final "Message" of the conference stated the same concern in a slightly different manner.

> At all times Christians must keep the ultimate goals clearly in view but they have equal responsibility to mark out attainable steps toward these goals, and to support them. An idealism which will not accept the discipline of the achievable may lose its power for good and ultimately lend aid to forces with whose purpose it cannot agree.[35]

In effect, the "Message" stated that the Dumbarton Oaks proposals were not good enough to satisfy the churches, but they were good enough to support as "an important step in the direction of world cooperation."[36]

The results of the Cleveland Conference provide important evidence that the Protestant churches were not guided by a naive idealism; rather, here they were exhibiting a pragmatic understanding of realistic issues. Indeed, these were church leaders who, at Cleveland, were able to avoid the ever-present temptation to personify either of the two poles Reinhold Niebuhr defined as Christian moralism and Political Pharisaism.

> A final contribution of the Christian faith is its understanding of the relative, partial and partly corrupt character of all human standards of justice. We must seek justice according to our best human insights; but all these insights contain elements of positive corruption.... The Christian moralists will have nothing to do with such a peace because of the taint of sin which will be upon it. But the Political Pharisees (and all political morality tends toward Pharisaeism [sic]) will call it a righteous and just peace and will accentuate the injustices in it because they will have no contrite recognition of the corruption which their own egotism has introduced into it.[37]

The success of the Commission to Study a Just and Durable Peace in fulfilling the original directives assigned to it by the Federal Council is impressive. Much of the credit for this accomplishment belongs to John Foster Dulles. As Bennett asserts, "It was a Dulles Commission."[38] Dulles's understanding of the "complexity of international affairs" led the church to the middle position of calling for a new international order "with effective but limited powers."[39] He was one of the first Americans of this time to call for such an organization and, through the work of the commission, one of the most influential in promulgating the idea. Frederick Nolde, a fellow church leader known for his consistent realism in political matters, commented that, concerning world order, "what Dulles was after at the time was revolutionary."[40] John C. Bennett described Dulles's contribution to the concept of a realistic limited world organization:

> I've always said that I thought that it's very interesting that the American churches never went in heavily for world government, because of the influence of Reinhold Niebuhr and John Foster Dulles. Niebuhr providing, perhaps, the broader rationale, but Dulles also having this intuitive sense of the way things developed, that they didn't develop by fiat ... it was a

rather empirical movement toward world order that rejected shortcuts, like world state—and, of course, he [Dulles] rejected all pacifist short cuts.... And the establishment of the United Nations itself, was a major goal. But I think the improvement of it and the perfecting of this kind of world order was also hoped for—not, as I say, in terms of some kind of panacea. The panacea had been pretty well discounted, as I say, by Dulles's influence and by Niebuhr's.[41]

Dulles' Worldview

The prophetic Protestantism of John Foster Dulles served as the standard by which he measured present events and developments. Yet this is not the same as saying that he expected historical attainments that would be equivalent to his vision of the ideal. He did believe, however, that it was important to point to present deficiencies in order to make progress toward the ideal.

During the years 1937-1945, Dulles devoted his capacity as a thinker to the task of defining a norm for international morality. Indeed, the problem of international morality represented a lifelong concern for Dulles. Yet the moralism he espoused in these years "was not the kind of hardened moralism that many...felt later on when he was dividing the free world from the slave world and so on."[42] Rather, it was a moralism that served as an ideal type embodied in what Dulles called the moral law. This particular brand of moralism had no concrete representative among the world of nations. Every nation falls short of recognizing and incorporating into its international policy the concept of "the universal brotherhood of man," which is the heart of the moral law.[43]

The Dulles Commission dealt with the moral law most explicitly in its "Statement of Guiding Principles." The first two principles are concerned directly with this subject.

> We believe that moral law, no less than physical law, undergirds our world. There is a moral order which is fundamental and eternal, and which is relevant to the corporate life of men and the ordering of society.
>
> We believe that the sickness and suffering which afflict our present society are proof of indifference to as well as direct violation of the moral law. All share in responsibility for the present evils. There is none who does not need forgiveness. A mood of genuine penitence is therefore demanded of us—individuals and nations alike.[44]

Throughout this period of his life, Dulles expressed an international ethic that is quite similar to H. Richard Niebuhr's description of cathekontic ethics, the ethics of the "fitting response." Niebuhr writes that such an ethic should find itself led by experiences to the

> notion of universal responsibility, that is, of a life of responses to action which is always qualified by our interpretation of the actions as taking place in a universe, and by the further understanding that there will be a response to our actions by representatives of universal community, or by the generalized other who is universal, or by an impartial spectator who regards our actions from a universal point of view, whose impartiality is that of loyalty to the universal cause.[45]

The fact that the leadership and population of each nation view their particular ideas as right, or universally applicable, constitutes the major obstacle to realizing a world of nations that will heed the moral law as the norm for international policymaking.[46]

On the one hand, Dulles asserted the existence of a universal moral law. The heart of the moral law, which all nations should heed, consisted of the recognition of humankind's interdependence and thus reflected ultimate concern for the general welfare of the human race. On the other hand, and equally important, Dulles urged all individuals, including those in political power, to realize that no single nation possessed ideals synonymous with the dictates of the moral law. "We must not be dogmatic," he told the messengers gathered at the 1945 Cleveland National Study Conference, "our particular ideals and sense of vital interest are not the only ones in the world."[47]

Dulles often emphasized that the nature of the politician's job required both a quest for power and a concern for the national interest. Dedication to the universal welfare of humankind strikes most politicians as an intrusion from the outside. At most, it can only be a secondary concern. "The political leaders of each nation, " wrote Dulles, "have, in law, a duty only to their own people. The welfare of others in no wise restricts what they may do."[48] However, the task of the individual citizen is different from that of the political leader. The American people—especially the Christian audiences he addressed—should, according to Dulles, try to press universal concerns on their political leaders. Thus, out of their mandate to serve the expressed needs of the people, political leaders might occasionally transcend normal behavior by including other than merely national concerns in their policy decisions.

Dulles, as an "internationalist" rather than an "isolationist" during this period, tried to pursue policy that was in the American national interest from within the context of attempting to understand the needs of the other peoples in the world. For him, such a position was one of "enlightened self-interest."[49] In assuming this posture, Dulles represented what Kenneth W. Thompson has described as the "realist" perspective in international affairs.

> International politics, as politics within national communities, is lived at the point of convergence of particular and universalistic interests. If this is something less than abstract love and justice, it is more than a totally self-centered narrow nationalism. Sometimes, in politics, as in life, enlightened self-interest is man's highest moral attainment.[50]

Out of this commitment to enlightened self-interest, Dulles did not attempt to cloak American concern for national interests with simple moralizing, as he was prone to do in later years. Rather, he argued that

> moral distinctions, though pleasing to those who draw them, are hard to sustain in fact, and I know of no historic reasons to justify our approaching these problems of international relations with the complacent assumption that we are party to a clashing of the forces of good and evil, and that solution is to be found in the moral regeneration of those who hold views contrary to our own.[51]

Dulles considered these aspects of national and international human affairs in *War, Peace and Change*, his first book (1939). His focus was on presenting the problem ("what is") and proposing the solution ("what ought to be"). Presenting this contrast occupied Dulles for most of his life, though his definition of the problem measurably changed after 1945.

The Problem: Understanding "What Is"

Human Nature. One of the most consistent themes expressed by Dulles throughout this period warned American Christians that "any human order is bound to be finite and fraught with evil."[52] Though Dulles rarely used the word "sin," he was highly cognizant of its existence in the context of international problems. He aptly described the heart of the problem when he wrote that "man is by nature selfish."

> Whenever life assumes a form which involves consciousness there is an awareness of needs and a desire to satisfy them. Selfishness in this sense is a basic human instinct.... The fact that human beings, all selfish, are in contact with each other inevitably brings dissatisfaction.[53]

Human selfishness, Dulles elaborated, is combined with a tendency toward "gregariousness." One's needs cannot be satisfied in isolation. Since the desire to satisfy selfish needs is a driving force in human nature, the desire for association with others who can satisfy those needs is overwhelming. Therefore, communities are formed. Human beings begin to meet the needs of their neighbors, not out of a spirit of self-sacrifice, but rather out of the expectation that their own personal needs will be met in return. One must be able, through personal contact, to see the gratification that results from personal action. That is why, wrote Dulles, "discontent beyond our ken is apt to be a matter of indifference."[54]

As the borders of one's community begin to solidify, one begins to see it as the only moral community. Thus, one group's dissatisfaction leads to a wish to acquire at another group's expense. Such forced acquisition is justified by the members of the acquiring community through reference to their perceived "righteous" standing. The selfishness of humanity comes through ever more dangerously as the selfishness and self-righteousness of the community.[55] In this way, the national deification process begins.

Nationalism. Dulles defined nationalism as "that form of patriotism which personifies the nation as a living being endowed with heroic qualities, who lives bravely and dangerously in a world of inferior, and even villainous, other nation personalities."[56] Why is the need to deify the state so enticing? Dulles believed that the explanation "lies in the failure of the churches to provide mankind with a loftier means of satisfying its spiritual cravings."[57] Human beings, according to Dulles, demand a creed through which they can achieve spiritual exaltation. Sounding like Freud, he expressed the following presupposition concerning human nature.

> Aware of his own finite character, and his inadequacies, man seeks self-exaltation by identification with some external cause or Being which appears more noble and more enduring than is he himself.[58]

Dulles differed from Freud in that he viewed this longing for self-exaltation as proof that human beings need to maintain a vital connection with God in order to become whole. Thus the search for identification with some higher entity should logically end in a relationship with God. However, "religious leaders have seemed unable to make vital and gripping the concept of God as revealed by Christ." Because of the decline of "vital" religion, "the false gods of nationalism have been imagined to fill the spiritual need which most men feel."[59] The state becomes "an incorporeal being endowed with perpetuity and possessed of qualities which seem noble and heroic."[60]

Not only did religious leadership encourage deification of the nation through failure to direct the spiritual cravings of the human race to God, but religious leaders, according to Dulles, were equally guilty of a far more serious charge: they identified righteousness with one or another national cause. "In many churches," Dulles told his listeners in 1939 at the United Christian Convention in Hartford, Connecticut, "the national flag and national anthem today replace the Christian symbols."[61]

As Dulles expressed it, the drift toward "rendering unto Caesar that which is God's" was disconcerting. Devotion to an ideal, coupled with willingness to sacrifice, is among the finest of human traits; however, warned Dulles, when the ideal itself is unworthy of such devotion, the sacrificial action should be considered dangerous.[62] Dulles urged the churches to educate themselves regarding the dangers of nationalism. "Too often, " he cautioned,

> spiritual and secular motives become unconsciously mixed, and it requires unusual practical experience to detect the pitfalls which the worldly constantly prepare to secure for themselves the appearance of church benediction.[63]

Throughout 1940 and 1941, Dulles consistently warned Christians to avoid the temptation of falling under the influence of political leaders who "seek to advance the national self-interest by identifying it with righteousness."[64] The "extraordinary parallelism between moral judgments and national self-interest" leads to an international policy that is offensive to other nations and only serves to endanger the peace.[65]

"What Ought To Be":
Suggesting a Solution for the Problem

In his years of close association with the ecumenical movement, Dulles attempted to do more than simply point out the obstacles to international peace. Dulles believed that, with proper education and direction, nations could begin to overcome these problems. In order for any solution to be effective, it must further the potentiality of bringing world nations together in a forum that would make the attainment of political solutions possible. Equally as important to Dulles was the concept of a world organization that would not try to perpetuate the status quo. "That," Dulles said, "would be stultifying." Therefore, part of a realistic assessment of world affairs must necessarily promote the need for orderly processes of change.[66]

In the vocabulary of Dulles, one of his most beloved phrases was "peaceful change." Peace, if it is to be lasting,

> must also take account of the fact that life is essentially dynamic, that change is inevitable, and that transformations are bound to occur violently unless they are provided ways of peaceful change.[67]

In his thinking concerning the concept of peaceful change, Dulles found his inspiration in the writings of the French philosopher and Nobel Prize winner, Henri Bergson. Echoing the illustrious French philosopher under whom he once studied, Dulles came to view all reality as being in a constant state of flux.[68] While he was associated with the churches, Dulles consistently expressed his conviction that the static forces of the world needed to give some satisfaction to the dynamic forces of the world. In other words, the satisfied nations would need to learn to live with a certain degree of insecurity.[69] "Change," he asserted,

> is the one thing which cannot be permanently prevented and the effort to perpetuate that which has become artificial will inevitably break the person or nation committed thereto.[70]

The commission's Guiding Principle "Number Six" expressed the same idea in yet another way: "Nor must it be forgotten that refusal to assent to needed change may be as immoral as the attempt by violent means to force such a change."[71]

Dulles acted on the assumption that "the demand for change at its inception is generally moderate and largely justifiable."[72] This caused him to exhibit a sincere concern for the rights of the inhabitants of what is now referred to as the Third World. He was one of the few public leaders calling attention to the poverty and economic distress of that area. Furthermore, Dulles insisted that the political leadership of the satisfied nations recognize the legitimacy of the dynamic impulse and become willing to accept the change that accompanies it. One of the realities demanding change is that in several parts of the world the population is larger than the natural resources readily accessible for that population. This unfortunate circumstance was due largely to the fact that "the natural bounties which God has provided for the benefit of mankind are not apportioned in accordance with the national boundaries which man has drawn."[73]

In order to "reconcile" peacefully the "different interests and different ideals" of their nations, international political leaders must realize that negotiation "is not a process of coercion but of reason."[74] Dulles de-emphasized the use of force as a solvent to world problems. He openly disagreed with Secretary of the Navy Frank Knox and others who believed that peace consisted in having with England the power to coerce the rest of the world. This kind of alliance "would be bound to the maintenance of the status quo."[75] To the poorer nations, "a federation of the so-called democracies would ... appear as the banding together of the well-to-do." There could be "nothing more hopeless, more sure to fail."[76] A world police force of the sort that Secretary Knox proposed would only "create great antagonisms throughout the rest of.the world."[77] Dulles opposed having the United States or any world power playing such a role.

The ultimate goal of the political solution, and thus the task of political leadership, is that of "striking a fair balance between static and dynamic, to prevent the growth of violent tendencies on the part of great numbers."[78] In order for this goal to become a reality, a flexible "body of international law adequate to settle or dissipate the political, economic and ideological strains" among nations must be developed. Naturally, international cooperation must precede the development of a flexible body of international law. Thus the formation of some kind of international organization is an integral part of the political solution.[79] In this context, every nation's ideals and goals would be subject to the checks and balances of an international organization that, as a result, might contribute in a more meaningful way to finding fairer solutions to the world's problems.

This concern was uppermost in Dulles's mind as he prepared to attend the United Nations Organization Conference in San Francisco in 1945 as a legal adviser for the American negotiating team. Dulles hoped to see the development of an international organization dedicated to bringing the nations together in an atmosphere where tough negotiation and compromise might become a reality between national sovereignties hoping to get what they perceived as necessary for their security and economic interests. On this point, Dulles's position is illustrative of the heart of realism in general.[80] Yet, Dulles's realistic approach had its own characteristic emphases.

The Prophetic Realism of John Foster Dulles

The complex prophetic realism of John Foster Dulles, during these years, is best summarized by breaking it down into at least three basic realistic observations. Each of these observations served as the foundation upon which Dulles constructed a corresponding prophetic dimension in order to remind hearers who were self-righteous and complacent that they had not "arrived" yet. The three realistic observations, along with their respective prophetic dimensions, really form an integrated whole. Each depends upon and clarifies the others; no one of them stands alone. Together, they form the philosophical framework for Dulles's commitment to cooperation among nations in international relations.

The first component of Dulles's realism arose from his recognition that nations, in their foreign affairs, act out of concern for their own national interests. Every good government is expected to protect what it perceives as the best interests of the nation it is appointed to serve. Most nations are not anxious to recognize obligations beyond their own interests. Political leaders are mainly concerned with pursuing those that seem to safeguard the particular interests of the country they serve.[81]

The prophetic expression accompanying this first realistic observation advised political leaders and their constituencies to avoid the temptation to cloak pragmatic and essentially selfish actions with moral pretense.[82] Since all foreign policies naturally arise out of selfish concerns, moral pretenses are unnecessary, even dangerous. They can only lead to an unhealthy self-righteousness that inevitably results in feelings of hostility and distrust among other nations affected by such policies. Such feelings, in turn, result in foreign actions and attitudes that pose a new threat to the national interest.[83] Dulles expressed in this regard a belief very similar to the Niebuhrian concept of the dualism in humankind. Good and evil are present in every person, and much more present in every nation. Therefore, self-righteousness is synonymous with hypocrisy.[84] The world is populated by people who are both good and evil, not by people who are good and people who are evil. The latter dichotomy is false. During the war years, Dulles emphasized that peace involved more than merely defeating one's enemies. The unfortunate conditions, out of which people tending toward evil emerge, needed strong emphasis. Merely eradicating the people who are victimized by destructive conditions could not be viewed as a final solution.

Occasionally, generally perceived moral principles happen to coincide with the national interests. On such occasions policies emerge from what Dulles referred to as "enlightened self-interest."[85] These rare occurrences should be recognized as the highest attainment for a nation's policies. However, such recognition should be given with full understanding that national interest, not moral commitment, was the determining factor in formulating the particular policy in question.

Though the role of the political leadership in any given country is dictated by a dedication to national-interest considerations, Dulles equally emphasized the prophetic need for a country's general population to press universal concerns upon its government. Such an expression might force government leaders more actively to seek policies where national-interest considerations will coincide with internationalist concerns. Policies born from such a coincidence serve to increase trust among nations and improve the potential for future concurrence between national interest and moral principle.[86]

The fact that leaders from each nation act out of concern for particular national interests naturally leads to the conclusion that no one nation's policies are synonymous with the moral law. This realization constitutes Dulles's second realistic observation. During his tenure with the churches, Dulles maintained that national policies were rarely either right or wrong. International relations were much too complex to be grasped by such a simple approach. No nation is ever entirely righteous or pure in its policies since national-interest considerations are inherently selfish.

Based on this observation, Dulles repeatedly emphasized his prophetic belief that each nation's foreign policy ultimately should be judged by something outside itself. For Dulles, the moral law was the ultimate judge standing over and above each nation's policies. Rooted in God, its concern was universalistic. Every individual nation must be held accountable for activities that affect the world community. Thus, each nation's policies must be subjected to realistic, objective standards.

This involved granting that, national interests aside, no nation possessed the inherent right to act with impunity. Nations periodically need to be reminded of the universality and interdependence of humanity. During the late 1930s and early 1940s, Dulles struck just such a prophetic note.

Dulles's third realistic observation naturally follows from the first two. Since nations are motivated by national interests, and since no one nation can completely embody the moral law in its policies, it follows that the interests of one nation will quite often conflict with the interests of other nations. Dulles, therefore, consistently stressed the need for balancing the competing interests of nations. No nation embodies absolute truth; therefore, international relations should foster temporary coalitions among nations and encourage each nation to choose between the lesser of two evils in particular situations.

For Dulles, the United Nations could not play the role of a world government with the power to enforce one system of values at the expense of other systems of values; rather, he hoped it would provide the forum wherein competing value systems could negotiate differences, each acting as a check or balance against the others. Peace for the world depends upon such a check and balance system, argued Dulles, simply because national political leaders are primarily concerned with the extension of power, either for themselves or for their nations. Due to the selfish nature of existence, Dulles fervently pressed for the development of the United Nations. Out of hard-fought compromise and accommodation among nations, he hoped there might arise a sense of trust and a system of values that nations could begin to hold in common.[87]

Based on this realistic understanding of the complex world of nations and their competing value systems, Dulles again emphasized a prophetic corollary: Christians, he said, must be willing to accept practical situations that fall short of their ideals. He feared that the power of Christian idealism might thwart American acceptance of a meaningful role in a new world organization. Thus, as particularly exemplified by the Cleveland National Study Conference, Dulles and his commission actively worked to counteract such idealism.

These three couplets of realistic observation and prophetic expression provided the theological grist from which Dulles ground out his worldview from 1937 to 1945. His experience in international affairs and the respect he earned as a thinker among the religious leaders of the Federal Council of Churches enabled him to make a significant impact on the political thinking of the churches during those eight years.

Conclusion

Anyone who lived through the Eisenhower presidency, and who paid any attention to the conduct of foreign affairs during the seven years

John Foster Dulles headed the State Department, might legitimately wonder, given the picture painted of the man thus far, what happened to the realist? The John Foster Dulles who was secretary of state is best remembered for his moralistic and self-righteous conduct of foreign affairs. The realism of these earlier years was seemingly absent.

Likewise, the prophetic dimension of his speech, which reminded America that God judges as well as shapes a nation, gave way to a more priestly style. The early Dulles's transcendent God was replaced by God "the friendly neighbor" who was on the side of Americans in the struggle between good (democracy) and evil (Communism). In the words of a contemporary observer, A. Roy Eckardt, penned in late 1954, "the God of judgment [had] died."[88] What caused his demise?

Immediately after World War II, Americans were experiencing unprecedented affluence and international prestige. Then, suddenly, Americans were faced with the Cold War. Former allies had become enemies. Such changes require interpreters. Dulles, increasingly involved as a leader in civil affairs, became one of the major leaders interpreting new events for an alarmed and worried public. In the process of fulfilling that role, Dulles's personal philosophy underwent a transformation.

The religious reasons behind his change are most certainly rooted in the practical questions raised by Soviet behavior. As Dulles sought answers to the many crises that developed in the post-war world, he consistently confronted the antireligious, clearly materialistic, nature of the Soviet Union. The more he studied this particular dimension of Soviet ideology, the more he became convinced that the Soviets were bent on the destruction of all religious expression. Since, for Dulles, commitment to the moral law was a religious commitment, he came to view Soviet attacks on religion as direct attacks on the moral law. Conversely, since the United States defended religious expression and religious freedom, he came to understand American policy as a defense of the moral law.

This process of reasoning led Dulles, borrowing John Smylie's terminology, to merge the traditional purpose of the church with the purpose of the nation. In the face of the very real crises of post-1945, America assumed the role of God's redemptive agent in the world.[89] This process was made easier by the way Dulles analyzed Soviet behavior. The Soviet dedication to antireligious materialism made American commitment to religious principles seem pale by comparison. He developed a renewed appreciation for the religious heritage of the American republic – a heritage that seemed to have resulted from the permeation of Christian principles in the democratic institutions of American government. Since he viewed the principles as the primary foundation for American democratic institutions, Dulles saw no contradiction in his developing identification between the moral law and American policies.

In an important way, the Cold War acted as a revelatory event for America. Dulles's reaction to it exemplifies its impact. He saw in its development a new incarnation of the will of God for the world. It revealed God's purposes for the nation and provided the nation with a clear mission to fulfill in much the same way as the American Revolution did. As Dulles interpreted this revelatory event, he used it to call for American rededication to the fulfillment of this mission. Soviet behavior caused Americans to take stock of themselves and particularly caused Dulles to call for spiritual revival in America. He called Americans to return to faith in God and in democratic institutions as instruments of the divine will. The power of the Soviet threat was a reminder to Americans of their general tendency to take American institutions for granted and a warning about where such apathy might lead them.

History always tends to be a harsh judge. From the perspective of nearly sixty years later, it is always easy to criticize. Church leaders like Reinhold Niebuhr and John C. Bennett certainly maintained their prophetic and realistic voices in the Cold War era, but they had possessed a solid and studied theological grounding that Dulles lacked. Dulles's quest for an ideal world beyond the present one should not, in itself, be faulted. His commitment to bringing that world into being showed dedication and sacrifice. Yet from the point of view of prophetic Protestantism, during the years after World War II, Dulles failed to distinguish between the universal he sought and the policies of the country he served.

His ideological expressions as secretary of state were more than merely his way of providing window dressing for an otherwise conventional approach to world events. Indeed, his moralistic rhetoric, though occasionally embellished for political effect, fundamentally revealed the true nature of the man behind it: a determined Calvinist who was transformed as events led him to translate his tradition's long-held belief in the reality of a moral universe into a belief in the moral virtue of his own nation. Thus, as John Foster Dulles assumed the office of secretary of state, his new vision of the task ahead resembled the earlier perspective of Josiah Strong, who once wrote: "Not America for America's sake; but America for the World's sake."[90]

Notes

[1] Dulles's father, Allen Macy Dulles, was a liberal Presbyterian minister who was greatly influenced by the Social Gospel movement. For an accounting of how early religious influences in the home affected John Foster Dulles, see Toulouse, *The Transformation of John Foster Dulles: From Prophet of Realism to Priest of Nationalism* (Macon: Mercer University Press, 1985): 3-26.

[2] John W. Foster served as the forty-ninth secretary of state under Benjamin Harrison, 1892-1893. Robert Lansing, the only Democrat in the Republican clan, served as the fifty-seventh secretary of state under Woodrow Wilson, from 1915-1920.

[3] Van Dusen noted that Niebuhr and Dulles "had a great respect for each other.... I don't think that we felt, in the context in which we saw him, that Dulles was conservative at all. I would say he was a moderate liberal.... Among his closest legal colleagues, he was regarded as, if not a radical, a liberal" (Henry P. Van Dusen, interview, 41,43 – the transcripts of all interviews cited are part of The John Foster Dulles Oral History Collection housed along with the Dulles Papers at Princeton University as part of the Seeley G. Mudd Manuscript Library. All transcripts have been read and approved by the interviewees. Interviews cited hereafter were conducted by Richard Challener in 1965 unless otherwise indicated).

[4] See Toulouse, *Transformation of John Foster Dulles*, chapters 8-10, for an accounting of this change.

[5] According to Tillich, the Protestant principle "is the theological expression of the true relation between the unconditional and the conditioned or, religiously speaking, between God and man.... It is the guardian against the attempts of the finite and conditioned to usurp the place of the unconditional in thinking and acting." See Paul Tillich, *The Protestant Era*, abr. ed. (Chicago: The University of Chicago Press, Phoenix Books, 1957): 163. This Protestant principle is also referred to as the "prophetic protest" of Protestantism (see ibid., 230).

[6] John Foster Dulles, "The Problem of Peace in a Dynamic World, " *Religion in Life* 6 (Spring 1937): 207.

[7] Dulles discusses the influence of the conference upon him in each of the following addresses: "As Seen by a Layman," *Religion in Life* 7 (Winter 1938); "The Churches' Contribution Toward a Warless World," *Religion in Life* 9 (Winter 1940); and "The Churches and World Order," and "Faith of Our Fathers," --both these essays are published in *The Spiritual Legacy of John Foster Dulles,* ed. Henry P. Van Dusen (Philadelphia: The Westminster Press, 1960). See also *Federal Council Bulletin* 24 (January 1941): 6. Both Lillias Dulles Hinshaw and Avery Dulles, his daughter and son, emphasize the impact of Oxford upon his life. See their respective interviews in the Oral History Collection. E. Raymond Platig, in his dissertation, goes so far as to view

Dulles's involvement with the churches after Oxford as the result of a recent "conversion" to Christianity. According to Platig, this conversion was a natural outgrowth of Dulles's previous commitment to a utilitarian ethic. Dulles became a professing Christian, writes Platig, because after Oxford he came to feel that "Christianity was socially useful" (see E. Raymond Platig, "John Foster Dulles: A Study of His Political and Moral Thought Prior to 1953 with Special Emphasis on International Relations" [dissertation, University of Chicago, 1957]: 130). Platig's terminology is insufficient; it dismisses the sincerity of Dulles's previous religious attachments.

[8] John C. Bennett, interview, 22.

[9] John Foster Dulles, "As Seen by a Layman," 18-19, 22. See also "The Churches' Role in Developing the Bases of a Just and Durable Peace," 16, 28 May 1941, p. 8, Dulles Papers housed at Princeton University (hereafter DP), Box 20. "I am anxious that the remainder of my life shall more effectively serve the cause of international peace than has the past. Therefore, I have increasingly sought the fellowship of Christians, believing that practical results can best be achieved by the cooperation of those who possess the spiritual qualities Christ taught."

[10] John Foster Dulles to W. W. Van Kirk, 13 June 1940, DP, Box 19.

[11] This statement is not to be confused with another by the same title that was released on 22 January 1940 over the signatures of several churchmen including Dulles.

[12] For further information, see *Federal Council Bulletin* 24 (January 1941); *Biennial Report of the Federal Council of the Churches of Christ in America* (1940) (hereafter referred to as *Biennial Report*); and "Policy during the War Urged on Churches, " *New York Times* (11 December 1940).

[13] *Federal Council Bulletin* 23 (January 1940): 2.

[14] The phrase, "a just and durable peace, " was Dulles's. On 16 November 1943, upon request of the commission, a vote was taken to change the name to read simply "Commission on a Just and Durable Peace" *(Annual Report of the Federal Council of the Churches of Christ in America* (1943): 153. Hereafter referred to as *Annual Report).*

[15] Representatives from each of the following bodies were "invited to become members of the commission: the International Council of Religious Education, the Foreign Missions Conference of North America, the Home Mission Councils, the National Council of Church Women and the United Stewardship Council, the Church Peace Union and the World Alliance for International Friendship through the Churches." *Biennial Report* (1941): 214.

[16] *Annual Report* (1941): 94.

[17] Richard Fagley, interview conducted by Richard D. Challener, 1964, 27.

[18] Richard Fagley, interview, 35; and John C. Bennett, interview, 4. Roswell Barnes, interview conducted by Philip A. Crowl, 11.

[19] Ronald W. Pruessen mistakenly stated that the commission eventually had "several hundred members." In actuality, its membership never exceeded one

hundred. He is evidently confusing participants at National Study Conferences with actual members of the commission. See Ronald W. Pruessen, *John Foster Dulles: The Road to Power* (New York: The Free Press, 1982).

[20] *Annual Report* (1941): 122.

[21] On the general question of whether the whole of the commission's work accurately represented Dulles's own thinking, Cavert said, "I would hazard the guess that they [commission statements] weren't very far from expressing the main trend of Dulles's own thinking.... He really looked to some of the other people - the more theologically trained people - to formulate what you might call the specifically religious approach, but he was always watching not to let them get sentimental or superidealistic. He wanted them to have their feet on the ground" (Samuel McCrea Cavert, interview, 18-19*).*

[22] This is contrary to Mulder's statement that the principles were issued for the first time with the six pillars in 1943 (John Mulder, "The Moral World of John Foster Dulles," *Journal of Presbyterian History* 49 (Summer 1971): 170). The *Christian Century* commented on the "Guiding Principles" statement in the following manner: "We hope most of all that the substance and significance of this document may be borne in on those who head the government of the United States, for it speaks a word which they can ignore only at the nation's peril." "The Churches and the Peace," *Christian Century* 59 (18 March 1942): 342.

[23] *Biennial Report* (1942): 42.

[24] "The study "Conference on the Bases of Peace," *Federal Council Bulletin* 25 (April 1942): 9.

[25] *"Annual Report* (1943): 97.

[26] *Annual Report* (1943): 108. Richard Gould-Adams on p. 42 in his *The Time of Power: Reappraisal of John Foster Dulles* (New York: Appleton-Century-Crofts, 1962) incorrectly dates the six pillars as being issued in 1941 as a response to the Atlantic Charter. Gould-Adams is thinking of the "Long Range Peace Objectives. " The six pillars were not written as a response to the Atlantic Charter. They appeared close to one and a half years after that document.

[27] John Foster Dulles, "Six Pillars of Peace, " *Christianity and Crisis* 3 (31 May 1943): 5.

[28] When Roosevelt read the "in principle" part of the six pillars, he quipped that he could see that the Dulles group had given the statement a great deal of thought. (Memorandum, 26 March 1943, DP, Box 22).

[29] John Foster Dulles, Letter to the commission membership, 12 March 1943, DP, Box 22.

[30] Reinhold Niebuhr, "American Power and World Responsibility," *Christianity and Crisis* 3 (5 April 1943): 4.

[31] Henry P. Van Dusen, "The Six Pillars of Peace," *Christianity and Crisis* 3 (22 March 1943): 1.

[32] For details describing these conferences, see Toulouse, *The Transformation of John Foster Dulles*, 72-82.

[33] John Foster Dulles, "America's Role in the Peace, " *Christianity and Crisis* 4 (22 January 1945): 2. Also published under the title "Collaboration Must Be Practical, " *Vital Speeches of the Day* 9 (1 February 1945): 246-49, and under the title "Ideals Are Not Enough," *International Conciliation* no. 409 (March 1945): 131-41.

[34] *Federal Council Bulletin* 28 (February 1945): 3.

[35] "Cleveland Conference on a Just and Durable Peace," *Federal Council Bulletin* 28 (February 1945): 6.

[36] See John C. Bennett, "Editorial Notes," *Christianity and Crisis* 5 (5 March 1945): 2.

[37] Reinhold Niebuhr "The Christian Perspective on the World Crisis " *Christianity and Crisis* 4 (1 May 1944): 5.

[38] Van Dusen, interview, 11; Cavert, interview, 17. Bennett remembers that Dulles "didn't polarize things as much in regard to the war as he did later with regards to communism" (Bennett, interview, 4; see also 11).

[39] "Mulder, "The Moral World," 176. Here Mulder very astutely understands the importance of Dulles's contribution in this area.

[40] Frederick Nolde, interview, 9. For secular recognition of Dulles's commission and its contribution, see the following: Robert Divine, *Second Chance: The Triumph of Internationalism in America during World War II* (New York: Atheneum, 1967): 252ff. and idem, *Foreign Policy and the United States Presidential Elections, 1940-48* (New York: New Viewpoints, 1974): 91-92. Cordell Hull, *The Memoirs of Cordell Hull* (New York: Macmillan Company, 1948): 1625-26. "Truman and Dulles Exchange Letters, " *Post War World 3* (15 December 1945): 2: "If today we Americans have a clearer understanding of our place in world community - as I believe we have - it is due, in no small part, to the churches' advanced position in international thinking taken by the Federal Council" (Letter, President Truman to John Foster Dulles, 6 November 1945).

[41] Bennett, interview, 4-5, 11; see also Barnes, interview, conducted by Philip A. Crowl, 21.

[42] John C. Bennett, interview, 11. Earlier in the interview, Bennett stated the following: "And I want to keep saying that the same churchmen who had accepted him would have been very critical of the hardening tendencies that came later" (7).

[43] John Foster Dulles, "As Seen by a Layman," 41.

[44] John Foster Dulles, "Statement of Guiding Principles," *Biennial Report* (1942): 42-45. See also "Introductory Statement" in *A Just and Durable Peace: Statement of Political Proposition* (New York: Commission on a Just and Durable Peace [hereafter CJDP], 1943).

[45] H. Richard Niebuhr, *The Responsible Self. An Essay in Christian Moral Philosophy* (New York: Harper and Row, 1963): 88. Emphasis is that of Niebuhr.

[46] His first major written work, *War, Peace and Change* (New York: Harper and Brothers, 1939), published the year after the fall of Paris, resulted from devotion to these issues The editorial staff of *Christianity and Crisis*, made up of men like Reinhold Niebuhr and John C. Bennett, regarded the work as "an excellent analysis of the basic principles which must underlie a new world order." *Christianity and Crisis* 2 (23 February 1942): 7.

[47] John Foster Dulles, "America's Role in the Peace, " *Christianity and Crisis* 4 (22 January 1945): 5.

[48] John Foster Dulles, "Christianity in This Hour," 13, 21 April 1941, DP, Box 20; and "The Churches' Role in Developing the Bases of a just and Durable Peace," 16, 28 May 1941, DP, Box 20. See also John Foster Dulles, *War, Peace and Change*, 117-118, where he explains that there are "valid reasons" for such a mandate: "It is a sound principle of international practice which bids each nation avoid interference with the internal affairs of another."

[49] This was one of his favorite expressions. See, for example, *The Six Pillars of Peace: A Study Guide* (New York: The Commission on a Just and Durable Peace,. 1943): 30. For a particular example of how he applied this idea to policy, see John Foster Dulles to Hamilton Fish Armstrong, 18 March 1940, DP, Box 19.

[50] Kenneth W. Thompson, *Ethics, Functionalism, and Power in International Politics: The Crisis in Values* (Baton Rouge: Louisiana State University Press, 1979): 22.

[51] Quoted in Pruessen, *The Road to Power*, 102, this excerpt is from an address entitled "The Relation of France to a Program of World Reconstruction," undated, but probably in 1924. See also John Foster Dulles to L. L. Summers, 5 January 1921, DP, Box 4.

[52] John Foster Dulles, "Christianity: Solvent of World Conflict," *Social Progress* 33 (January 1943): 5. See also the widely circulated statement that was presented to the Atlantic City biennial meeting of the Federal Council, where Dulles admonished Christians never to fail "to remember that all human institutions are finite and prone to error." ("The American Churches and the International Situation," 3, 19 December 1940, DP, Box 19.) Still another example of his awareness concerning this issue may be found in John Foster Dulles, "A Christian World Hope, " *The Presbyterian Tribune* 60 (November 1944): 3. John Mulder commented that Dulles's "speeches to church groups and his statements as chairman of the Commission rarely contained references to sin." Mulder pointed out that "Dulles never seemed to comprehend Niebuhr's insistence on the ambiguity involved in all ethical decisions, the dimension of finitude and fallibility in all human institutions, and the degree of self-interest, self-preservation, and self-righteousness implicit in every exercise of power." When this statement is used to describe the Dulles who emerged

after 1945, its truth is verifiable. However, when used in the context of his work with the churches, as Mulder used it, the description proves somewhat inaccurate. John Mulder, "The Moral World of John Foster Dulles," 180. See also Townsend Hoopes, *The Devil and John Foster Dulles* (Boston: Little, Brown and Company, 1973): 35.

[53] John Foster Dulles, *War, Peace and Change*, 52, 6-7.
[54] Ibid., 17.
[55] The ideas expressed in this regard are quite similar to those of Reinhold Niebuhr, *Moral Man and Immoral Society* (New York: Charles Scribner's Sons, 1932).
[56] John Foster Dulles, *War, Peace and Change*, 57-58.
[57] John Foster Dulles, "The Churches' Contribution toward a Warless World, " *Religion in Life* 9 (Winter 1940): 38.
[58] John Foster Dulles, *War, Peace and Change*, 6.
[59] John Foster Dulles, "The Churches' Contribution," 38. See also John Foster Dulles, *War, Peace and Change*, 64.
[60] John Foster Dulles, *War, Peace and Change*, 114-15.
[61] John Foster Dulles, "The Churches' Contribution, " 39. See also John Foster Dulles, "As Seen by a Layman," 37.
[62] John Foster Dulles, *War, Peace and Change*, 117.
[63] John Foster Dulles, "As Seen by a Layman," 43.
[64] John Foster Dulles, Statement, 8 April 1940, DP, Box 19.
[65] John Foster Dulles, "United States and World of Nations," 14, 27 February 1940, DP, Box 19.
[66] John Foster Dulles, "Appraisal of United States Foreign Policy," 9, 5 February 1945, DP, Box 27.
[67] John Foster Dulles, "Peaceful Change," International Conciliation no. 369 (April 1941): 493.
[68] One can find the basis for much of what Dulles wrote concerning change in Henri Bergson, *Creative Evolution,* trans. Arthur Mitchell (New York: Henry Holt and Company, 1911).
[69] Ibid., 30-33.
[70] Letter, John Foster Dulles to Thomas M. Debevoise, 30 April 1940, DP, Box 19.
[71] John Foster Dulles, "Statement of Guiding Principles, " 44. See also, "The American Churches and the International Situation," 19 December 1940, DP, Box 19.
[72] John Foster Dulles, *War, Peace and Change,* 144.
[73] John Foster Dulles, "The Problem of Peace in a Dynamic World, " *Religion in Life* 6 (Spring 1937): 192.
[74] John Foster Dulles, "Our Vital Peace Decision," *Vital Speeches of the Day* 12 (15 October 1945): 7.
[75] John Foster Dulles, "Long Range Peace Objectives," 4, 18 September 1941, DP, Box 20.

[76] Letter, John Foster Dulles to Under Secretary of State Sumner Welles, 24 July 1941, DP, Box 20.
[77] Letter, John Foster Dulles to Reverend Bradford S. Abernethy, 15 October 1941, DP, Box 20.
[78] John Foster Dulles, *War, Peace and Change,* 32.
[79] Ibid., 151.
[80] For a detailed analysis of Dulles's role in San Francisco, see Toulouse, *The Transformation of John Foster Dulles,* ch. 7.
[81] See John Foster Dulles, "Christianity in This Hour," 13, 21 April 1941, DP, Box 20; "Churches' Role in Developing the Bases of a Just and Durable Peace," 16, 28 May DP, Box 20; and John Foster Dulles, *War, Peace and Change,* 117-18.
[82] See, for example, "Article for the *New York Times Sunday Magazine,"* 7 August 1945, DP, Box 26; to F. Earnest Johnson, 16 April 1941, DP, Box 20; John Foster Dulles, "United States and the World of Nations, " 14, 27 February 1940, DP, Box 19; John Foster Dulles to Henry S. Coffin, 20 May 1940, DP, Box 19.
[83] John Foster Dulles, "United States and World of Nations," 14.
[84] John Foster Dulles to Henry P. Van Dusen, 18 March 1940, DP, Box 19. See Reinhold Niebuhr, *Moral Man and Immoral Society: A Study in Ethics and Society* (New York: Charles Scribner's Sons, 1932).
[85] See John Foster Dulles, *Six Pillars of Peace: A Study Guide Based on "A Statement of Political Propositions"* ed. with an intro. by John Foster Dulles (New York: Commission to Study the Bases of a Just and Durable Peace, 1943): 30; and John Foster Dulles to Hamilton Fish Armstrong, 18 March 1940, DP, Box 19.
[86] See, for example, John Foster Dulles, "As Seen by a Layman, " *Religion in Life* 7 (Winter 1938): 18-22; "The Problem of Peace in a Dynamic World," *Religion in Life* 6 (Spring 1937): 207; "The Churches' Contribution toward a Warless World," *Religion in Life* 9 (Winter 1940): 31; "Christianity in This Hour," 21-22.
[87] See John Foster Dulles, "Our Vital Peace Decision," *Vital Speeches of the Day* 12 (15 October 1945): 7.
[88] A. Roy Eckardt, "The New Look in American Piety," *Christian Century* 71 (17 November 1954): 1396.
[89] John E. Smylie, "National Ethos and the Church," *Theology Today* 20 (October 1963): 313-21.
[90] Josiah Strong, *Our Country: Its Possible Future and Its Present Crisis* (New York: Baker and Taylor, 1885): 218.

Chapter 4

Herbert Butterfield and the Limits of Christian Realism

Malcolm R. Thorp

Herbert Butterfield is viewed as one of the most important Christian realists of the Cold War period. He was a proponent of power politics and balance of power. Yet he was also concerned about morality in the relations among nations and he thought that Christianity had something unique to offer in international affairs. As he stated, "I cannot accept the self-interest of a nation as the final objective for either an individual or a people." And, he continued, "we should do our thinking (even in I[nternationa] R[elations]) with the idea in mind that "nothing save human souls really counts or really exists in the world."[1] Certainly his position on morality (as we will see) is not entirely in keeping with mainstream realist thought. Indeed, while many of Butterfield's views do fit into discussions with other Christian realists, there are issues where he appears to be outside the pale of such, thus raising the issue of boundaries between realism and moralism in international affairs.

Any analysis of Butterfield's position on Christianity and international affairs must begin with his views on human nature. In addition to his scholarly career as Professor of Modern European History at Cambridge University, Butterfield was a life-long Methodist and, for many years a local preacher in the Cambridge area. Butterfield came to believe that man's nature was sinful; Butterfield believed as a result of the Fall of Man, human nature was defective.[2] From this primeval event, mankind acquired defective wills, thus resulting in the perpetuation throughout the generations of a propensity towards egotism and self-righteousness, a situation affecting not only individuals but also groups and nations. As he stated the case, human nature was "built on the side of a volcano," and therefore needed to be kept in check by the countervailing forces of civilization at all times. But, in spite of durations of relative peace and tranquility, efforts to keep egotism in check inevitably breakdown. Hence the human family has been subjected to a recurring series of predicaments where the worst aspects of our nature at least momentarily triumph over the good. Thus there can be no long lasting stability in human relations. Butterfield said:

> No matter what the period in which we find ourselves there is a sense in which life is the same — every generation has to rescue the world from the sins and errors of its predecessors, and every generation seems to have the feeling that it will be lucky if it can just keep its head above water. Providence puts the human race in a certain predicament and virtually says to all of us 'See it you can find your way out of that'.[3]

The realities of the human predicament made it absolutely imperative that mankind learn to cooperate with Providence. To him, the world is a place for soul making, where individuals have the freedom of choice to shape their eternal destinies.[4] Butterfield believed that history takes place in a field in which every action has a moral significance.[5] Thus, "In Him we live and move and have our being."[6] It is necessary for individuals to choose the right and live in accordance with the divine will. Still it is individuals who make these choices, and history as we know it is shaped by their actions, either for the good, or for evil.

One of Butterfield's most distinctive insights was the idea that the history of the ancient Hebrews was fundamentally of the same texture as our own.[7] "That is the history of a nation whose stories of violence and conflict, treachery and war, or worldliness and cupidity, could be told just like the story of any other nation."[8] Key to this perspective is the idea of a promise offering greater things to the human family. He describes the role of God among the ancient Hebrews as an extremely close and intimate relationship:

> Conceiving of God as a person who was very close to them, very closely involved in human affairs, they walked with him, they conversed with him, they wrestled with him on ethical issues, sometimes with frankness that is quite startling. Above all, they established an intimacy with him, realised him as a spirit, knew that he was inside them, and that if you plunged to the depths of the ocean you would find him there as well. It is this God who exists in the very inwardness of things that we have to have in mind when we

think of God in history.[9]

Yet, the tragedy of history has always been our deviation from the promise. Butterfield's perspective was always based on the notion of human free will, and our responsibility for creating the past.[10] To him, we cannot blame Providence for the misfortunes that we have constantly created from the beginning of human history.

Thus, Butterfield believed we always make our own history through the choices we make, leading to both exceptional creative achievements, but also unfortunately to carnage and destruction. But God is nevertheless directly involved in human events, breaking into the story as the divine judge, convicting us of our sins and shortcomings, but at the same time offering us a new and ever greater promise of a better and renewed life out of the tragedies of our past. As Butterfield stated, the greatest insight into human history was God's presence in the story of mankind, fulfilling the promise, "but fulfilling it at a higher attitude than men had in mind."[11] "The crucial issue," to Butterfield, "concerns the God who can be a Presence, for in the depths of us he stands as the voice of conscience within us; he speaks to us in our loneliness and may rescue us from the dominion of past sins. He draws us to a higher righteousness and the New Testament ideal of love."[12] Thus the role of Providence is to convict men of their sins, to win them over, and to free men from the slavery to their past. God is always with the process of events, even though Butterfield was insistent about human responsibility for the tragedies of the past.

But, although Butterfield identified with the Old Testament view of the Promise, he also incorporated a New Testament perspective into his views. Obviously he was convinced through his experiences in life that the human family is under divine guidance, not chance happenings. Thus, "the ultimate faith is the belief that all things will have a final reconciliation —a final share in the redemptive purpose of Christ."[13] In one of his most moving passages he outlines the meaning of New Testament love to the historical process: "...the spectacle of Christian humility, the knowledge of forgiveness of sins—furthermore, the astonishing power of these things and the way they came to be vindicated over long periods of history—are like something supernatural imposed on the whole drama."[14] The purpose of the historical process since the Resurrection continues to be the same: "He [Christ] has a project to convict men of sin, to win them from their sins, to take away the burden of them, and free men from slavery to their own past."[15] God is love and, like a leaven comes to influence the course of worldly events in ways that we mortals cannot totally fathom.[16]

Because of the human predicament, however, cooperation with

Providence also meant efforts to keep human cupidity in check. There must be the use of force for maintaining order and stability in both domestic and international affairs. As a young man, Butterfield was shocked by the actions of normal, law-abiding citizens in 1919 during a policemen's strike in Liverpool. With the forces of law and order absent, citizens resorted to looting and a myriad of other crimes that would not have happened if policeman had been present. This incident was important in shaping his attitude towards the realities of power and the need to keep human excesses under control with at least some element of force.[17] At the same time, however, he believed that there needed to be a balance between force and the ethical order. Power should not be excessive to the point where human values were suppressed by brutal and unreasonable use of force.

It is significant that Butterfield lived through many of the dark periods of the twentieth century. As a young student, he witnessed the disasters of trench warfare on the western front during the first World War. At Cambridge University in the 1920s, he studied under the diplomatic historian, Harold Temperley, who was an outspoken critic of the 1919 peace settlement at Versailles. Butterfield shared his views, and decried the failure of the great powers to reestablish a viable international order following the defeat of Germany.[18] Many of the new leaders of Europe lacked substantive education in diplomacy and were prone to accept utopian visions of a peaceful world without considerations of power. Butterfield wrote about the misapprehensions of statesmen in 1919, which to him reflected how imperfectly the political experience had been handed down by that generation of statesmen. Some generalities about diplomacy and balance of power were transmitted, but "construed as empty banalities because the inner knowledge had been lacking."[19] Instead, the leading nations attempted to prevent future calamities through unilateral disarmament and, in some cases isolationism, thus leaving a power vacuum which was instrumental in the rise of ruthless dictators who were not committed to maintaining peace and stability, such as Mussolini, Stalin and Hitler.

Butterfield couched his opposition to Hitler as a form of barbarity that put him outside of the international order. He did not want to use the term "evil," to describe Nazi brutality, but rather he saw the dictators as a threat to civilized values.[20] Even after Hitler's rise, Butterfield believed that western statesmen failed to create countervailing systems of power to counteract the huge buildup of arms by the dictators in the late 1930s.

While asserting that he was "almost a pacifist," Butterfield supported efforts to destroy Nazi power in Europe because of the inhumane aspects of Nazi tyranny that he saw as a threat to Western values. Nor did he think Stalinist Russia to be morally much better than the Nazis. Both the Soviet system under Stalin and the tyranny of the Nazis were seen by Butterfield as evidence of the breakdown of civilization and the re-emergence of barbarism in Europe, not unlike what the world experienced with the breakdown of the Roman Empire.[21] Nor did the defeat of Nazi Germany and Japan lead to an end to barbaric atrocities, as the world plunged into Cold War conflict, which in turn lead to new conflicts, such as the Korean conflict and the Vietnam war. This latter development Butterfield opposed as the arrogance of US power.

Thus Butterfield commented on the *general* tendencies in world events throughout his life, which he saw in a mixture of both secular and religious terms, but he often omitted *specific* incidents in his analysis. For instance, Butterfield wrote little about the Holocaust, perhaps the worst episode in the modern world with the systematic, scientific extermination of at least six million people. His only comment was that, out of the horrors of World War II (like the pattern of the Old Testament) came the rebirth of the nation of Israel. In his analysis, God had made the best possible end to tragedy, given the reality of the human predicament.[22]

Science vs. Morality

After enduring the two major wars of the twentieth century, Butterfield concluded that the deadliest features of modern warfare were "the hatred, the viciousness, the refusal to compromise" that reached the level of threatening the very fabric of civilization as we know it.[23] Out of this fear, coupled with his historical interest in diplomacy—especially in eighteenth century Europe—Butterfield came to develop his position on how conflicts could at least be reduced, if not entirely eliminated.

"I always pleaded," Butterfield asserted, " for a 'scientific' rather than a 'moralistic' attitude to international affairs...I want to see the reassertion of the traditional Old World handling of these matters (the development of a quasi-scientific treatment inaugurated in the eighteenth century)."[24] What did Butterfield mean by a "quasi-scientific" approach? "There is a point in discovering what I shall call "laws" even when these are true only in the conditional sense—true, for example, with the provision "other things being equal." It is something to be able to discern such laws even if they are valid only as representing a tendency or a bias in events—a factor which the wise politician will therefore want to take into account.[25]

Butterfield believed there are certain historical tendencies in the pattern of events that can enable scholars to think about political and historical developments on a higher level than otherwise would be the case. Out of such reflections might come the unfolding of historical laws or postulates that would be useful in shaping the future course of affairs.

Butterfield developed a series of such postulates that he thought applicable to shaping policies among nations. One factor that appeared to Butterfield to be a "scientific" premise was the dangerous aspect of power in international affairs. "Power," he postulated, "will not consent to be a mere instrument. It acquires purposes of its own. It certainly tends to corrupt. It turns politics into the exercise of will." This premise applies to all situations where power is exercised; there is always to potential for abuse even in democracies, political majorities or churches.[26]

To him, the aim of diplomacy is to provide a *modus vivendi*, the maintenance of an international order such as will allow the higher objects of life to be decided by the play of reason and the voice of public opinion.[27] This is something that does not come naturally, but requires, he believed, methodical thinking, the readiness to pursue problems beyond the realm of rough common sense, and the determination not to be excluded by moralistic prejudices from the analysis of anything relating to the establishment of a stable system of power. He believed in balance of power as the only viable approach to establishing an international order where 'rights' among nations might be maintained, which is the best that can be offered given his disbelief in the possibility of an ultimate system of international justice. Within the system of order created by the balance of power all systems, creeds and ideologies would be properly embraced.[28]

Butterfield contended that there are only two choices available—world empire (such as Rome) or balance of power. Because of the containment of human liberty and possibilities of tyranny, no statesman has advocated a return to conditions found under Rome. Consequently, balance of power and the sense of an international community are important for maintaining order in the world.

In 1945 the realities of power were too obvious to be ignored. He feared a state system that represented two vast agglomerations of technological power confronting one another with little capacity for human understanding.[29] Moreover, from early in the Cold War he came to fear the arrogance of power on the part of the United States as much as Soviet aggrandizement. Over time, he saw the possibility of Russia moderating her posture, but he feared that the Americans were too caught up in a Cold War crusade against Communism.[30] Indeed, Butterfield exhibited a life-long fear of systems of power based on ideological conflict because each side tended to view its adversary as a great mass of evil. It is better, he averred, to cast diplomacy within the perspective of concrete issues of power rather than ideological concerns. Thus, to him, Communism was not the real enemy, rather it was Russian aggression.[31]

Cold War balance of power had its own difficulties. An equilibrium established between two super-states is the most intense but also most precarious form that the balance of power can assume. Irrespective of this consideration, the former apostles of such a system came to attach some importance to the establishment of subordinate regional balances. They would have regarded the freedom of European states as more secure today if there had also been a balance within the compass of the continent itself.[32] Fearing U.S. domination, Butterfield suggested that a regional system with the ability to cooperate with America, perhaps like NATO, could veto actions that were not deemed in the interest of the balance of power system, thus providing greater stability for Europeans and the world.

Another "quasi-scientific" premise that Butterfield deduced from his historical studies was the idea that "more than anything else, fear is the cause of war."[33] Butterfield used a number of examples to demonstrate how fear created an atmosphere where politicians were caught up into an almost inescapable predicament in which real issues became secondary to the uncertainty and the suspicions produced at the time of crisis. According to Butterfield, one of the clearest examples of how fear led to predicament was the outbreak of the civil war in England in 1642. In using this example, he was not interested in the political and constitutional issues that had initially motivated tensions between King Charles I and Parliament. Instead, Butterfield urged that we focus attention on the actual crisis that resulted in the outbreak of war. What mattered was that the situation in early 1642 had deteriorated to the point that the royalists and the parliamentarians stood in hostile opposition to each other, with both sides being driven to the brink of war by fear, willfulness, and misunderstanding. Butterfield likened the situation to a Chinese puzzle, complete with interlocking pieces: "Each [side] beset by the devils of fear and suspicion...and each side locked into its own system of self righteousness." In this atmosphere of despair, both of the contending factions lost sight of the issues that originally produced the crisis, and were driven irrationally into doing battle with their "wicked opponents." Hence, Butterfield wrote that it takes a historian to come later and "tell the poor royalists and roundheads what they were fighting about in the first place." Butterfield also asserted that the issue of personality—in this case that of Charles I—has little to do with the predicament. The "goodness or badness" of the king was nothing more than a "fringe issue" that is of little consequence to the actual dynamics of the predicament. To Butterfield, the real issue was how fear came to motivate both sides to the extent that they were incapable of rationally analyzing the crisis and finding avenues of compromise.[34]

But does Butterfield really provide "scientific" insight into the origins of conflict? Insight, perhaps, that would enable practitioners of international affairs to develop meaningful precepts that might lead to crisis management in times of potential conflict? Most historians would dismiss his contention that the English Civil War in 1642 was the result of irrational fears on both sides which prevented the resort to last minute diplomacy. Nor would they argue that issues and personalities were unimportant to an understanding of the actual breakdown. Moreover, most historians would not agree with his example of the diplomatic stalemate in July 1914, where (according to him) war resulted from an inescapable predicament when politicians on all sides somehow lost sight of the issues and were consumed by irrational impulses to the extent that war came to be the only avenue of escape.[35] To view conflict from the model provided by Butterfield tends to distort the historicity of the actual circumstances and, curiously enough (given to his premise that it is individuals who make history) causes us to lose sight of the complicated nature of human behavior. The best that we can say of Butterfield's ideas on the predicament is that fear, as he has described it, might be an element in some patterns of conflict, but it not a recurring phenomenon that would give us "quasi-scientific" insight necessary for us to assume that "all else being equal" conflicts will invariably produce a dominion of fear.

In a more limited sense, perhaps, Butterfield's adage that armaments race have potential for unintended consequences (because they create an escalation of fear and insecurity) has some useful application, although this is certainly not a new or "scientific" idea. In such a situations of elevated tensions caused by armaments races, tensions can dramatically increase, but usually this does not in itself produce war. Thus his views on fear merit some consideration, in spite of the fact that he did not really provide a covering law for either students of international relations or historians.

If Butterfield's "scientific" approach has only limited application, are his views on morality and politics perhaps more useful? Butterfield decried the influence of idealists in international affairs and believed the best statesmen were educated practitioners well trained in the historical realities of power who could see the realities of power and avoid ideological excesses. Butterfield favored men who were hard boiled practitioners, seasoned by deep, insightful understanding of the past as well as practical experience in the management of power. Real statesmanship requires the ability to hold in one's mind a jungle of relevant details, yet also be able to understand complicated issues. Such a person needs to have an education rich in humanistic and historical understanding. Too often, however, he thought that it was possible to produce a kind of political man who seems to have no inside, no depth of humanity or internal life.³⁶

Kenneth Thompson, one of the leading commentators on Butterfield's views on international affairs, echoed Butterfield's position, arguing that foreign policies put forth by religious people too often became entangled with patriotic fervor and vested interests and hence come to represent absolute truth. Such people's knowledge and skill levels are usually far behind that of professional diplomats.³⁷ While Thompson certainly echoes Butterfield's position here, a problem with his analysis, is that Butterfield certainly believed in inserting religious values into international affairs. Foreign policy, as Thompson fails to show, is never morally neutral. Moreover, if diplomacy is the art of compromise and reconciliation, then one's values as a Christian most certainly should be manifested in the political process.³⁸

According to Alberto Coll, in another important study on Butterfield, the higher the statesman's moral idealism the more likely he was to claim moral sanctity for his politics and decry the alleged immorality of those who oppose him. "Men who claimed to be the bearers of absolute morality in politics, a Woodrow Wilson or a Gladstone, fell prey to self-righteousness more readily than those statesmen, such as Churchill and Richelieu, whose regard for the moral law was accompanied by the knowledge that their own hands and purposes were inevitably soiled in the rough-and-tumble of the political world." In another passage, Coll writes that "No political cause, however noble, could succeed without the use understanding of power no quest for power, however unscrupulous, could achieve lasting results without at least a tacit appeal to moral justification."³⁹

But is Butterfield's view on power less realistic than Coll admits? In a real way, Butterfield shies away from a strictly realist posture with his fundamental distrust of power. To be sure it is a useful instrument to keep human cupidity in check, it is a necessary evil. But his message is that we should always be suspicious of power. Hence, as Vice Chancellor of Cambridge University, Butterfield was always glad of the sixty miles that separated the university from the politicians in Westminster. Butterfield was prone to attack the arrogance of all political and ecclesiastical institutions. Thus, my quibble with both Coll and Thompson is subtle but important for a Christian understanding of the issue. Butterfield wrote that "Charity requires of us a vivid appreciation of the needs and predicaments of other men. It is incumbent upon us to have compassion for all human being and to see them apart from the organizations and systems in which they are imprisoned. Even religion, he warned, can become "degraded into the service of vested interests and strategic considerations.⁴⁰

To be sure, religion can produce self-righteousness that hardens into inflexible idealism. Butterfield wrote extensively about this problem: "When I hear some men talk of a special political ethic ... or a separate political morality, I cannot fit this anywhere into my thinking, nor do I understand for a moment what it means."⁴¹ Like other realists, Butterfield believed that the choices we make are more often than not between actions that are either less moral or more moral. Most political decisions must take into account the grey areas of human behavior and make assessments on the best alternatives for all parties concerned. Moreover, as Butterfield contended, realistically the "morality" of states can best be achieved when it is allied with self-interest. On the other hand, "In any country and any period there will be idealists who ignore the limiting conditions and to be in almost standing opposition to the practitioners of international politics." Such people may, he averred, raise the standard of human behavior, but they fail as statesmen."⁴² Still, spiritual ideals and the western doctrine of liberty and our high valuation of personality offered an important opportunity to change the course of the Cold War. "At the moment," he wrote at the height of the Cold War, "it is respect to our ideals rather than our armaments that we are found wanting."⁴³

Morality is not one thing for the statesman and another thing for the rest of mankind. There is no such thing as a separate political ethic. Butterfield said:

> The statesman, like the professor or the poet, will constantly be confronted by the alternative between an act that is more moral and another that is less moral; but we can hardly admit of any fundamental difference between the quality of the decision in these cases, or the ethical principles involved. And in particular I don't see why in politics the virtues which I associate with the Christian religion should be suspended—humility, charity, self-judgment and the acceptance of the problem Providence sets before one; also a disposition not to direct affairs as a sovereign will in the world but to make one's action a form of co-operation with Providence.⁴⁴

To be sure, statesmen, poets, university professors and ministers must all (on occasion) must make decisions not necessarily between absolute good and evil, but between lesser evils or partial good. Still, there is a morality involved in such decisions that cannot be denied.⁴⁵ "We should do our thinking (even in international relations) with the idea in mind that "nothing save human souls really counts or really exists in this world."⁴⁶ Obviously this posture is a moral one that certainly raises questions about extolling the virtues of practitioners of *realpolitik*, such as Richelieu, Frederick the Great, or a Bismarck, as if the decisions they made could somehow be justified by a political reality devoid of moral imperatives.

While moral considerations are admitted by Butterfield to be valid in the field of politics, at the very heart of his approach was the idea of self-righteousness. This requires considerable introspection in order to avoid being pharisaical. It is best to ask if we ourselves may be wrong in some of our considerations. It is necessary to put ourselves in the shoes of the other party, trying to see our opponent's case the best we can, better than he is even able to make for himself. Thus, Butterfield argued, in foreign affairs, "I don't see why (at the highest level of our thinking at least) the theological virtues of humility and charity should be suspended. And the real negation of both politics and diplomacy (as well as religion) is to say that our view shall prevail, whatever it costs the world." The condemnation of other human beings in the political arena is certainly problematic where our judgments are so gravely intertwined with our own self-interests, thus often blinding our efforts to comprehend the reality of issues at hand.[47]

While such a position in theory is admirable and might apply to virtually all aspects of human relations, in practice few of us mere mortals might have conquered the ways of the world necessary for the proper application of such saintly conduct. Regardless of such failings, however, the real issue presented for our consideration is its implication for international realism. Such an admonition might really have been more fitting for a Gladstone with his religious view of politics and commitment to moral imperatives rather than the secular idols of the realists, such as Richelieu, Bismarck and Churchill. What I am suggesting here is that if one is committed to Christian realism, as Butterfield most certainly was, then one could certainly find more appropriate historical examples to exemplify the virtues of this position than provided by Butterfield, Thompson or Coll.

"Just War" and the Nuclear Dilemma

One area of Butterfield's thought that has received little attention are his studies on Grotius and the Just War theoreticians of the early modern period. In spite of his contention that he was nearly a pacifist, Butterfield conceded that under certain conditions Christians were justified in taking up arms. These included self-defense and defending the interests of the weak against the over mighty. Furthermore, in certain situations, Christians can resort to limited wars in defense of the international order.[48]

Following the arguments laid out by Hugo Grotius, Butterfield contended that international theory since the sixteenth century has recognized that victims of aggression, when waging war in self-defense, are on a different moral plain than their assailant. Butterfield went one step further by stating that under certain conditions Christians can fight to right a wrong, but never to punish sin. What he meant was there must be a definable moral reason for going to war, not simply because we believe the enemy to be evil.

In all situations leading to potential war, however, Butterfield said that nations considering the justness of war should stand back from the issues and consider the good of the entire world. The vindication of the rights of a single country is justifiable only if it serves to secure the better establishment of the whole system of rights for all countries. Nevertheless, borrowing from the theory of Vittoria, he gave credence to the concept that a war that is just and lawful in its own right might be unlawful because of collateral circumstances. Greater evils should not come out of the war than the evils which the war was intended to avert. War can only be morally justified if such conflicts result in limited collateral damage to civilian populations. At the conclusion of such hostilities, "Just War" theorists such as Pufendorf argued that the power winning a "Just War" might rightfully take steps to rectify the original injustice that led to war, and even demand more guarantees to prevent future aggression. On all occasions, however, as Seneca stated, "Man is not to use man prodigally"—destruction of the enemy is not the justified purpose of conflict.[49]

Butterfield's view on the role of force in international affairs was clearly circumscribed. Building on the ideas of the early modern theorists of Just War, Butterfield argued that a moderate use of force might be justified on grounds that the refusal to do so might create a situation in which tensions increased to the point of creating a colossal explosion.[50] He feared the freezing of the status quo if every resort to force was considered taboo. Consequently, the use of force might be used in order to prevent the much greater use of force. A moderate use of force might even be justified on grounds that the refusal to do so might create a situation in which tensions could increase to the point of creating a colossal explosion.[51]

When considering the issue of human rights, Butterfield argued that it was certainly true that the severities imposed on mankind by insensitive governments—especially by revolutionary elites and those determined to impose superiority over racial and ethnic minorities—may be particularly revolting by western standards. Nevertheless, governments, both past and present, have been prone to use such situations as pretexts for going to war, while their real aim was self-aggrandizement. Butterfield's approach, however, offered no immediate hope for the amelioration of racial and ethnic difficulties created by "insensitive governments," excepting what might be achieved through the normal diplomatic process.⁵²

In other situations involving human rights, Butterfield discussed the principle of "abstention," a principle attached to Just War theory which involves a careful consideration of the consequences of actions and the possibility of non-resolution due to the collateral damage that might occur through direct intervention to solve such issues. Butterfield asserted that "abstention" might be said to promote the good of mankind and allow the rectification of odious conditions over a long period of time and avoid the problems associated with direct intervention in an effort to solve human rights violations. Butterfield reminds us that wars or punitive military action to rectify wrongs tend to produce more human suffering than the evil they attempt to eradicate. Still he does lay open the possibility of calculated action. Thus he did condone the possible use of force to resolve such issues if it can be shown that such actions do not promote undue suffering among the weak and defenseless. His position also suggests the possibility of sanctions (economic and political) against powers that are in gross violation of human rights. But, he also suggested that the approach of applying sanctions to eradicate human rights violations has traditionally been ineffective, if not disastrous.⁵³

Nonetheless, Butterfield was not willing to go beyond this position that supported limited actions in favor of eliminating human rights violations. His views, we have seen, were clearly motivated by his approach toward Just War and the possibility that more harm could be done by direct action than through quiet diplomacy and the possibility that over time issues could be resolved short of war. On the other hand, we have also demonstrated that Butterfield believed that the Nazi regime represented such a direct threat to human rights that war could not be avoided.

When it came to the issue of nuclear weapons, Butterfield was likewise influenced by Just War theory. From the beginning of the atomic age Butterfield was concerned about the bomb's potential for the destruction of civilization. Butterfield was not alone in this fear but, to him, the unlocking of the secrets of the atom for military purposes represented "the second fall of Adam." In a statement written in 1950, Butterfield asserted that the dropping of the atomic bombs on Japan had been a mistake.⁵⁴ He later reflected that he was especially disturbed by the way in which the atomic bomb was developed during the war. The impetus for creating such a terrible weapon moved with such momentum that it gave no time for human reflection on the consequences of the use of such weapons.⁵⁵

With the coming of the Cold War and development of the hydrogen bomb, as well as intercontinental ballistic missiles, Butterfield was fearful that both sides in the Cold War could be driven by what he referred to as the "dominion of fear." There is always the possibility that nuclear weapons can find their way into the hands of desperate men or morally bankrupt characters such as a Hitler. In such conditions nuclear weapons pose a danger to all sides of the spectrum, and there is the possibility of a disastrous war, maybe even leading to a nuclear winter and an end to civilization as we know it. This is an argument in favor of blocking nuclear proliferation. But still there is no certainly that in the future such potentially disastrous circumstances could become a reality.

Butterfield believed that in "normal" circumstances no rational leader would use such weapons. But he feared that even minor issues could escalate into potentially lethal conflicts due to the "dominion of fear." Butterfield hypothetically postulated that the Soviet bloc on the one hand and Western nations on the other were absolutely equal in virtue and the moral qualities of statesmen on both sides are reasonably high—perhaps not saints—but modestly virtuous men. Both sides were desirous that no harm should come to their nations and were moved by reasonable levels of national self-interest. "We will assume," continued Butterfield, that they have just those faults which men can have who feel themselves to be righteous and well-disposed—both sides anxious to avoid war, but each desperately unsure about the intentions of the other party; each beset by the devils of fear and suspicion, therefore; and each side locked into its own system of self-righteousness." Even though both sides might possess only ordinary amounts of human willfulness all of the ingredients could be present for a grand catastrophe. Through acute fear of what the other side might do, and the inability of both sides to resolve such tensions, it is possible that a preventative nuclear first strike could occur that would then engulf the world in a terrible holocaust.[56]

Butterfield's hypothesis, based on a moral reading of such a situation, is a possibility, albeit an extremely remote one. Still, in situations such as the Cuban missile crisis, there was the potential that thermalnuclear war could have resulted if last minute compromises had not lead to an easing of tensions. But, it could be argued, this is where the factor of the nuclear deterrent comes into play, making the possibility of massive retaliation such an important factor as neither side in a situation involving the "dominion of fear" would possibly ever consider the use of such weapons.

And, even then, rational men might balk at unleashing such a nuclear Armageddon by considering the welfare of the world above any issue of national self-interest.

Butterfield, however, continued to be concerned about the remote possibility that nuclear weapons could be used. From the Christian perspective of Just War, nuclear weapons will always produce immeasurably more harm than good and therefore are useless in any effort to rectify wrong. From this perspective there was no mundane objective, even the saving of civilization, that justified the infliction of so much destruction on innocent victims. Hence, a cause might well be just, but waging war could be unjust because of the indiscriminate methods of destruction that are employed. Theoreticians of Just War have clearly condemned the use of such warfare that would occur in a nuclear conflict: "It is time that we really faced the question whether the whole conception of judgment, and the whole idea of the vindication of righteousness, which are involved in this notion of nuclear war are consistent with Christian teachings."[57]

As a result, Butterfield first came out with the premise that nations of the Western world should announce that they would neither use the hydrogen bomb nor further manufacture any such weapons.[58] On this premise, Butterfield agreed to publish a pamphlet entitled, "Human Nature and the Dominion of Fear," for the Campaign for Nuclear Disarmament (CND) in 1962. Early on in the CND campaign Butterfield participated in various Christian action groups in Cambridge, and was at least nominally associated with the local CND activities surrounding the abolition of nuclear weapons. In the 1964 parliamentary elections, the CND was a vocal minority group in the hustings campaigns. By then, however, Butterfield had disavowed the political tactics of the CND, such as large organized public protests at Trafalgar Square and elsewhere as well as orchestrated media campaigns aimed at convincing the British public of the dangers of nuclear weapons. Instead, Butterfield came to see the most viable approach for a Christian simply to bear witness:

> When I contemplate the New Testament and then consider the question of actually dropping the hydrogen bomb for any mundane purpose whatsoever —or indeed, of course, for any supra-mundane purpose—I ask myself whether I ought not to cut through those centuries of subtlety, those fabulous chains of reasoning of the kind which have led both to persecution and the theory that we can escape historical responsibility for it.[59]

Thus, Butterfield concluded that Christians faced with this particular evil in the world ought to look back to first principles (i.e., concepts of New Testament love toward our fellow man) and then simply bear witness to the world of these principles. This, he thought, might have a lasting effect on the world.

As he probed into the problem of nuclear weapons, his convictions led him even further. In a letter to the Reverend John Stacey on 11 April 1963 Butterfield asserted his belief that a nation, such as Great Britain, ought to suffer whatever the other party (i.e. the Soviets) may do, even suffering the effects of megaton bombs without retaliation, the guilt being, he contended in sending the bomb, not in receiving it. Furthermore, he stated that such a nation should accept all the consequences that would follow from the losing of such a war. In other words, there would be no resistance to the aggressor, simply submission to the reality of the situation.[60] As Butterfield clarified his position, he asserted:

> It is not legitimate for him [the Christian] to argue that by unilateral action of this kind his country will be reducing the risk of actual suffering or military defeat. Perhaps it would be a beautiful thing if a country which had the power to abjure the nuclear weapon would have all the risks and undertake that policy for the sake of an improvement this might produce in the world situation, a recovery of confidence.[61]

To accomplish this end Butterfield believed that a statesman of strong stature and integrity—perhaps a modern day Bismarck—was required, who could perhaps break the nuclear stalemate through adroit diplomacy, negotiating with the other side in good faith, showing the Soviets that nations of the West were taking a calculated risk for the benefit of mankind, a risk that ultimately would benefit the Communist world as well as the western democracies.

Butterfield recognized that the elimination of the deterrent factor might place a nation in such a position of inferiority that it would be unable to conduct a real kind of diplomacy if the other powers chose to keep their nuclear arsenals. Because weapons are used more often for diplomatic "pull" in negotiations, such a renunciation would be tantamount to giving up one's trump card in advance, thus risking the possibility of winning. Nonetheless he believed the risk worth taking: "I always thought that an avowed renunciation of the nuclear weapons might perhaps [allow] a chance to do good—just as being a great gesture of faith; but even this couldn't be the kind of thing on which one could go to one's fellow-citizens with a promise of immunity."[62]

Butterfield's approach to the nuclear stalemate might have some plausibility if confined to a single nation, say the United Kingdom. Such a country could develop conventional forces for limited military purposes and renounce (if this were really possible) deterrence within the nuclear umbrella, which, seemingly, Butterfield came to advocate. It is doubtful, however, if such an approach would have any impact whatsoever on the overall nuclear stalemate. By projecting oneself as a "suffering servant" for mankind on the issue of the abolition of nuclear weapons it is highly unlikely that such a denunciation would have any positive effect on convincing other nuclear nations to follow suit. Maurice Cowling trenchantly criticized Butterfield's approach: "It seems to me a sentimental perversity rather than an act of Christian initiative to suppose that the devil or the Russians would likely be affected by announcements of the sort that Butterfield was demanding."[63] Indeed few would agree with Butterfield's premise, "We will not bow to your gods, though you destroy us with the hydrogen bomb."[64] For our purposes, however, Butterfield's approach does look like old-fashioned moralism rather than hard-boiled realism. And, from the perspective of Just War, is it correct to place innocent civilians at risk by unilaterally denouncing the bomb when the idea of deterrence to create a stalemate could possibly lead to reduction and perhaps ultimate disarmament? But, we should also remember that Butterfield called the advent of nuclear weapons the "second fall of Adam" which means that nuclear knowledge will never disappear; there will always be a nuclear threat in the world. This in itself is a cogent argument in favor of nuclear diplomacy which can only occur in a situation in which all nations having such weapons are willing to negotiate for reductions.

The Limits of Christian Realism

One of the most intriguing questions concerning Butterfield's approach to international affairs is the issue of where were the limits of his views on Christian realism? To be sure, Butterfield argued in favor of a "scientific" approach to international affairs which involved the application of rules and dictums of statecraft largely taken from the eighteenth century masters of balance of power theory. Thus he believed the only viable way of creating a stable world was through the creation of an international order committed to maintaining balance of power arrangements. All competing powers within such a system would seek to uphold and maintain the system even if this meant modifying and restraining their individual concepts of self-interest. Moral issues and human rights, he believed, could best be achieved within a system of balance of power where competing concepts of morality can be recognized, and trade-off can be made without collapsing the system itself. Such a system could best be created and maintained by practical statesmen, such as a Bismarck, who would approach issues from the perspective of *realpolitik* rather than moral consideration. It is within such a system, he argued, that legitimate grievances could be best adjudicated without the resort to war.

While labeling himself a near pacifist, Butterfield recognized that force was necessary both in domestic and international affairs. He asserted that human nature, such as it was, must be put in check by force, and that even normal, law abiding citizens, as well as states, if not confronted with the possibility of force, often become worse than they otherwise would be. Yet Butterfield also believed, as we have seen, that the self-interest of a nation is never the final objective of politics. If we read Butterfield carefully we find that he always came back to New Testament concepts of love that he deemed all-important to the Christian. Thus Christians should constantly bear witness, not in an aggressive way by public rallies and protests over moral issues, but with the idea in mind that nothing save human souls really exists in this world. When Christians fail in their efforts to promote a better world, either because of entanglements of power or through materialism, they should always return to the first principles of the New Testament for revival and renewal.

The issue that causes the most difficulty when we consider Butterfield's position within the tradition of Christian realism, however, was his stance on nuclear weapons. From the early 1950s Butterfield came to the conclusion that nuclear weapons represented such a profound threat to civilization that it would be better for a nation, such as Great Britain, to unilaterally denounce such weapons, even if this mean suffering the horrors of the nuclear attack without retaliation or occupation by a nuclear nation through intimidation. There is no evidence, at least in Butterfield's voluminous papers, that he ever abandoned this position. Simply stated, the nuclear issue represented such a profound threat to civilization that he placed this issue in a special category by itself, outside the confines of his views on balance of power diplomacy. This is perhaps the only way to reconcile what is otherwise an incongruous aspect of his thought, although this is not so strange when we consider that he always thought in moral and ethical terms.

In final analysis, Butterfield's "scientific" approach to politics, coupled with his views on the need to keep human cupidity in check through constant application of power, establishes his credentials as a Christian realist. But at least some of his views do not clearly fit with others of realist camp. It could be argued, in spite of all that he said to the contrary, he was a moralist who viewed the world from this perspective. His deeply held views on the sanctity of the human personality led him to fear for the world that had succumbed to the "second fall" of Adam. Although he put his trust in Providence, he still believed that something should be done about this terrible dilemma. He was convinced that if Christians collectively put their minds together, along with their faith, maybe some way out could be found for the human family. While we might applaud

Butterfield's search for a solution, it would appear that he, like so many others (including Christian realists), have not been able to solve the problem that nuclear knowledge has beset upon the human family. Indeed, we might even speculate that nuclear proliferation since Butterfield's death in 1979 has put the world in even greater peril and that we are no closer today to an ultimate solution.

Notes

[1] Cambridge University Library. Butterfield Papers, Box 31, untitled, 14.

[2] For a discussion on his views concerning human nature, see Malcolm R. Thorp, "The Inescapable Predicament: Sir Herbert Butterfield's Views on the Human Dilemma," *Fides et Historia*, 16 (Fall, 1983): 7-17 and Malcolm R. Thorp, *Herbert Butterfield and the Reinterpretation of the Christian Historical Perspective*, Studies in Religion and Society, vol. 40 (Lampeter: Edwin Mellon Press, 1997): 99-119.

[3] Herbert Butterfield, "A Historian Looks at the World We Live in," *Religion in Education* 18 (1951): 43.

[4] Herbert Butterfield, *Christianity and History* (New York: Scribner's, 1950): 76.

[5] Butterfield, *Christianity and History*, 68.

[6] Cambridge University Library, Butterfield Papers, Box 92, "Christianity," Untitled, 27.

[7] Butterfield, "The Christian and the Biblical Interpretation of History," in C. T. McIntire, ed., *Writings on Christianity and History* (New York: Oxford University Press, 1979): 185.

[8] Butterfield, "God in History," in C. T. McIntyre, ed. *Herbert Butterfield Writings on Christianity and History* (New York: Oxford University Press, 1979): 16.

[9] Butterfield, "Originality of the Old Testament," in C. T. McIntyre, ed. *Herbert Butterfield Writings on Christianity and History* (New York: Oxford University Press, 1979): 94.

[10] Butterfield defined his position on history as the interplay of various forces: "I suspect that the play of human free will on one hand, the working of law in history on another hand, and - then, again - the operation of chance - are all embraced together in His Providence, the world and all its history lying in the hollow of his hand." Butterfield Papers, Box 66, "Papers on Christianity, Divine Judgment in History," 21.

[11] Butterfield, "God in History," in McIntire, 6-7.

[12] Butterfield Papers, Box 14, "Can Christian Thinking Make a Contribution to Any Age," Untitled, 1.

[13] Butterfield Papers, Box 92, "Christianity, typescript for Christmas number of *Methodist Recorder*, 3.

[14] Butterfield Papers, Box 92, "Christianity," Unpublished paper, "How the New Testament Has Influenced the Process of History," 8-9.

[15] Herbert Butterfield, "The Crucifixion in Human History," *British Weekly* 126 (6

April 1950).
[16] Butterfield presents a picture of "God presiding over this world of tumult and violence, of cupidity and fear, of struggle and cross-purposes - presiding over it and drawing upon it like a magnet, drawing men by the Lord of Love." Butterfield, *History and Human Relations*, 52.
[17] Herbert Butterfield, *Discontinuities between the Generations of History*. Rede Lecture, 1971 (London: Cambridge University Press, 1972): 24.
[18] Butterfield Papers, Box 15, "Rede Lecture," 16.
[19] Butterfield Papers, Box 15, "Rede Lecture," 16.
[20] See Butterfield Papers, Box 31, "Comments on Grotian Conception of Just War," 2, especially n. 2.
[21] According to Butterfield, "Many of the cruelties and the degradation of personality are at the same time a feature of what we have called modern barbarism, wherever the phenomenon may appear; and it is possible that there is no cure for this save peace and a continuity of development, during which men may grow in reasonableness. It is modern technique and organization, rather than any change in the quality of human nature - save, possibly such change as the technical developments themselves almost inevitably produce - which have altered the scale of atrocities in the modern world." Herbert Butterfield, *Christianity and History* (New York: Scribner's, 1950): 143-4.
[22] Butterfield, "God in History," in C. T. McIntyre, ed. *Herbert Butterfield Writings on Christianity and History* (New York: Oxford University Press, 1979): 8.
[23] Herbert Butterfield, *Christianity, Diplomacy and War* (London: Epworth, 1953): 26.
[24] Butterfield Papers, Box 18, "Rockefeller, Personal Material Retained," Letter to Peter Savigear, 16 February 1970.
[25] Herbert Butterfield, *International Conflict in the Twentieth Century: A Christian View* (London: Routledge and Kegan Paul, 1960): 52-3.
[26] Butterfield Papers, Box 80, Notebook, "From July 1968-", np.
[27] Butterfield Papers, Box 69, untitled, 23.
[28] Ibid, 78.
[29] Butterfield, "Reflections on Predicament," *Cambridge Journal* 1 (1949): 13.
[30] Butterfield Papers, Box 3, Moral Framework of International Relations, notebook.
[31] Butterfield Papers, Letter Box "T", Butterfield to Charles van Doren, 20 February 1952.
[32] Butterfield, "Morality and International Order," 351.
[33] Herbert Butterfield, *International Conflict in the Twentieth Century*, 89.
[34] See Thorp, *Butterfield*, 112-13.
[35] Butterfield Papers, Box 92, "Christianity," Paper for Christian Action, 5.
[36] Butterfield Papers, Box 69, Paper for BBC conference, 3.
[37] Kenneth W. Thompson, "The Transcendent and the Relative in Morality and Foreign Policy," in Kenneth Thompson, ed., *Herbert Butterfield: the Ethics of History and Politics* (Washington, D.C.: University Press of America, 1980): 115.

[38] Butterfield wrote: "Surely the field where we are continually forced back on the question: 'what is wrong with human beings?' is the field of international affairs. Christians have something to contribute here, because the factor which both sides are continually leaving out of account is the factor of self-righteousness - a problem with which the pagan ethic, however noble, seems particularly unfitted to deal." Butterfield Papers, Box 92, Christianity, Paper for Christian Action, 3-4.

[39] Alberto R. Coll, *The Wisdom of Statecraft: Sir Herbert Butterfield and the Philosophy of International Politics* (Durham: Duke University Press, 1985): 94 and passim.

[40] Thorp, *Butterfield*, 32.

[41] Butterfield Papers, Box 69, Rockefeller Foundation Paper, 1-2.

[42] Butterfield, "Morality and the International Order," 343.

[43] Butterfield Papers, Box 73, "Western Policy of Colonialism," 18.

[44] Butterfield Papers, Box 5, "Morality and the Historical Process in International Affairs," unpublished paper, 1-2, 33.

[45] According to Butterfield, "the condemnation of other human beings is particularly questionable in that political realm in which our judgments are so gravely entangled with our interests. Our problem in fact can only be brought under control if at the beginning of our argument we see ourselves involved in man's universal sin..." Butterfield Papers, Box 5, "Morality and the Historical Process in International Affairs," untitled, 8-9.

[46] Butterfield Papers, Box 31, "Comments on a Grotian Conception of Just War," 14.

[47] Butterfield Papers, Box 5, "Morality and the Historical Process in International Affairs," 33.

[48] Butterfield Papers, Box 2, "Just War."

[49] Butterfield Papers, Box 9, Christianity in European History, Revision "Christianity, Diplomacy and War," A3.

[50] Butterfield Papers, Box 31, Rockefeller Committee Reports, "Comments on ... Grotian Conception," 8.

[51] Ibid.

[52] He also realized that in a stalemate among superpowers both sides might prolong abuses because neither side gives primacy to justice. Seemingly he is admitting that this can be one of the weaknesses in balance of power theory. See Butterfield Papers, Box 92, "Christianity in European History," Paper for Christian Action meeting, 23 September 1959, 9.

[53] Butterfield Papers, Box 5, "Morality and the Historical Process in International Affairs," 35-36; Thorp, *Butterfield*, 169-70.

[54] Butterfield Papers, Letter File "S", Butterfield to H. W. Heckstall-Smith, 6 December 1950.

[55] Butterfield, *Human Nature and the Dominion of Fear, Christian CND pamphlet no. 3* (London: CND, 1962): 7.

[56] Herbert Butterfield, *History and Human Relations* (London: Collins, 1951): 18-19.

[57] Butterfield Papers, Box 9, Christianity, Unpublished paper for Christian Action

Meeting, 6-7.

[58] Butterfield, *Human Nature and the Dominion of Fear*.

[59] Butterfield Papers, Box 92, Paper for Christian Action, 2-3.

[60] Butterfield Papers, Letter Box "S".

[61] Butterfield Papers, Box 66, Papers on Christianity, "Christianity and International Relations," 26 December 1966.

[62] Butterfield Papers, Box 28, "Current Writings on Christianity," untitled.

[63] Maurice Cowling, *Religion and Public Doctrine* (Cambridge: Cambridge University Press, 1980): 249.

[64] Butterfield Papers, Box 9, Christianity in European History, "Revision of Christianity, Diplomacy and War," A4.

Chapter 5

Martin Wight: Politics in the Era of Leviathan

Daniel Young

Perhaps no one has thought more deeply about international society, and the tension between order and justice, than the English scholar Martin Wight (1913-1972).[1] Exceedingly well read in many fields, he refused to fence the discipline of international relations into a small academic box, as many of his contemporaries in the United States were attempting to do. Rather, he believed that the study of world politics could not be divorced from its context in history and ideas. Wight was, in Hedley Bull's words, "a very orthodox Christian—a devout Anglican."[2] His writings ultimately cannot be fully understood apart from his faith.

Wight was not a prolific writer, at least in terms of publication. From his posthumously published material, however, we can see a penetrating mind constantly at work, never satisfied with a particular formulation of a position. Reading his writings is simultaneously immensely instructive and exasperating, as the reader is never quite sure where Wight stands.

Most discussions of Wight classify him as a Grotian, that is, as representing an intellectual position that emphasizes the concept of an international society. In this chapter, I highlight that there was more than Hugo Grotius influencing Wight's position. I contend that Wight's intellectual position may be called *Whig realism*. This position is an outgrowth of his Christian realism as modified by what he called the Whig tradition, "the tradition of constitutional government which descends from Aristotle through Aquinas to Locke and the Founding Fathers of the United States."[3] Notably, Wight quotes Edmund Burke at least as often as he quotes Grotius.[4]

Was Wight a realist? Hedley Bull and Carsten Holbraad contend he was not, if we consider realism to be the belief that international politics is merely the politics of force.[5] However, realism generally has a more subtle meaning. In an oft-cited essay, Robert Gilpin states that

> political realism must be seen as a philosophical disposition and set of assumptions about the world rather than as in any strict sense a "scientific" theory. Although a realist perspective itself may give rise to testable hypotheses and more systematic theories, political realism itself, as Richard Rosecrance once aptly put it, is best viewed as an attitude regarding the human condition. Unlike its polar opposite, idealism, realism is founded on a pessimism regarding moral progress and human possibilities.[6]

If this is a satisfactory definition of realism, then Wight certainly qualifies. On this view, realism is a *philosophical* disposition that contrasts with idealism as to the possibilities of "moral progress and human possibilities." It is important to recall that the seminal realists Reinhold Niebuhr and E. H. Carr are doing political theory. In particular, they are putting forth one philosophical anthropology (generally called *realism*) to oppose another philosophical anthropology (generally called *idealism*). Wight himself was aware of this. "All political theory presupposes some kind of theory about human nature, some basic anthropological theory."[7] This realist-idealist divide on anthropological assumptions persists in international relations theory to this day.[8]

Was Wight a Christian realist? Like Niebuhr and Herbert Butterfield, Wight drew on Augustine at a time when this perspective had its heyday following World War II, a period Roger Epp calls "the Augustinian moment."[9] Unlike Niebuhr, Wight was less overt about it, confining his more explicit remarks to religious forums. But it informed his theorizing.

> Wight, while less explicit in many of his writings, was arguably the most Augustinian of the three [Niebuhr, Butterfield, Wight] in his strict separation of earthly and heavenly cities, his comparison of current concentrations of power in 'neo-pagan' states with the biblical Babylon, and his warning that Christians should prepare for the catacombs in the coming apocalypse. Wight also cited Augustine's denial of progress in the domain of secular history and the earthly city against latter-day

manifestations of 'pelagianism' or 'liberal optimism,' which bore some responsibility for twentieth century cataclysm.[10]

What distinguishes Wight from other Christian realists is that he came to hold a more liberal or "Whig" notion of practical morality. In his most representative essay, Wight contrasts a "political ethics" position to *Realpolitik*, pure expediency where moral considerations are irrelevant, and *Fiat justitia et pereat mundus*, let justice be done even if the world perish. Wight states that a "political ethics" position "assumes that the upholding of moral standards will in itself tend to strengthen the fabric of political life. These assumptions seem to lie within the province of philosophy of history, or belief in Providence..."[11] The heart of the difference between Wight and realists like Niebuhr and Hans Morgenthau is that for Wight, to do right was not always self-defeating.[12]

Wight's thought was always evolving. This evolution displays a probing of different traditions' ability to capture adequately the ever-changing realities of international politics.[13] This chapter will highlight three transitions. His earliest political writing (1936) takes the position of Christian pacifism. By 1940 however, it seems he had modified his pacifism to that of a personal vocation for he spoke more in terms of just war theory. By the late 1940s his voice is that of the classic Christian realist. In the 1960s, however, Wight apparently found useful the terminology of Catholic political thought, and as I will show, the pacifism of his youth lurks as well.[14]

Biographical Overview

Wight earned a degree in history at Oxford University. After graduating in 1935 he began a lifelong affiliation with the Royal Institute of International Affairs. There he assisted the historian Arnold Toynbee on his twelve-volume *A Study of History*.[15] Toynbee included Wight's often-critical commentary in footnotes to Volume VII.[16] Wight even authored two substantial appendices.[17] Wight returned to Oxford for eight years (1941-1949) researching African colonial issues, publishing four works on this topic.[18]

During this time he also published a seventy-page book entitled *Power Politics* (1946), a landmark realist text that was his breakthrough work.[19] In 1949 he joined the International Relations faculty at the London School of Economics. Here he developed an influential lecture course on the "three traditions" of international theory.[20] In the late 1950s, Wight and Herbert Butterfield founded the interdisciplinary

British Committee on the Theory of International Politics, which gave rise to the "English School" of international relations theory. The Committee included notable scholars such as Hedley Bull (international relations), Michael Howard (military history), and Donald MacKinnon (theology and philosophy).[21] Invited by Hans Morgenthau, Wight spent the academic year 1956-57 as a visiting professor at the University of Chicago. In 1961, he joined the faculty of the new University of Sussex, as dean of the School of European Studies. He died in 1972, apparently of a heart attack.

The Three Traditions

At this point a brief discussion of the "three traditions" is in order. There is a distinctly philosophical cast to Wight's theorizing about international politics. Most books that he reviewed for the journal *International Affairs* appeared in the "Philosophy and Politics" section. Typical examples are Eric Voegelin's *The New Science of Politics* and R. G. Collingwood's *The Idea of History*. Furthermore, Wight introduced his lectures on international relations theory with an explicit statement of philosophical intent. "By 'international theory' is meant something corresponding to political theory...international theory is the political philosophy of international relations."[22]

In 1939 E. H. Carr published *The Twenty Years' Crisis*, the most powerful restatement of the contemporary realism-utopianism debate. In his lectures Wight moved beyond this dichotomy, classifying international relations theory into three traditions: *Realism*, *Rationalism*, and *Revolutionism*. Each tradition emphasizes a particular facet of international relations. Wight identifies Realism with Machiavelli (and Hobbes), Rationalism with Grotius (and Locke), and Revolutionism with Kant (and Marx). Wight also occasionally refers to a pacifist *Inverse Revolutionism*, epitomized by the Quakers and Gandhi.[23]

Machiavellians or *Realists* emphasize international anarchy, power politics, and warfare, particularly as they are dissociated from ethical considerations. "It is the doctrine that conflict is inherent in relations between states...To use the word Realism implies an affirmation about what is real, what is reality...For the twentieth-century man, Realism means a frank acceptance of the disagreeable aspects of life. Realism, therefore, is violence, sin, suffering, and conflict..."[24]

Grotians or *Rationalists* emphasize diplomacy and commerce. In published writings Wight also refers to it as a "constitutional" or "Whig" tradition.[25] Wight explicitly connects the Grotian tradition and natural law theory, referring to it as "the broad middle road of European thinking":

> To call this tradition Rationalist is to associate it with the element of reason contained in the conception of natural law. The belief in natural law is a belief in a cosmic, moral constitution, appropriate to all created things including mankind; a system of eternal and immutable principles radiating from a source that transcends earthly power (either God or nature).... Reason means the capacity to know this natural law and the obligations it imposes; this law (of justice) is "written in his heart."[26]

Kantians or *Revolutionists* emphasize the concept of a society of states or family of nations. However, this is not just a vague feeling of the "brotherhood of man." Rather this brotherhood had to be concretized in political form, regardless of circumstances.

> The Revolutionists can be defined more precisely as those who believe so passionately in the moral unity of the society of states or international society, that they identify themselves with it, and therefore they both claim to speak in the name of this unity, and experience an overriding obligation to give effect to it, as the first aim of their international policies. For them, the whole of international society transcends its parts; they are cosmopolitan rather than "internationalist," and their international theory and policy has "a missionary character."[27]

Wight's three great historical examples are the Reformation, French Revolution, and Russian Revolution. "It is worth noting that all Revolutionism is of a Christian pattern, whether Rousseauite or Marxist: the patent is Christian, and perhaps the responsibility too. The ancient world has no tradition of political thought comparable to Revolutionism."[28]

Wight's lectures explore these traditions' views on human nature, international society, relations with "barbarians" (those considered "outside" international society),[29] national interest, diplomacy, the causes of war, and international law.[30]

In *International Theory* Wight described the interaction of the traditions as follows.

> There is overlapping and indistinctiveness between the three traditions. Each tradition can be subdivided into two or more, and they dove-tail; thus Grotians and Machiavellians agree in being Realist, in accepting the facts of the world of politics, although they differ in what they bring under the heading of 'fact'. Grotians and Kantians agree in being idealist, in pursuing ideals in the world of politics, although they differ in their

estimate of the power of ideals and in their method of obtaining them. A conflict between the traditions lies in the emphasis placed on the importance of facts as against ideas, and of men as against ideals.[31]

Wight goes on to note that

> The Grotian and the Kantian agree that history has a purpose and meaning. The Kantian may regard history as the totality of mankind surging forward and individuals getting trampled underfoot, while Grotians see history as a field in which individuals find their several purposes or meanings and are sceptical about the meaning of the whole; but at least they agree in a sense of history as dynamic, and the individual as having responsibility in it. The Machiavellian however regards history as static or cyclic, and the individual scrapes what corner or burrow in life he can.[32]

Furthermore,

> Although they disagree in their theory of history, the Machiavellian and Kantian agree that politics have their origin in sin; they believe in the Augustinian doctrine of the state as...punishment and remedy against sin...In a secularized version, this comes down to Machiavelli and Hobbes, who find the origin of the state in the badness of men; its essential purpose is to *restrain* men, whether from greed, violence, or folly...Kantians see it in a special way, as the rapacity of a special set of men.[33]

To what extent can this "sinful" nature of politics be changed? The Machiavellian says it *cannot* be changed. The Kantian says it *can* be changed. "Against them both is the Grotian (Aquinas as against Augustine), who believes that political life is natural to man, and needed for his proper development."[34]

Finally, in terms of ethics, the Machiavellian and Kantian agree on the primacy of consequences, "yet Grotian magnanimity often judges men by their nobility of character rather than their political correctness or success."[35]

Wight's detached examination of these traditions makes it tough to pin down his position. Partly this was for pedagogical purposes, but he also refused to pigeonhole himself because he saw merit in each tradition. However, he was most sympathetic with the Grotian tradition, finishing his lecture series by saying:

> You will have guessed that my prejudices are Realist, but I find I have become more Rationalist and less Realist through rethinking this question during the course of giving these lectures. If I said Rationalism was a

civilizing factor, Revolutionism a vitalizing factor, and Realism a controlling disciplinary factor in international politics, you might think I was playing with words, but I hope I have shown that there is more substance to international theory than that.[36]

Wight's Early Pacifism

The first aspect of Wight's religious thought I will discuss is his early pacifism.[37] By the outbreak of World War II the Peace Movement had failed through incoherence. Pacifists finally realized that Hitler could not be overcome through goodwill, and either began to support military options or retreated into a consistent apolitical pacifism, without illusion as to its efficacy.[38] Wight apparently took the latter approach, and sat out the war as a conscientious objector.

In essays and lecture notes written in the 1950s and 1960s, he is quite critical of the pacifist position. His comments on pacifism indicate some disavowal, although he never explicitly repudiated it. In fact, few of his students and colleagues knew of his pacifist past. Apparently it was mentioned at his funeral, to the great surprise of many. His widow notes that he never put the pacifism article on his curriculum vitae.[39]

As Wight shifted to a more Grotian outlook, so too apparently did his view of war. But he did not entirely repudiate his pacifist past, for it lurks in his late work. His earlier articles "Christian Pacifism" (explicitly) and "The Church, Russia, and the West" (latently) reveal a mode of thought drawn from classical Christian pacifism of the Anabaptist strain, with a sharp distinction between the symbolic cities of Jerusalem and Babylon. Although apparently Catholic-leaning in his theology, in this area Wight shows clear affinities with Anabaptist theology.

Anabaptist thought closely identifies the state with Babylon (also symbolized as "the beast" Leviathan), an idolatrous entity that worships its own power and glory. The state is founded upon and maintained by violence or the threat thereof. In contrast, the gospel message is one of peace, epitomized by Christ's nonviolence in the face of Roman power. The church is to attempt to live as the "peaceable kingdom." This compels the Christian to remain outside the coercive and idolatrous "beast", as the state was irredeemable. The state held the power of the sword, the Christian should not kill; therefore political life was off-limits to the Christian.[40]

In 1936 he contributed an article defending Christian pacifism to *Theology*, a leading English journal of Anglo-Catholic persuasion.

The core of pacifism is the belief that it is never right to take human life. It is nothing to do with quietism in the sense of immoral apathy and passivity. It is not the organization of mass-cowardice. It does not condemn all use of force. It does not assert that there is nothing worth fighting for. It does not make an unconditional surrender to evil. It does not belief in peace at any price. Its basis is not utilitarian.[41]

Wight goes on to base this thesis on the following conclusions from the gospels.

> (1) The message of the Incarnation was a message of peace...which challenged and survived any violence or catastrophe...(2) The new commandment of love was absolute because the Incarnation, through its derivative the Church, gave everyone the possibility of fulfilling it.[42]

Any force used must be redemptive, to aim at the restraint and rehabilitation of the offender. Killing rules out the possibility of redemption; it is irrevocable and implies that the offender is irredeemable. But such knowledge is not available, for who can look inside the human heart and see that change is impossible? Hence, killing is forbidden. Furthermore, since Christ was a pacifist, so all Christians must be pacifists. If Christ is the epitome of humanity and the church is the "body of Christ" then Christ's pacifism is normative. "To accept such a position means a complete reorientation of social and political values. What is called civilization has always been based, to a much greater extent than most people care to consider, on the arbitrary termination of one man's life by another."[43] But what about the dominant tradition of Christian thinking on war, set forth most notably by such luminaries as Augustine, Aquinas, Vitoria, and Grotius? Unfortunately, Wight argued, such a doctrine was a compromise on the gospel, a capitulation to the temptations of worldly power, having more to do with Stoic legal thought than the Sermon on the Mount.

> The root of the just-war doctrine was the contention that the morality binding on individuals was not binding on the State, and that the Christian prince might do things in his official capacity which were forbidden to him as a man. To the Christian pacifist this dualism is no legitimate development from the Gospel, but an attempt to lower its standards.[44]

Since the attempt to formulate a just war doctrine is compromised from the start, it is unworkable. It demands less than it should.

To demand perfection will always evoke a response from the divine in man, while the demand for a standard that makes concessions to human frailty has already undermined its own authority. Our Lord's demands were absolute, the Church's have too often been qualified.[45]

Any just war doctrine reflects a politically compromised church, a church attempting to protect its privileged position. An example is the Church of England, which has succumbed to "ecclesiastical Hegelianism" in justifying British imperialism as the movement of God in the world. Hence, according to this logic, it is right to war to protect the empire. The logical outcome of just war theory is that nearly any war can be declared just and so "any relation between force and morals has been lost for centuries."[46]

Wight concluded with a statement about the futility of warfare combined with a typical Anglo-Catholic socialist theme.

Military and political warfare is the result, in the modern world, of the continual economic and financial warfare which is the dynamic of bourgeois society; and the Christian pacifist is a pacifist in both spheres. He shares the ideals of the Communist, who uses class-war as the instrument of social justice, and of the orthodox theologian, who condones war as the instrument of international justice; but he believes that their ideals are belied by their methods, for violence breeds no lasting peace.[47]

It is the methods of Gandhi that will bring triumph, as they brought triumph in the early years of the Christian Church, before it obtained political power from Emperor Constantine. The Christian pacifist should not expect too much, however. Secular pacifists overestimate their own effectiveness because they take insufficient account of human evil. "The amount of evil in the world remains pretty constant; and my refusal to fight will not obliterate the doctrines of *Mein Kampf* nor change the state of mind of its author." Rather, change occurs over the long run.[48]

After this, Wight wrote nothing more explicitly advocating pacifism and indeed is often quite critical of it. Possibly this was through the influence of Niebuhr's critique of pacifism. In a dialogue between pacifists and just war advocates, written in 1940 for a school newspaper, he took the part of just war, using many Niebuhrian arguments.[49] In that dialogue Wight (under the guise of the character "Michael") asserts: "It is perfectly clear that the life of absolute goodness exemplified by Christ and his immediate followers is a vocation, of which everybody is not immediately capable."[50] That is, in a sinful world, Christians in public service may need to use lethal force in the service of justice, but other Christians are called to witness to the coming "peaceable kingdom" when swords are beaten into plowshares. Roger Epp argues on this basis that Wight had come to view his pacifism as vocational.[51] While any assertions about Wight's later pacifism are educated guesses, I believe this to be a sound interpretation.

Wight's Christian Realism: Post-War Neo-Augustinianism

The four dominant figures in the post-war revival of Christian historical thought were Herbert Butterfield, Arnold Toynbee, Reinhold Niebuhr, and Christopher Dawson.[52] Butterfield and Toynbee were Wight's collaborators and mentors. Wight often quoted Dawson and he praised Niebuhr's books. Many of the phrases and concepts of these thinkers surface in Wight's work, particularly when writing for religious audiences.[53]

A particularly English contribution to this scene was the Anglo-Catholic movement within the Church of England, which emphasized the transcendent, the importance of sacrament, and the transnational character of the Christian Church. It criticized the Church of England for merely saying "amen" to state policy. It was also characterized by an emphasis on the concrete, tradition, and prejudice, and was suspicious of the abstract. Wight clearly fits into this mold, with his rather Burkean critique of revolutionism's abstraction.[54] Wight's archetypal Christian realist phase is manifested in his use of Augustine and apocalypse to analyze history. It is markedly present in his 1948 article "The Church, Russia, and the West."

Post-Christendom and Leviathan

In this article Wight undertakes the Augustinian task of setting the pressing concerns of the moment into a larger perspective. He writes:

> We have the double task of analysing the crisis in historical terms and of assessing it in theological terms. The latter is much the more important: it includes the former in a way in which the former does not include *it*, for it means reconsidering the nature of the Church's action in history and politics.[55]

Wight starts the article by addressing the emerging Cold War. "Our conflict is fratricidal. It is a continuation, in another form, of the ancient conflict between Byzantine and Latin Christianity." He downscales the historical novelty of the Cold War conflict: same foes, new names. However, something has changed in this ancient rivalry. "But Russia and the West are not longer Christendoms; they are post-Christian civilizations; for Christendom, Eastern and Western alike, is dead."

> Let us try to define our terms: what do we mean by Christendom? Something like this: a society in which 1. the majority are practicing Christians; 2. the Church is therefore the most venerated and influential of all institutions; 3. the Church itself is vigorous and uncorrupted — and are we to add, united? 4. social and political organisation is therefore saturated with Christian presuppositions. These conditions are no longer found anywhere in the world.[56]

Wight contended that because of the failure of Christendom, secular substitutes like Marxism and bourgeois liberalism rose in its place. Moreover, and crucially, these secular substitutes had a different quality: they were the children of Leviathan. Wight seemingly saw the history of "the Christian era" as the attempt of the church to tame the state. With the decline of Christendom the state was unbound: God was privatized and the state was answerable only to itself. Hence, there is no God but Leviathan and Hobbes is his prophet. The two post-Christendoms had expanded to rule most of the earth. In this post-Christian world anti-Christs preached an anti-gospel: power and conquest.

> Thus the evangelical command, that repentance and the remission of sins should be preached in Christ's name among all nations, has received an inverted and terrifying fulfillment: there is no nation and no part of the earth that lies beyond the range either of the American business man or of the Communist Party organizer.[57]

What did this mean for the church? Did it mean a simple reversion to pre-Constantinian conditions?[58] Is there an analogy with Israel's exilic and post-exilic periods? Is there some synthesis of new insights with the experience of Christendom? Wight refuses to answer, but states that they are the kind of questions that must be asked.

Furthermore, the crisis was not merely a post-Christian phenomenon. It had its roots in Christendom, in events such as the Crusades. Christendom was reaping what it had sown.

> We are bound up today in the conflict between Russia and the West, because we are burdened by the heritage of sin which in Hindu philosophy is known as *Karma* — our corporate destiny decided by the sum or our

corporate actions in the past. We have inherited the sins of schism and war, of reunion unaccomplished, of the necessity for the Reformation and the Reformation's failure, of the apostasy of Christendom. Recognition, understanding, above all repentance, these alone can free us.[59]

These failures of our civilization mean we have a price to pay: we live in the era of Leviathan.

> Russia and America are the last two Great Powers within the Westernised system of sovereign states. And the characteristic of that system, after centuries in which the Church has had no influence upon its development, is the emancipation of power from moral restraints. Leviathan is a simple beast: his law is self-preservation, his appetite is for power.[60]

In the end, Wight thought that World War III was inevitable and that it would be fought "with the smallest moral restraint."

The Christian Dialectic of History: Augustine and the Two Cities

Wight argued against a "dying liberalism" based on Pelagianism and secular progressivism.[61] Hence, we do not muddle through history by well meaning actions. Nor did Wight find any "secular theory of progress" in the Bible. Rather, he found judgments on actions: "purification through catastrophe and redemption through suffering, the rediscovery in our individual lives and our corporate histories of resurrection and passion after death."[62] This liberalism was being replaced among Christians and non-Christians alike either by philosophies of despair such as existentialism, or by "submission to Leviathan": the various versions of totalitarianism. As they were perversions of Christianity, they held special appeal to Christians who would likely hang on to them longer than would non-Christians.

> The distinction between sacred and secular history is the stuff of our argument — between history as process only and history as purpose, between history aetiological and history teleological. If we use one metaphor we may say that secular and sacred history interpenetrate; if we use another, and perhaps a truer one, we will see secular history as the surface of the time-process, dead and glassy, and sacred history as the same time-process transparent against the light of eternity, the sum of all the depths of destiny. It is the distinction between St. Augustine's two cities, the earthly city which is built by love of self to the contempt of God, and the heavenly city which is built by the love of God to the contempt of self. The two cities are always mixed up in this world, but

there is a rhythm in their interaction, and sometimes it is their coincidence and sometimes their divergence that is more apparent.[63]

The replacement of inefficient tyrannies by efficient tyrannies demonstrates the meaninglessness of cyclical history. If that is all there is, then history is meaningless. The role of the church is to bring the whole thing under judgment, by proclaiming the appearance of God in history, in the incarnation of Christ.

The Christian View of the Meaning of History

Are the only options a delusional liberalism or totalitarian-inclined despair? As people move from optimistic liberalism to despair, Christianity has a point of contact. This despair is in a sense healthy, as it is realistic. Despair leads to humility, and hence to the possibility of repentance. The following summary is so crucial to understanding Wight's interpretation of history that I will quote it in full.

> The theory of history to which the Church has always been committed, and from which only in the last century perhaps some churches allowed their attention to be distracted, is the Biblical theodicy. History is not an autonomous process which secretes its own meaning as it goes along, like a cosmic endocrine gland. (This view of history as an autonomous process, by the way, is hard to separate from determinism and the denial of man's moral freedom). History is a process with an author, who lies outside it, that is to say outside time. It had a beginning and will have an end, both of them determined by its author; and it is only in relation to what lies outside itself that it has a meaning. But it is a process whose moving force is the moral freedom of the human individuals involved in it; and consequently its meaning is identical with *judgment* by the author, a verdict on the exercise of that freedom both general and particular, a sifting of the good elements from the bad. After an agelong preparation and expectation, at a certain point in the historical process (a point defined in the Creed by the reference to Pontius Pilate) meaning and judgment appeared inside history, with the incarnation of history's author. The meaning thus made apparent was God in human terms. But the judgment was *implicit* judgment, in that the forces of unmeaning history immediately rushed in upon the incarnate meaning to destroy it, thereby inadvertently passing judgment on themselves. This point was the fulfilment of history, since the meaning of history was there shown; but there still remained an epilogue in which that meaning might be fully proclaimed — the epilogue in which we live. And with the end of the epilogue history will end too: our air bubble in eternity will collapse. We imagine the end of history as the last event of the temporal series; we know it doctrinally as the Second Coming of Christ; but in the sense in

which we are considering it, it is the final verdict by the author of history, the act of *explicit* judgment, which will separate the evil from the good and afford the ultimate meaning.[64]

Wight goes on to discuss three important implications of this view of history. First, the second coming was immanent but beyond human understanding (a "concentrated intellectual paradox" but "morally simple"). In an argument that parallels Eric Voegelin, the end of human history was beyond human understanding. Because it was beyond human knowledge, speculations about it were foolish; believers were simply to live in obedience and service, as if each day were the last. We may not understand the grand scheme of things, but we do know our moral responsibilities. Quoting John Henry Newman, Wight speaks of all times being equally distant (and equally near) from the coming of Christ. This doctrine prevents one from believing that one's own time is the fulfillment of history (or at least a great leap forward) or in Wight's words "that history increases in importance as it approaches ourselves."

The second implication was the continued coexistence of good and evil, not a gradual perfection of things. "The notion that the Christian Era should be a period of the gradual perfection of men and society is the opposite of what we find in the New Testament."[65] In a sermon preached at Great St. Mary's, Cambridge, Wight quoted Jacques Maritain:

> I think that the two immanent tendencies intersect at every point in the history of the world and affect everyone with their momentary complexes: one tendency draws upward everything in the world which participates in the divine life of the Church, which is in the world but not of the world, and follows the attraction of Christ, the Head of the human race. The other tendency draws downward everything in the world which belongs to the Prince of the World, the head of all the wicked.[66]

These two tendencies interact throughout history, with increasing tension between them until God in a final act of judgement triumphs over antichrist.

The third implication was the recurrent pattern of crisis and redemption, judgment and the giving of life. "The archetypal pattern of the Incarnation, the Crucifixion, and the Resurrection is repeated continually in all human lives and all human situations."

Wight saw current threats of massive destruction as judgments on a dissolving Christendom.

...judgment on war, which is no longer a purposive and preservative activity governed by the doctrine of the just war, but has become an indiscriminate social convulsion; judgment on the state, in the form of an impending world state which may well be a more frightful concentration of tyrannical power than any we have yet experienced; judgment on nationalism, which has long been a form of idolatry that was denounced by the prophets of the Old Testament; judgment on revolution, which has been swollen into the decisive fact of contemporary secular history, and has produced a giant debased substitute for the Church.[67]

The primary task for the church then is to recognize these judgments on itself, repent, and take hope. "As the present crisis deepens and the historical prospect grows darker, their meaninglessness and terror will increase for everybody except the Christian. The Church alone knows all about this; — has been here before; — this is where she comes in."[68] According to this view, the church is the bearer of sacred history but is not identified with it. Mystically, *she* is one with Christ. Institutionally, *it* repeatedly fails at its vocation and has done so since day one. Ironically, its *institutional* dominance led the failure of its mission. In its mystical form, alienated from the surrounding pagan culture, it attracted adherents, eventually being made the state religion. This establishment diluted its witness as the speaker of truth to power, leading to the downfall of Christendom.

Just as in *The City of God* Augustine deconstructs the alleged splendor and glories of imperial Rome, so Wight deconstructs not only the failures of the modern age, but also the alleged splendors and glories of Christendom. The answer is not nostalgia, but repentance. The clock could not be turned back, but one had to learn from the errors of the past. "Maybe you can't change what has passed, but you can change all the meaning of what has passed."

In his sermon Wight gave a similar argument.

The whole of the pattern on the tapestry we shall never see, of course, in this life. But even the partial vision cannot be steadily maintained, because we ourselves are part of the tapestry we scrutinize, and the degree of firelight is determined not only by our own efforts but also by what God permits us, and it may be that he sees that it is good and necessary for us as actors in history, which after all is our real business, that we should walk a great deal in darkness in the place of dragons and covered with the shadow of death.[69]

Obedience arises out of catastrophe, just as the account of Abraham immediately follows the story of the Tower of Babel.

For Toynbee, the Incarnation demonstrated that history had meaning despite its apparent meaninglessness. This was because God affirmed the world by becoming part of the created order, thus showing that history was not a mere cycle. Earth was an unruly province of the kingdom of God; the Incarnation demonstrated that it was not outside of God's jurisdiction. But Wight admonished Toynbee for missing the point of the Incarnation and its eschatological significance: God himself in history. Ultimately all history was sacred history.[70] Likewise, "both Butterfield and Niebuhr emphasize the Old Testament at the expense of the New Testament, and seem to undervalue the doctrine of the Church...neither sees the historical rôle of the Church as the instrument of the Kingdom, the bearer of sacred history."[71]

Apocalypse as Political Commentary

However, helpful or insightful into the sovereignty of God this scheme was, it was insufficient. It did not discuss the hiddenness and inscrutability of God. We cannot stand outside of history and see its shape. At first glance it might seem that Wight thought that Christendom was a political failure, successful only in changing a few hearts.

Given a post-Christian era, Wight urged on his readers a renewed focus on apocalyptic literature as a source of political thought. He did not take a "predict-the-future" reading of such literature. Rather, apocalypse was a specifically Jewish literature written in response to particular political situations. They were addressed to particular religious communities under pressure from a dominant and pagan empire (whether Babylon or Rome). Despite that, the lessons taught were lasting, addressing permanent problems.

An important motif that recurs in apocalyptic literature is that the struggle between good and evil is a cosmic one. The book of Revelation portrays God as conqueror while the saints do nothing. They are exceedingly passive; they live their lives in obedience and service and die their deaths of martyrdom. It is left to God to crush the dragon. No human act can overcome evil, only an act of God. Hence there is a deflation of human ambitions to remake the world. Part of this of course is due to the social location of the Christians to whom this literature was addressed. They were a small, persecuted sect. They had little access to the levers of power except to some minor local officials.

In post-Christendom, the era of Leviathan, the church no longer had a privileged place. It had to metaphorically retreat to the catacombs. The church would have to shift its emphasis from that of Romans 13, where

St. Paul emphasizes government's role in administering justice, to that of Revelation 13, in which the self-glorifying, conquest-loving Roman Empire is symbolized as a multi-headed beast (or Leviathan) with blasphemous names on its forehead. Wight seems to have in mind that the bestial state is an archetype that emerges repeatedly in history and that the church will have to react accordingly. Just as John of Patmos adapts the apocalyptic imagery from the Jewish experience with Babylon, so Wight thinks that John's insights are relevant today. Just as the Jewish people outlasted Babylon, so the church outlasted the Roman Empire and other imperial challenges, and so it can outlast post-Christendom.

For Wight Christian eschatology had to relate Christian political thinking; its influence had to become conscious. If that occurred it might take the following form.

> First, by throwing the Church back upon the task which is at once the center and the circumference of its attempt to build a Christian civilization: the proclaiming of the gospel of the crucified and risen Christ. Then, by applying the call to repentance with which the gospel was first heard among men *to itself*, the Church to the Church. For within the Church too there are the tensions of history, the struggle between nature and grace; and the historical Church has its share of guilt for the collapse of Christendom. Here its task now may be to see how its own position carries some degree of determination, some inescapable accumulation of retribution due.[72]

Wight and Theological Hope: The Crushing of Leviathan

Given this analysis, Wight argued, we should not be optimistic, but we can be hopeful. "There is a way of foretelling the inevitability of disaster which is theologically responsible and informed with — not optimism, but with hope."[73] Wight has been criticized as being a pessimist. In political terms this is probably accurate. A favorite Wight maxim was that war is inevitable, but particular wars are avoidable.[74] However, like Augustine, Wight was ultimately hopeful. He wrote:

> Ruthlessly realistic analysis is not incompatible with hope, for hope is a theological not a political virtue. 'Humanly speaking' inevitable, we say, but this omits the humanly incalculable factor of God's grace. And even if it is not God's purpose to intervene, it does not invalidate hope, because the object of hope is not particular things God may allow in history, but God himself.[75]

Augustine was hopeful because he believed that through the death and resurrection of Christ God had defeated evil. Despite the continuation of many evils, its power had been decisively broken. The rest of history was a mop up operation.

> And we must remember that Christianity, like Judaism, differs from all the other great religions, in being founded upon a concrete historical disaster. The first was the Captivity of the Chosen People in Egypt. The second—when the lens had been focussed down from a ring of light to a burning pinpoint, from a nation to an Individual—the second disaster was the Crucifixion of the Messiah. But God led his people up out of Egypt, and the Messiah rose from the dead. If we believe in this, all subsequent catastrophes are so to speak anticipated. The catastrophic nature of history continues — that is simply a matter of looking at the record — but history is a sea-serpent whose back has been broken, even if it seems to us to be thrashing about more violently than ever.[76]

Using Isaiah's imagery, Wight evokes God's crushing of the coiling sea serpent Leviathan.[77]

Whig Themes in Wight's Thought: Power and Right

In the 1960s Wight shifted from typical Christian realist themes to language more typical of Catholic political thought. He uses concepts such as *perfect community* and *natural law*, while at the same time his earlier pacifist strain shadows his thought. Wight's commentary on ethical issues implied a trustee theory of political morality not normally associated with realism.

Following the historian William Stubbs, Wight begins both editions of *Power Politics*, his most realist text, by highlighting the shift from "right" to "power."

> 'Medieval history' said the historian Stubbs, 'is a history of rights and wrongs; modern history as contrasted with medieval history is a history of powers, forces, dynasties and ideas...Medieval wars are, as a rule, wars of rights; they are seldom wars of unprovoked, never wars of absolutely unjustifiable aggression; they are not wars of idea, or liberation, or of glory, or of nationality, or of propagandism.'[78]

Wight goes on to comment that this sense of unity had been thoroughly weakened by the rise of the independent state, so that "international society" has become merely the sum of its parts. Wight summarizes in one of his last writings: "Prescriptive rights were sacrosanct, and power politics were conducted in a litigious and not a doctrinal or ideological idiom."[79]

This concept accounts for the persistent Leviathan theme in Wight: the modern state as an organization of power emancipated from right. Perhaps we can say that although power is largely the determining factor, Western culture has never quite escaped the notion of right. Wight's work can thus be seen as exploring the efficacy of the residue of the idea of right. "Powers will continue to seek security without reference to justice, and to pursue their vital interests irrespective of common interests, but in the fraction that they may be deflected lies the difference between the jungle and the traditions of Europe."[80]

Criticisms of the Idea of International Society

Wight's fullest statement of his Whig or Grotian phase is a 1966 essay "Western Values in International Relations."[81] Significantly, he referred to it as the *Whig* or *constitutional* tradition, not the *Grotian* tradition. In fact, to the best of my knowledge, Wight *never* used the term *Grotian* in a work published in his lifetime.[82] "The primary questions of international theory concern the nature of international society and of international law." To examine that nature assumes that international society exists. There are, Wight says, two extreme views opposing this position. First, some legal positivists deny the existence of international society. Machiavelli and Hobbes are the most formidable examples. Legal positivism is closely associated with realism. If international society is a fiction, then legal positivism is true, that "the basis of international obligation is purely contractual." Legal positivism, the orthodoxy of international legal philosophy, recognizes no international society except the society of sovereign states. Thus it denies the existence of an effective international society.[83]

At the other extreme are the cosmopolitans, who hold that the society of states is unreal in the sense that it "conceals, obstructs, and oppresses the *real* society of individual men and women, the *civitas maxima*." Thus "international society is none other than the community of mankind." The problem is that this community is latent and not realized. Nature made man the only rational animal, so therefore it intends the rational faculties to be fully developed. It is the task of the rational intellect to make it real. This was the argument of Kant and Hegel.

Cosmopolitans hold various opinions on how the society of states will dissolve into the cosmopolis: a universal acceptance of some standard, a global federation, or perhaps a messiah-state will lead or compel the other states into all righteousness. These various views have implications for how international law is viewed. Either international law and municipal law are not that different, or cooperation is impossible because some are elect and some are reprobate.

> Like Turgot before him and like most thinkers since, Kant clarified or simplified the mysteries of Providence into a perceptible linear movement of history that would bring about, irrespective of individual human strivings, the fruition of collective human aims. Hence the belief, common in varying degrees to the Huguenots, the Jacobins, Mazzini, President Wilson, and the Communists, that the whole of diplomatic history has groaned and travailed together until now, and that the community of mankind, like the kingdom of God, is the glory that shall be revealed, is within reach, is at hand.[84]

There is a great deal to be unpacked within that comment. As I noted above, Wight's three great historical examples of revolutionary movements are the Reformation, the French Revolution, and the Russian Revolution. The Huguenots were the French Calvinist branch of the Reformation, the Jacobins were the French Revolutionaries, and the Communists of course led the Russian Revolution. Hence Wight includes all three of the great revolutionary movements. The sentence in which these names appear alludes to Romans 8:18-25.

> For I consider that the sufferings of this present time are not worth comparing with the glory that is to be revealed to us. For the creation waits with eager longing for the revealing of the sons of God. For the creation was subjected to futility, not willingly, but because of him who subjected it, in hope that the creation itself will be set free from its bondage to decay and obtain the freedom of the glory of the children of God. For we know that the whole creation has been groaning together in the pains of childbirth until now. And not only the creation, but we ourselves, who have the firstfruits of the Spirit, groan inwardly as we wait eagerly for adoption as sons, the redemption of our bodies. For in this hope we were saved. Now hope that is seen is not hope. For who hopes for what he sees? But if we hope for what we do not see, we wait for it with patience.

Wight's point is that the revolutionists have taken an eschatological concept and immanentized it; they are impatient. The world is indeed groaning in travail, and it ultimately shall be revealed in glory, but Wight cannot agree with anyone who says that it is at hand; it unwarrantedly projects on to the historical process an eschatological and christological character.

This text, among others, gave rise to a tension in Christian political thought, and hence in Western political thought, and it shows in Wight, although perhaps not consciously. Regarding the "first fruits" reference in the above extract, in Christian theology the resurrected Christ is called the "first fruits" of the creation reconciled to God. However, he is only the first fruit; the tree has not come to full fruition. The tree metaphor implies growth and increase. There is tension between "already" and "not yet." "Already" because Christ has definitively triumphed over evil: there has been a qualitative change in history. Hence there are transformative possibilities; the endless cycle of human futility has been broken. Perhaps Third World liberation theologies highlight this aspect.

But human evil still exists; the divine plan, inscrutable to all, has not been completed. Christian realists like Niebuhr highlight this "not yet" aspect in an attempt to discredit overly ambitious political programs. In a different realist vein, Thomas Hobbes argues against Puritans and Catholics that the kingdom of God is wholly "not yet," that it is totally irrelevant to the present. He seeks to confine religion to personal piety and liturgical observance, draining them of public import. Both forms of realism are susceptible to quietism (passive resignation to the status quo) or to cynicism. On the other side, the revolutionist sees the transformative possibilities in the inklings of the *civitas maxima* as the first fruits but diverges from the Pauline approach by supposing it can be made fully manifest by human design. Wight's Whig tradition seeks a middle ground between these two pitfalls; rationalism is reformist.[85] Hence, key thinkers for Wight are Aquinas, the Spanish neo-scholastics, and Grotius. While these theological themes elements are not dominant in Wight's thought, they do conform to the *via media* approach that Wight ascribes to the Whig tradition.

Wight's Idea of International Society

Wight analyzes international society in a language derived from natural law theory.

> Between the belief that the society of states is non-existent or at best a polite fiction, and the belief that it is the chrysalis for the community of mankind, lies a more complex conception of international society. It does not derogate from the moral claims of states, conceding that they are, in Suarez's phrase, *communitates perfectae* (exercising valid political authority); but it sees them as relatively, not absolutely perfect, and as parts of a greater whole. It does not see international society as ready to supersede domestic society; but it notes that international society actually

exercises restraints upon its members. Such a conception lacks intellectual conciseness and emotional appeal. The language in which it is stated is necessarily full of qualifications and imprecision.[86]

Wight sympathizes with the natural law thesis that international society is bound to arise out of the recognition of each state's incapacity to fully provide for its citizens' flourishing; the state is only *relatively* perfect. The premise (unstated by Wight) is that we have a common human nature and common interests, so there can be a *common* good, so there can be an international society.

> International society, then, on this view can be properly described only in historical and sociological depth. It is the habitual intercourse of independent communities, beginning in the Christendom of Western Europe and gradually extending throughout the world. It is manifest in the diplomatic system; in the conscious maintenance of the balance of power to preserve the independence of the member communities; in the regular operations of international law, whose binding force is accepted over a wide though politically unimportant range of subjects; in economic, social and technical interdependence and the functional international institutions established regularly to regulate it. *All these presuppose an international social consciousness, a world-wide community sentiment* (Italics mine).[87]

This picture of international society

> does not easily accommodate the strict doctrine that the only international persons, the only subjects of international law, are states. In international legal practice there have always been anomalies, and it has seemed that the law of diplomatic privilege, of extradition, of piracy, of prize, have regarded the individual as the subject of rights and duties, enforceable by or against him...[88]

Where did the dominant doctrine of exclusive state-personality come from? Wolff and Vattel replaced the medieval and Grotian idea of the *jus gentium* (law of nations) as the basis for international law and replaced it with the quasi-Lockean notion of state-as-rights-bearer.

> An earlier tradition saw the princes and subjects of different states as all bound together by the obligations of the *jus gentium*... Nor was this tradition entirely eclipsed by the orthodox doctrine of state-personality. Perhaps it might be said that it survived among the lawyers who saw international law rather as a legitimate child of political philosophy than as a recalcitrant vassal of legal science.[89]

Wight's project seems to be to try to recover this "earlier tradition." Wight's use of the Whig tradition seems to be a protest against the "orthodox doctrine." As we will see, the orthodox doctrine of state personality is defective because it ignores the state's trustee role. Sovereignty is a tool, not an end in itself. Natural law concepts provide some limits on state sovereignty.

Lurking here also it a debate between legal naturalism ("an earlier tradition") and legal positivism ("legal science"). The former conceived of law inherently bound up in moral norms. The "law of nations" (customary practice) provided the normative content for international law. Legal positivists attempted to construct a science of law distinct from moral philosophy. A law was a law because of certain characteristics it possessed, such as being a command backed by threat of force. International law hardly possessed this characteristic.

The Maintenance of Order

If there is no international society, Wight continues, then international relations are indeed Hobbesian: the war of all against all and a zero-sum game. All state action is purely self-help to the detriment of other states.

> If there is an international society, however, then there is an order of some kind to be maintained, or even developed. It is not fallacious to speak of a collective interest, and security acquires a broadened meaning: it can be enjoyed or pursued in common. Foreign policy will take some account of the common interest. *It becomes possible to transfer to international politics some of the categories of constitutionalism* (Italics mine).[90]

This assumes an ontological view that Wight claims for the Whig tradition. This ontological view, that *ultimately* the universe is orderly and peaceful, and hence evil is parasitic on good, fits Wight's theologically informed theoretical perspective. Wars are fought to obtain peace. Here he cites the supposed arch-realist Augustine in support.

> Whoever gives even moderate attention to human affairs and to our common nature, will recognize that as there is no man who does not want to be joyful, neither is there anyone who does not wish to have peace. Even those who make war desire nothing but victory, desire, that is to say, to attain peace with glory...Wars are waged with the desire for peace, even by those who take pleasure in exercising their warlike nature in ...battle. So it is obvious that peace is the end sought for by war.

Everybody seeks peace by making war, but nobody seeks war by making peace. Even those who interrupt the peace in which they are living, have no hatred of peace, but only wish it changed to a peace which suits them better. They do not therefore wish to have no peace, but only one more suited to their mind.[91]

In the Augustinian perspective, peace is fundamental, and war is a perversion of peace, a mere seeking to find a peace to one's own liking.

The Whig treatment of war should illuminate this point. According to Wight, the Whig tradition has two basic tenets regarding war. "The first is that the object of war is peace, not vice versa. Peace is the norm, war the violation or exception."[92] This stems directly from Augustine. Wight writes that the Whig tradition is neither pessimistic nor optimistic about human nature, but sees our experience of human nature as a paradox.[93] The Whig tradition does not see life as the war of all against all:

> Both in its Christian and in its secular form, the Rationalist tradition appeals to reason. It affirms that besides being a sinful, pugnacious and irrational animal, man is also rational, and through his reason he can attain a considerable degree of success in adjusting his political and social arrangements. Society is not a picture of fools being duped by rogues, but of a largely successful field of co-operation between rational persons. The Rationalist is therefore a reformist, the practitioner of piecemeal social engineering.[94]

One major source of international law is Vitoria's defense of the American Indian against the Spanish conquistadors. This has to do with international society's treatment of "barbarians": those who are outside of international society. Burke's appeal to natural justice in the British treatment of India is another example. Hence justice is needed for order, and indeed Wight believes justice will strengthen order, since it is part of the moral fabric of the universe. Intervention is an occasional necessity, although unfortunate because it conflicts with the right of independence. Why might intervention be justified?

> ...in a moral scale, to maintain the balance of power is a better reason for intervening than to uphold civilized standards, but to uphold civilized standards is a better reason than to maintain existing governments.
>
> These principles postulate the existence of an international society of which states are the immediate but men the ultimate members. In such a society, there will be social duties not only towards the states but also towards the individuals whom the states represent and for whom they exist. Moreover, the members will have the capacity in some degree to

reconcile their own interests with those of others and to attain to the idea of a common interest.[95]

To what moral scale is Wight referring? Wight's discussion implies natural justice and the notion of states as trustees. If so, self-preservation is not the only duty of statesmen. Rather, there are duties to all humanity. Wight quotes from Grotius: "Kings, in addition to the particular care of their own state, are also burdened with a general responsibility for human society."[96]

International Morality

Wight contends that the concept of *international morality* best represents a pattern of ideas representing Western values. The areas discussed are (1) the place of the individual conscience in international politics, and (2) the notion of the ethical limits to political action.

First he discusses the realists, who are Hobbesians. "The school of American realists in political theory who acknowledge Reinhold Niebuhr as their patriarch are accustomed to argue that it is only in national life and institutions that ideals such as justice, freedom and equality have a concrete meaning."[97] Hobbes writes in *Leviathan*:

> For these words of good, evil, and contemptible are ever used with relation to the person that useth them, there being nothing simply and absolutely so, nor any common rule of good and evil to be taken from the nature of the objects themselves, but from the person of the man (where there is no commonwealth), or (in a commonwealth) from the person that representeth it...[98]

Also,

> To this war of every man against every man, this also is consequent: that nothing can be unjust. The notions of right and wrong, justice and injustice, have there no place. Where there is no common power, there is no law; where no law, no injustice.[99]

If one is not satisfied with such a Hobbesian view, where does one find the concrete meaning of ideals other than in national institutions or some messiah-state? Wight contends that one finds it in the heroic sacrifice of the individual who defies the state.

> Two ideas are bound up in this answer. There is a positive denial that ideals are concretely embodied in social institutions, and the strength of

the denial grows in proportion to the strength and exclusiveness of the claim. And this denial is made, not in the name of some political or social institutions against others, but in the name of the non-political against them all.[100]

Here we find hints of the pacifism of Wight's youth, which held up a non-political ideal of God's "peaceable kingdom" as an eternal rebuke to all temporal powers.

Wight argues that the term *political* does not quite capture the full ramifications of the idea of obligation. These ideas "contain the paradox, that the health of the political realm is only maintained by conscientious objection to the political...It is clear that the natural law tradition is the soil out of which these ideas have sprung."[101] In very subtle ways, the ensuing discussion carries on some of his concerns from his overtly pacifist days.

Wight discusses some of the natural law characteristics of Western thought as it relates not only to the relation of citizen to state, but to the politician in relating political responsibilities to moral duties.

> The vitality of the natural law ethic might be looked for, not only in the encouragement it may give to ordinary men to criticize their rulers, but also in the encouragement it may give to rulers themselves to break free from political categories, to deny the finality of human institutions...What we are concerned with here is not so much the doctrine of natural law (whatever that is), as a certain ethical temper which may be regarded as its residue or hangover. Cicero's one eternal unchangeable law, the same at Athens as at Rome, the same in the future as now, may be an archaic fancy, or the archaic expression of something true.[102]

Wight's examples of statesmen who thought in this fashion are Burke, Lincoln, Bismarck, Gladstone, and Churchill, who sensed themselves as in some way, and in varying degrees of humility, "instruments of Providence."

> It might be thought enough to say of the natural law ethic that it survives in an awareness of the moral significance and the moral context of all political action. But the moral context is focused more precisely where it is seen as imposing prohibitions on political action—at the point where the politically expedient and the morally permissible come into conflict.[103]

Responding to the skeptic who thinks the dramatic moral veto on immoral action is non-existent, or at least exceedingly rare, Wight contends that European civilization has given rise to the idea of *political ethics*. "There was no Greek Grotius." The ancients' international ethics, such that it was, was either about the statesman's personal honor or the justification of humane action on grounds of expediency.

> Perhaps it is a characteristic of medieval and modern Europe that, in contrast to classical civilization, it has cultivated this middle ground, and developed the conception of a political morality distinct equally from personal morality and from *Realpolitik*...
> It might roughly be said that it was left for medieval thinkers to explore the doctrine that governments are stewards for their peoples and for future generations, having duties analogous to trustees; and for modern thinkers to explore the doctrine that these duties are owed, not only by each government to its subjects, but by one government to another, and by one people to another.
> The cultivation of this middle ground, and the discovery of political morality, seem peculiarly related to Western values. Political morality is different from personal morality, as the moral duties of a trustee are different from the one who acts on his own behalf.[104]

International ethics then considers *prudence* to be the paramount moral virtue. But note that prudence is not merely modest intention or the downscaling of great ambition, as it is often used in discussions of foreign policy. It is not mere pragmatism. Rather, prudence is a *moral* virtue that takes on added import when the actor is conceived of as a trustee. The trustee must take into account the moral sense of those the policy will affect, as well as his or her own moral sense. Thus Burke argued that British imperial policy either uplifted or degraded the British constitution. Hence, there is no distinction between domestic and international politics. If so, political expedience "is softened into prudence, which is a moral virtue."

> Therefore the characteristic fruit of the natural law ethic in modern politics is not so much the dramatic moral veto on political action (though this is always held, as it were, in reserve) as the discovery of an alternative positive policy which avoids the occasion of the veto—an *alternative* policy, because it embodies the notion of a middle course, of a permissible accommodation between moral necessity and practical demands.[105]

Two extreme positions opposing this "political ethics" view are *Realpolitik*, pure expediency where moral considerations are irrelevant, and *Fiat justitia et pereat mundus*, "let justice be done even if the world perish." Wight ends his essay with the following:

130   *The Christian Realists*

Between lies the moral sense we have been considering. It can reach the point of uttering a moral prohibition in politics. But it assumes that moral standards can be upheld without the heavens falling. And it assumes that the fabric of social and political life will be maintained, without accepting the doctrine that to preserve it any measures are permissible. For it assumes that the upholding of moral standards will in itself tend to strengthen the fabric of political life. These assumptions seem to lie within the province of philosophy of history, or belief in Providence, whither it is not the purpose of this paper to pursue them.[106]

The heart of the difference between Wight and realists like Niebuhr and Morgenthau is that for Wight, to do right was not always self-defeating.

Contingency of the Western Tradition

Wight held this natural law view of international society in conscious tension with the recognition of its Western derivation, but does not discard it as merely contingent. Rather, he thinks it has some ontological validity ("the archaic expression of something true"). His 1946 work *Power Politics* is a realist classic. But in the underdeveloped concluding chapter there is a shift. Wight begins to discuss states' common interests and common moral traditions in terms of natural law. The Western states-system expanded to take in the whole globe but the entire matrix of Western culture, including the natural law tradition, did not so expand. Furthermore, in the West itself the natural law tradition in its classic form declined in influence. Thus whatever moral system did inhibit the pursuit of power was rendered almost, but not entirely inert.[107]

Power, Justice, and Peace

The contemporary political scene of Leviathans destroying one another horrified Martin Wight. His shifts from one theoretical tradition to another betray an attempt to find a satisfactory reconciliation of justice and power politics. However, in all of Wight's writings, the reader tacitly finds the ancient Christian idea of an *ultimately* peaceful universe governed by divine providence. For Augustine, peace is fundamental. In other words, evil is a corruption of good, not an independent thing of its own. Hence, violence was parasitic on peace for its existence. Thus, Wight could assert that doing right would strengthen the moral fabric of the universe.[108] Closely linked with this is Augustine's concept of *tranquillitas ordinis*: the peace of right order.

In contrast to the Hobbesian realist view of peace, an Augustinian peace is not the mere absence of warfare without reference to justice. Instead it includes the concept of justice, for, to paraphrase Augustine, an unjust peace is no peace at all.

Wight explicitly links the Whig tradition with this peaceful ontology. Recall from above that Wight described the Whig view as including a "cosmic, moral constitution"[109] and wrote: "The Rationalist writes about international relations in terms of the metaphysical question: he is concerned with the essential nature of affairs" and goes on to quote Suarez on the physical, political, and moral unity of the human race.[110] As I noted above, Wight sees the Whig view of warfare resting on this: wars are fought for the end of peace, at least hypocritically. In sum, Wight was the Whig realist for whom faith and his understanding of international life compelled him to take a middle ground when considering the problem of war and the goal of peace: "Powers will continue to seek security without reference to justice, and to pursue their vital interests irrespective of common interests, but in the fraction that they may be deflected lies the difference between the jungle and the traditions of Europe."[111]

Notes

[1] I would like to acknowledge my debt to the writings of Roger Epp and Scott Thomas in illuminating aspects of Wight's thought.
[2] Martin Wight, *Systems of States*, ed. Hedley Bull (Leicester: Leicester University Press, 1977): 11.
[3] Martin Wight, "Western Values in International Relations," in Herbert Butterfield and Martin Wight, eds., *Diplomatic Investigations: Essays in the Theory of International Politics* (London: George Allen and Unwin, 1966): 89.
[4] For example, in the index to *Power Politics*, Burke has eight entries, Grotius has one.
[5] Martin Wight, *Power Politics*, ed. Hedley Bull and Carsten Holbraad (Leicester: Leicester University Press, 1978; reprint, Leicester: Leicester University Press, 1995): 18.
[6] Robert G. Gilpin, "The Richness of the Tradition of Political Realism," in Robert O. Keohane, ed., *Neorealism and its Critics* (New York: Columbia University Press, 1986): 304.
[7] Martin Wight, *International Theory: The Three Traditions*, ed. Gabriele Wight and Brian Porter (New York: Holmes and Meier, 1992): 25.
[8] See Charles W. Kegley, "The Neoliberal Challenge to Realist Theories of World Politics: An Introduction." In Charles W. Kegley, Jr., ed., *Controversies in International Relations Theory: Realism and the Neoliberal Challenge* (New York: St. Martin's, 1995): 4-5.

[9] Roger Epp, "The 'Augustinian Moment' in International Politics: Niebuhr, Butterfield, Wight and the Reclaiming of a Tradition." *International Politics Research Papers*, No. 10. Aberystwyth, UK: Department of International Politics, University College of Wales, 1991).

[10] Epp, p. 3. "Apocalypse" here refers to a nuclear World War III.

[11] Wight, "Western Values," 131.

[12] Cf. Morgenthau: "Political ethics is indeed the ethics of doing evil." *Scientific Man Versus Power Politics* (Chicago: University of Chicago Press, 1946): 202.

[13] Of necessity, this chapter will focus on Wight as a *Christian* realist. For analyses of other aspects of Wight's thought, see Hedley Bull's introductions to Wight's posthumous *Systems of States* and *International Theory*.

[14] This is ironic in that Niebuhr always found the language of Catholic natural law theory to be inadequate, a mere baptizing of historically contingent structures. See for example his discussion in "Augustine's Political Realism," in *Christian Realism and Political Problems* (New York: Scribner's, 1953): 132-3.

[15] These volumes were a project of the Royal Institute of International Affairs and published by Oxford University Press over the years 1934 to 1961.

[16] Wight indicated this was more out of intransigence; Toynbee would not have to alter his argument. Martin Wight, "Arnold Toynbee: An Appreciation." *International Affairs* 52:1 (January 1976): 10-12.

[17] "The Crux for an Historian Brought up in the Christian Tradition" and "Spiritual and Material Achievement: The Law of Inverse Operation in Italian Visual Art." In Arnold J. Toynbee, *A Study of History*, vol. 7 (Oxford: Oxford University Press, 1954).

[18] *The Development of the Legislative Council 1606-1945* (London: Faber and Faber, 1946); *The Gold Coast Legislative Council* (London: Faber and Faber, 1947); *British Colonial Constitutions 1947* (Oxford: Clarendon Press, 1952); and coauthored with W. Arthur Lewis, Michael Scott, and Colin Legum, *Attitude to Africa* (Harmondsworth, UK: Penguin, 1951).

[19] After Wight's death, Hedley Bull and Carsten Holbraad published a revised and expanded edition based on Wight's notes. All citations to *Power Politics* are from this version.

[20] These lectures were posthumously published as *International Theory*.

[21] Butterfield wanted Alasdair MacIntyre as well, but some members thought he would push the Committee away from a solid focus on ethics *and* international politics. See Scott M. Thomas, "Faith, History, and Martin Wight: The Role of Religion in the Historical Sociology of the English School of International Relations." *International Affairs* 77:4 (October 2001): 918. The Rockefeller Foundation, under the auspices of Kenneth W. Thompson, funded the Committee. See Tim Dunne, *Inventing International Society: A History of the English School* (New York: St. Martin's, 1998) for a complete account.

[22] *International Theory*, 1.

[23] For a brief overview, see Martin Wight, "An Anatomy of International Thought." *Review of International Studies* 13 (January 1995): 221-27.
[24] *International Theory*, 16.
[25] Wight, "Western Values," 90.
[26] *International Theory*, 14. The phrase "written on the heart" is St. Paul's (Romans 2:15).
[27] Ibid, 7-8. *Kantianism* may be a misnomer however, if Charles Taylor is correct. Taylor holds that Kant refuses to countenance any revolutionary action. See "Kant's Theory of Freedom" in *Philosophy and the Human Sciences* (Cambridge: Cambridge University Press, 1985): 330.
[28] Ibid, 109.
[29] Gabriele Wight, his widow, suggests that the "barbarians" chapter is the best starting point for reading Wight. See Roger Epp, "The English School on the Frontiers of International Society: A Hermeneutic Recollection." *Review of International Studies* 24 (December 1998): 56.
[30] In later years, the three traditions are further refined into subcategories. These include aggressive and defensive Machiavellians, realist and idealist Grotians, and evolutionary and revolutionary Kantians. These categories may be arranged in a circle, with revolutionary Kantianism shading into aggressive Machiavellianism. See *International Theory*, 158-63.
[31] Ibid, 158-59.
[32] Ibid, 161. This closely corresponds to William H. Dray's classifications of the patterns of history. The Hegelian or cyclical view equates to the Machiavellian tradition. The Toynbeean or progressive view equates to the Kantian tradition. The Niebuhrian or chaotic view equates to the Grotian tradition. See Dray, *Philosophy of History* (Englewood Cliffs, NJ: Prentice-Hall, 1964).
[33] *International Theory*, 161.
[34] Ibid, 161-2.
[35] Ibid, 162.
[36] Ibid, 268. Also in the reference work *Contemporary Authors*, Wight's politics are described as Grotian. Presumably he provided this information himself. (Thanks are due to Professor David Yost, who alerted me to this entry.)
[37] Wight was a good friend of Dick Sheppard, leader of the 1930s Peace Movement. See Thomas, "Faith, History, and Martin Wight," 911-3.
[38] See Adrian Hastings, *A History of English Christianity, 1920-1985* (London: Collins, 1986), chapter 21, for an historical overview of the English Peace Movement.
[39] David S. Yost, "Political Philosophy and the Theory of International Relations." *International Affairs* 70:2 (April 1994): 271.
[40] Christian pacifists are divided as to whether all service in the state is forbidden, or merely participation in the use of lethal force.
[41] Martin Wight, "Christian Pacifism." *Theology* 33, no. 163 (July): 12-21. I will set page citations in the text.

[42] Ibid.
[43] Ibid, 15.
[44] Ibid, 16.
[45] Ibid, 17.
[46] Ibid, 18-19.
[47] Ibid, 20.
[48] Ibid, 21.
[49] "War and the Christian Conscience." *The Haileyburian* (July 27, 1940): 203-7. Wight was headmaster of Haileybury from 1938-1941.
[50] Ibid, 203.
[51] Roger Epp, "Martin Wight: International Relations as a Realm of Persuasion." In Francis A. Beer and Robert Hariman, eds., *Post-Realism: The Rhetorical Turn in International Relations* (East Lansing: Michigan State University Press, 1996), 140.
[52] C. T. McIntire, ed. *God, History, and Historians.* New York: Oxford University Press, 1977.
[53] These and many of the other leading figures in the revival of a Christian theory of history were involved in the founding of the World Council of Churches. The journal of the WCC, the *Ecumenical Review*, had Wight on its editorial board. He contributed an article, "The Church, Russia, and the West" (discussed below), to its inaugural issue.
[54] This did not automatically translate into conservative politics, as Anglo-Catholics could be found at all points of the political spectrum. See David Nicholls, "Two Tendencies in Anglo-Catholic Political Theology." In Geoffrey Rowell, ed., *Tradition Renewed: The Oxford Movement Conference Papers*, (London: Darton, Longman, and Todd Nichols 1986): 149. Wight is not easy to pigeonhole as a conservative.
[55] Martin Wight, "The Church, Russia, and the West." *Ecumenical Review* 1: 1 (Autumn 1948): 25.
[56] Ibid, 26-27.
[57] Ibid, 28.
[58] The Roman emperor Constantine legalized Christianity in 313 and made it an official religion of the empire.
[59] Ibid, 29.
[60] Ibid, 30.
[61] Wight never defines liberalism, but he seems to mean progressivist Enlightenment liberalism
[62] Ibid, 36.
[63] Ibid, 34.
[64] Ibid, 38-39.
[65] Ibid, 41.
[66] Martin Wight, "God in History," Sermon preached in Great St. Mary's Church, Cambridge, 15.
England, February 4, 1951.
[67] Martin Wight, "The Church, Russia, and the West," 43.

[68] Ibid, 45.
[69] Martin Wight, "God in History," 29.
[70] Martin Wight, "The Crux for an Historian Brought up in the Christian Tradition," 738.
[71] Martin Wight, "History and Judgement: Butterfield, Niebuhr and the Technical Historian." *The Frontier* 1: 8 (August 1950): 301-14. This view contains elements of both the Anabaptist notion of the church as the peaceable kingdom and the Anglo-Catholic emphasis on the sacramental nature of the church.
[72] Martin Wight, "The Church, Russia, and the West," 44.
[73] Ibid, 32.
[74] Wight, *Power Politics*, 137.
[75] Ibid, 34.
[76] From a 1948 BBC radio address by Wight.
[77] Cf. Isaiah 27:1. "In that day, the Lord will punish with his sword, his fierce, great and powerful sword, Leviathan the gliding serpent, Leviathan the coiling serpent; he will slay the monster of the sea."
[78] *Power Politics*, 26.
[79] *Systems of States*, 159.
[80] *Power Politics*, 2nd ed, 293.
[81] The essay is a chapter in *Diplomatic Investigations*.
[82] Wight did of course use the word *Grotian* in his *International Theory* lectures. Even then, *Grotian* is a late development, replacing the term *Rationalist*. The latest version of the lectures seems to predate "Western Values" by a year or so. By comparing the lectures and "Western Values" on who are the paradigmatic thinkers of the tradition, it is abundantly clear that *Whig* and *Grotian* are coterminous in Wight's thought.
[83] "Western Values in International Relations," 92-93.
[84] Ibid, 94.
[85] *International Theory*, 29.
[86] "Western Values in International Relations," 95. In *International Theory*, he notes that the realist agrees with the international lawyers that the state is a perfect organization; "because the state is the final term of political organization. This is not Hegelianism, but a matter of fact. The state is the body that affords the protection and organizes the welfare of its members. The majority of states to today may well be tyrannical or corrupt, but would not the inhabitants of every state be worse off if that state dissolved altogether? Nobody is prepared to transfer the state's functions to an international body..." (139-40).
[87] Ibid, 96-97.
[88] Ibid, 101.
[89] Ibid, 102.
[90] Ibid, 103.
[91] *City of God* XIX, 12. Quoted in *International Theory*, 206.
[92] *International Theory*, 206.

[93] Ibid, 28.
[94] Ibid, 29.
[95] "Western Values in International Relations," 116.
[96] Ibid.
[97] Ibid, 120-121.
[98] *Leviathan*, ch. 6.
[99] Ibid, ch. 13.
[100] "Western Values in International Relations," 121.
[101] Ibid, 122-123.
[102] Ibid, 123.
[103] Ibid, 124.
[104] Ibid, 126-128. Here is a clear break from Hans Morgenthau, who condemns such a dual standard as incoherent and unsustainable. See *Scientific Man versus Power Politics* (Chicago: University of Chicago Press, 1946): 178-80.
[105] Ibid, 128.
[106] Ibid, 131.
[107] *Power Politics*, 290. This chapter is unchanged from the original *Power Politics*. Hence even in his earliest and most "realist" work the concern with natural law and its efficacy is present.
[108] In Greek thought violence was fundamental. Greek creation accounts are stories of the taming of chaos; there is continual creation through violence. It is no surprise Plato and Aristotle saw the *polis* as a fortress against the exterior chaos. The perfect *polis* still has to fight wars. Writers such as Nietzsche picked up on this Greek concept of "making through struggle." Notably, Hans Morgenthau was quite influenced by Nietzsche. (See Christopher Frei, *Hans J. Morgenthau: An Intellectual Biography* [Baton Rouge: Louisiana State University Press, 2001]). By contrast, in Genesis, God merely speaks, and it is so. The usual Mesopotamian mythological symbols of chaos, such as sea monsters, are merely described in passing as creatures like any other. When Augustine describes his vision of the City of God, he drew on the Hebrew conception of created order against that of the Greek concept of chaos. That is, all of the cosmos was *ultimately* in harmony. Sin or evil was merely a corruption of this harmony.
[109] *International Theory*, 14.
[110] Ibid, 22.
[111] *Power Politics*, 293.

Chapter 6

John Coleman Bennett in Contemporary Context

David McCreary

John Coleman Bennett (1903-1995) wrote for a period of about sixty years, but little of what he wrote seems dated. Whether he is dealing with church-state issues, social policy, foreign policy, the duties and privileges of a Christian citizen, or emerging theologies in the poorer countries, much of what he wrote from the 1930's on is still largely pertinent to our world. This is due to his perspicacious understanding of social issues and his balance in presenting opposing sides of an argument, not to mention an open mind. He is still close to us in time and his writing tends to present wider principles that abide in spite of changing historical conditions.

During his career, he stood in the shadow of Reinhold Niebuhr, his colleague and friend at Union Theological Seminary in New York City, with whom he shared many common assumptions and theological understandings of God, humanity, and history. Theologian John B. Cobb, Jr., regards him as the inheritor of Niebuhr's mantle.[1] There is truth in that claim.

In style, if not in substance, however, it would be wrong simply to identify Bennett as a campfollower of Reinhold Niebuhr. By his own account, Niebuhr appreciated Bennett's calm and considered style of writing which he found wanting in his own polemical approach and from which he thought he could learn. Niebuhr consciously used polemic to shake up the "comfortable" liberal optimists of the earlier part of the twentieth-century. Their easy idealism regarding pacifism, world government, and building the Kingdom of God through a moral society forced Niebuhr to fight for the recognition of "immoral society" as a permanent condition. This "Christian realism" about society had earlier precedent in Augustinian Christian thinking, to which in some ways he returned, had lost its hold on the church in the progressive optimism of a society intrigued with technological solutions and social engineering. Deeply in touch with the political and social realities of his time, especially the plight of the poor, Niebuhr emphasized the realities of power and economic inequality in the struggle for justice. There is little difference between Niebuhr and Bennett on this account.

To appreciate Bennett's unique contributions to the realist debate, we need to read him with our own problems, issues, and intellectual growth in mind. Today we no longer think with the optimistic mood that gave rise to world-saving panaceas. We are often despairing of any real advance in human kindness, justice, or solutions to intractable problems. It is easy to be cynical rather than realistic in the Niebuhrian sense. It is even possible to treat Niebuhr as a contributor to the general pessimism of our age, a conservative reinforcer of the status quo, rather than the advocate of justice and social change that he was. Christian realism, as Niebuhr and Bennett understood it, was not baptized Machiavellianism. It was the precarious attempt to walk a fine line between hope and despair, possibility and reality. In some ways, Bennett was better at this than Niebuhr.

If calm and considered was more Bennett's style, there is another respect in which Bennett contrasts to Niebuhr. Early in his career Bennett taught systematic theology, which is the full exposition of the Christian faith through its major doctrines. Niebuhr never had an interest in fully expounding the truth of the Christian faith. As a professor of "applied Christianity," he was more eclectic and narrow in his theological approach to issues. He selectively used the doctrines of sin, perfection, and grace as major themes in his ethical and social writings, or presupposed them in addressing secular audiences who learned from him. Bennett, as a systematic theologian, developed social ethics within the full range of Christian doctrine, including his understanding of the church and its place in society (ecclesiology), the nature, work, and person of Christ (christology), the role of the Holy Spirit in salvation history as an emancipatory movement (pneumatology), and the ultimate Christian hope (eschatology). The technical terms may seem arcane to those unfamiliar with the work of systematic theology, but in assaying the truth of Christianity, they are a permanent part of Christian thought through the ages. Bennett understood this and put his theological training to work in the service of "social salvation."

Finally, Bennett outlived Reinhold Niebuhr by a quarter century, a fact that allowed him to come into contact with, and contribute to, newer theological currents. To the charge, put to him by this writer as well as others, that Christian realism had lost its prophetic edge and, in the fight against fascism and communism, become a defender of the status quo, he was as adamant as he was indignant. "No," he said, "there are always new realities to be considered. We must be realistic about liberation and poverty and oppression as many liberation theologians are calling us to do."[2] Indeed, Bennett was more sympathetic to liberation theology than he was to its detractors in wealthy countries. Bennett observes, "More recently some neo-conservatives claim Niebuhr as one of themselves. Michael Novak in his able book, *The Spirit of Democratic Capitalism,* claims to be inspired by Niebuhr. His picture of Democratic Capitalism is not so bad but his complacency about what it is like in this country today and about its being the best road for all countries is fatuous."[3]

On the other side, Bennett also criticized a noted liberal theologian who took liberation theology to task because it was "witness" and not "theology" in the proper sense of the word. Theology, it was argued, has to do with the truth of the gospel, not the various ways it is witnessed to. While Bennett acknowledged that the distinction was probably accurate, he wondered how one could write a book about liberation theology and not mention once that the Latin Americans had a case against the United States.[4]

One mark of Bennett's thought is that it is always concrete rather than abstract, it is down-to-earth and to the point. As we survey his thought, particularly on sin and salvation, we will see that any abstract philosophical principles always find some exemplification in concrete experience and practice.

Bennett's Realism in the Currents of Contemporary Theology

Niebuhr and the Christian realists were often thought of as "neo-orthodox" theologians who shared common assumptions with the great twentieth-century Protestant theologian, Karl Barth. They were called "neo-orthodox" because of their rejection of the liberal theological school of Schleiermacher and Ritschl. The liberal theologian, Schubert Ogden, has aptly pointed out, that the term, "neo-orthodoxy," should not be understood as a restoration of Reformation theologies or any other orthodoxy. Orthodoxy does not produce neo-orthodoxy.

Liberalism produces neo-orthodoxy as a self-critical phase of its own excesses or mistakes. In the case of the earlier social gospel liberalism, the criticism was directed primarily at a facile optimism about perfecting society by human effort. Although neo-orthodox theologians found Augustine, Luther, and Calvin to be informative, they hardly wanted to return to a pre-critical age when science and historical criticism were only in their infancy, if existing at all. Karl Barth, Reinhold Niebuhr, and others could all agree that the Bible could be studied by historical-critical methods, that scientific evolution was fact, and that the Bible needed some form of "demythologizing" (i.e., a mytho-poetic interpretation or hermeneutics).

Nevertheless, Niebuhr and Bennett did not use the neo-orthodox label to describe their own work, even if others did. Both did use the phrase, "Christian realism," and that is probably a better designation because they felt Barth endangered social ethics by his own extremes. If anything, Bennett allied himself more with a critic of Barth, Emil Brunner, who not only balanced antinomies better, but also allowed a place for natural law and natural theology in a way that Barth did not. This provided Bennett with an opening to Catholic natural law teaching, while rejecting some of the legalistic and historically-bound versions of it. One of the burdens of Bennett's thought is to move between the antinomies of a fixed legalism with its rigidity toward social change and the nihilistic side of moral relativism that denies any common moral imperatives uniting humanity. The moral imperative lies somewhere in the balance between those extremes.

Theologically, then, Bennett accepts natural theology and general revelation as points of contact with the secular and non-Christian world. Christian faith in the revelation of God in Jesus Christ is not above rational understanding and criticism. Still, faith precedes understanding and arguments that might be put forth to support its truth. He is also following the lead of H. Richard Niebuhr in *The Meaning of Revelation*, that all truth is perspectival and therefore lacks universality.[4] On historicist, rather than obscurantist, grounds, Bennett sees no universal truth unaffected by the historical situation in which it is asserted. Christian revelation corrects, alters, or transforms natural theology through the historical forms by which that revelation is understood.[5]

While Christian realists are not noted as philosophers of religion or descriptive metaphysicians, Bennett is open to philosophies such as Alfred North Whitehead's process philosophy or philosophy of organism. Rational speculative systems are valuable both to science and to theology in interpreting their basic notions. In particular, the notion of God needs metaphysical exposition, though the Christian realists dwell more on the historical experience of divine encounter and human response than on the relation of God to the whole natural order. In this regard, Christian realism is closer to liberation theology than to process theology.

Since both liberation theology and process theology have overshadowed Christian realism since the 1970's, the connections among the three theologies is in order.

In assessing the place of Christian realism and liberation theology vis-à-vis process theology, Bennett sees three points of difference. First, "Both Christian Realism and Liberation Theology were from the beginning strongly political whereas political activism has only lately become an interest of Process Theology." Second, "There is no doubt that both Christian Realism and Liberation Theology are centered in history and have very little interest in nature. Process Theology would find this very one-sided and wrong." Third, "Neither Christian Realism nor Liberation Theology has the metaphysical confidence of all Process Theologians."[6]

Bennett appreciates in process theology a couple of things that make a contribution to the Christian realist position, as well as the concerns of liberation theology. First, process thought claims to speak of God's nature as it is in itself, not just as God is active in history. Realists and liberationists speak often about God's judging or liberating activity in history, but feel highly constrained about any metaphysical description of God. This is due in large part because both realists and liberationists were trained in the same European and North American schools and universities with their post-Enlightenment restrictions on the metaphysical use of reason.

The positive gain of process theology over Christian realism and liberation theology is a wider focus on creation as both history and nature rather than dividing the two and limiting theological discourse only to history. In practice, this means nature and non-human life have value in themselves and need liberation from oppression, exploitation, and injustice. In process thought, to be is to be a value, which is not simply utilitarian value for humans. Each being, from the simplest to the most complex, has intrinsic value. The love of God for all nature, human and non-human, finds expression in God's creative response to the world, bringing rich harmony out of chaotic forces.

Though Bennett did not develop his thought in light of Whitehead's cosmological theory, he did ally himself with the "radical empiricism" that underlies process philosophy. "Radical empiricism" is a term

William James coined for any view of experience that takes account of all experience, not just the five senses. It rejects the prejudice in favor of higher forms of experience found in the senses, seeking to include feelings, subconscious intuitions, religious experiences, memory as a direct experience of causality, and anything else he calls "the buzzing, blooming confusion." Radical empiricism contrasts with positivism or positivist empiricism by accepting a wider notion of fact than positivists are willing to admit in sticking to the deliverances of the senses, especially sight. Positivism renders religious statements meaningless by a dogmatic unwillingness to admit these wider dimensions of experience.

Bennett, however, does not want to use radical empiricism to introduce a philosophical defense of orthodox supernaturalism, the definition of "supernaturalism" depending on what one means by "natural." He defends instead God's divine imminence in nature and experience in a way common to theistic philosophers, such as Whitehead, James, and others. He writes:

> We can recognize these processes as the work of God if we already believe in the existence of the Christian God. Such a belief is not merely wishful thinking. It can be grounded in a philosophy of religion such as that which we find in E. W. Lyman's *The Meaning and Truth of Religion* or F. R. Tennant's *Philosophical Theology*. Such a philosophy is based upon man's whole experience of reality. It is confirmed by the intuitions of faith which come to those who are not mere spectators but who are loyal participants within the divine processes which we have described—especially men who have been persuaded and have become part of the process of persuasion and men who have been healed and have become part of the process of healing. The Christian revelation furnishes part of the data for the philosophy of religion and through it God persuades most powerfully and heals most fully.[7]

With Bennett's theological views stated generally, we now turn to the more specific issues of order and disorder in the world as they relate to human nature and affairs.

"The Mystery of Iniquity" Analyzed

In his 1935 work, *Social Salvation*, Bennett laid the foundation for his own understanding of the Christian faith, the human condition, and the Christian's hope. From the beginning of this preface to social action and amelioration of specific evils in society, Bennett recognizes the truth in St. Paul's statement, "The mystery of iniquity doth already work." (2 Thessalonians 2:7, KJV)   Bennett writes:

> There is no more baffling experience than to catch a glimpse of the contrast between what human life might be in this world and what it is. Apart from any limitations imposed by nature we seem to be caught in a vast network of evil that we are unable to overcome or escape. There seems to be an inherent wrongness in human life that corrupts and destroys. If the individual looks into his own soul without self-deception he will find there traces enough of this evil. But, if he looks at the destructive forces in society which lead to exploitation and war he cannot help feeling that they are more diabolical than any desires or attitudes which he can find in his own heart even though, whether he is their tool or victim, they could not go on without the consent of multitudes of people like himself. These evil social processes can be traced to no worse motives in our time than in any time but that does not keep them from being more destructive than they have ever been.[8]

Christian faith is more than just a cult of individual salvation so often proclaimed in various forms by the sectarian Christian churches, supposedly delivering us from the impurities of the world and its moral dilemmas. Christians have social responsibilities, though they have often failed to fulfill them. The beginning of Christian realism is penance regarding this fact by self-critical examination and correction. Bennett and Niebuhr would see this repentance as the appropriate Christian response to the abiding "sin" infecting all human institutions, including (and especially) the church. 'Sin,' in their definition, is an inordinate pride in human moral achievements issuing in self-righteousness. Thus, both Niebuhr and Bennett tend to criticize human beings at their best rather than at their worst. Even the best people will mess up.

This responsibility, though clear, is difficult to carry out. Just the fact that so many social problems demand an expertise that few Christians have makes appropriate Christian decisions difficult for the average person in the pew. These technical aspects are neutral issues in making Christian choices and they demand knowledge more than just good will. Even among experts there are fundamental disagreements of perspective, some of which lead willy-nilly to evil consequences regardless of intent. And who, in a privileged, rich, and powerful nation, can really understand the poor, the oppressed, the neglected, and the socially weak? We do not have the power of imagination, unless we are extraordinarily sensitive, to see beyond what surely remains invisible to most of us: that we are privileged, rich, and powerful, even though we may have little control over our government and its policies. These are major themes running throughout Bennett's writings.

One fundamental obstacle to social salvation is too simple a view of evil. "In the social thinking of Christians there is vagueness and oversimplification in the diagnosis of the particular social evils we face," he wrote in a preparatory volume of essays to the 1937 Oxford Conference on Church, Community, and State. "The usual form which this tendency takes is to reduce all evil to one root—sin. Even if some account is given of the specific, proximate causes of such evils as war and economic injustice these causes are not taken seriously, and emphasis is placed too soon on the fact of sin, which, since it can be used to explain everything, really explains nothing in particular."[9] The use of sin to explain away solutions to problems that demand critical analysis and creative imagination for their understanding and transformation becomes in effect the precondition for offering religion as an opiate. Marx's charge that religion is the "opiate of the people" only applies to those forms of faith that do not motivate one to "change the things that can be changed" (Niebuhr's "serenity prayer").[10] The Christian realist seeks to distinguish what can and what cannot be changed, not avoid change altogether. Dogmatic pessimism about the transformative possibilities of humans is just as unwarranted as the overly-optimistic belief in human and social perfectibility. By staying within the realm of specific facts, Bennett follows a more empirical path about the causes of social evils that have given rise to pessimism about the total human situation.

Obstacles to change, however, are many. First of all is ambiguity in the word, 'sin,' itself, which causes confusion from the outset. Even in the Bible, the word is not clearly defined and has a number of meanings. While noting the problem of definition, Bennett does not want to dwell on proposing an unambiguous meaning to the term. Rather, he would distinguish five types of experience that are clearly distinct and should not be lumped together under one word.

> 1. The attitude of religious humility which makes the best men unable to give themselves credit for moral or spiritual achievements, which makes them regard themselves as part of the world's wrongness, which creates a sense of unworthiness which is not necessarily related to any particular evil for which they are morally responsible.
> 2. The choices of men who are limited by an external situation which is beyond their control and which forces them to make tragic compromises with evil. Here we see the cumulative results of the evil choices of the past, which have created a present situation in which men of the best intentions face limited possibilities. Into the making of this inherited

external situation there have gone all the factors that will be discussed in this paper.
3. The choices of men who are living in the presence of far better possibilities than those which they choose to realize, but who are blinded by unavoidable ignorance which has for them external causes.
4. The choices of men who are living in the presence of far better possibilities than those which they choose to realize, but who are blinded by ignorance that is primarily the result of inertia, selfishness, and moral insensitivity.
5. The choices of men who are living in the presence of far better possibilities than those which they choose, but who deliberately and with full knowledge violate the standards of conduct which they know to be binding on them.[11]

If these five factors cover the variety of meanings of 'sin,' then we can proceed with the more concrete obstacles to social change, i.e., social salvation. Of course, most of us can cite examples from our own experience for each of the five types of evil Bennett lists. One example from Bennett's day is Germany and how to deal with the question of guilt for Nazi atrocities.

As a case of the first form of experience, German Evangelical Church leaders signed the "Stuttgart Confession" after the war, which took responsibility for much of the criminal Nazi atrocities and the war itself. "...We accuse ourselves that we didn't witness more courageously, pray more faithfully, believe more joyously, love more ardently."[12] While it is an important *mea culpa*, these leaders were the "good Germans" who had not fallen in line with the German Christians of Nazi persuasion. Some, like Bishop Lilje and Pastor Niemoeller, had served time in jail for their convictions and activities in the church. The statement was criticized by those who bore more responsibility than they owned for what came to pass in those years. However, it was a necessary step in reconciling not only the world church, but in bringing healing and reconciliation between Germany and its former enemies.

The Barmen Declaration of 1933 might be an example of a response to the second form of moral experience: prior choices weighing heavily on the present over which one had no control or responsibility. The totalitarian German imperial state is usually traced back to Bismarck and the Prussian unification of Germany on authoritarian and anti-liberal principles. Though not the direct or only cause of Nazism, that heritage weighed heavily on Germany in the twentieth-century. By the time theologian Karl Barth formulated the Barmen Declaration, basically defending the first commandment—to have no other gods before me—against Nazi idolatry, the die had been cast.[13] Some have criticized the declaration as ten years too late and only concerned with the freedom of the church, not human rights as such. Barth regretted later that it said nothing about the Jews and their positive role in Christian tradition. There is truth in this, but one wonders if the church could have done much at all after the Versailles treaty and its demand for heavy reparations, the high inflation, the depression, and a democracy that had only minimal support from the people.

In the third and fourth cases, evil produced by blindness resulting from ignorance of external causes, and ignorance resulting from inertia, selfishness, and moral insensitivity, many Germans in the inter-war years had very little political understanding of their situation because of these choices. Class interests often prevailed over universal interests. The result was a broad base of support for Hitler in his election and lack of protest after he assumed dictatorial powers. One observer called these people "normal Nazis," although not all Germans actually belonged to the party.

The fifth class of moral experience those persons exemplify who knowingly and cynically chose Nazism despite its violation of basic human rights and international standards of national conduct. The "criminal Nazis" we might call them.

While the German experience with Nazism has been a touchstone for modern reflection on ethics and the dilemmas of choosing a moral course of action, other historical experiences, such as choices in the U.S. over slavery or the displacement of American Indians could easily be substituted. In sum, Bennett recognized the moral ambiguity of various political dilemmas and pointed out that there were both objective and subjective factors which must be considered in moral decision-making.

Objective and Subjective Factors in Moral Decision-Making

The objective factors

Bennett recognized that in a world of knowledge vastly more specialized than it once was, no one can claim expertise in every specialty. Yet, technical knowledge is often part of moral decision-making. When we try to decide a moral issue on the basis of certain consequences flowing from a certain policy, the consequences often are not obvious to those of us who lack expertise in a particular field or lack farsightedness. We must rely upon experts, but experts themselves often do not agree.

The first objective factor is *the size and complexity of modern social problems.* As an illustration, let us take an issue that concerned Bennett and other Christian realists in the '30's and which still concerns us today: economics. Is the church competent to speak on economic issues? Bennett analyzes this issue into three questions regarding the U.S. economy:

What does capitalism do to persons?
What kind of economic order is just and desirable?
What kind of economic order is possible within the limits set by human nature and the structure of economic life?[14]

While the first two questions come clearly within the pastoral and prophetic work of the churches, the third question presupposes technical knowledge of economic systems and how they function. There may be differing ideas on how to avoid recurring depressions in the business cycle. Without consensus on that, furthering economic justice and avoiding economic misery bogs down in differing economists' prescriptions. Gaining some broad understanding of economics seems to be the first step in arriving at an answer to the other questions.

Lags in social development account for another form of objective factor. Immigration rates around the beginning of the twentieth-century were high, but the population was low compared to the total land available, the type of unskilled labor needed, and the number of jobs available. Today, that is no longer the case. Low-skilled immigrants compete with the working poor in this country, lowering wages for those who can least afford it. The expected doubling of the population within this century causes real concerns about the carrying capacity of the land. Yet, to say,"We are a nation of immigrants," as a precedent simply defines the nation in terms of immigration rather than defining the role of immigration today and its affects on the future.

The unpredictability of results is also an objective factor. Assimilating the American Indian to white standards gave the indigenous peoples access to a mainstream education and its advantages, but also robbed them of traditions and a spirituality that served as the common glue in their culture. Even though assimilationist policies are out of favor today, Native Americans nonetheless deal with the long-term unforeseen negative consequences of policies which might have been well-meaning, but proved otherwise.

The necessity of concerted action in dealing with problems. Bennett names several large subjects that fit this category, such as international economic injustice, reduction of armaments, and provisions for collective security. Various forms of discrimination and ecological destruction also demand the intervention of "big government," even though regulation is an affront to many economic individualists. He does not lightly dismiss the national government in bringing its resources and power to bear, when only national government can really deal with a problem. This is especially true in social services, education, and health care.

The positive bias towards evil embodied in institutions, movements, and social habits. Changing institutional behavior is more than just changing the individuals making up the institution—the point of Reinhold Niebuhr's *Moral Man and Immoral Society.* There is a difference in the way people feel and act as individuals and their behavior within institutions for which they bear responsibility and whose corporate culture and traditions they internalize. In light of the imminent war in Europe at the time Bennett wrote his article, he observed: "...We must consider as positively evil the vicious circle of which the last war was but one incident—the vicious circle of defeat and revenge, of hate and fear, of militaristic nationalism met by militaristic nationalism."[15] The cycle could have been broken with moral insight, foresight about the consequences, and courage to act by those in power.

The subjective factors

The subjective factors of moral decision-making that may lead to evil consequences demand some introspection to see in oneself, but can be obvious in the attitudes and actions of others or as others observe us. We notice the splinter in another's eye, but ignore the log in our own.

The subjective factors include: the pull of self-interest—the greater part of our deliberate choice of evil; provincialism which is the result of external conditions; specialization or a narrow focus on a particular method assumed to be more universal than it is; fatigue; theories which are honestly held but do not fit the facts of modern life; the existence of convenient facades for deceiving the self and others, including various ideologies; social inertia caused by aging; stupidity due to physiological changes, routine, and the educational process itself; inescapable limits of attention and imagination; becoming accustomed to suffering at a distance; emotional maladjustment of individuals; and the caution that is the result of the unpredictability of results.

In short, the "mystery of iniquity" is not just the result of something dogmatically asserted as "original sin," which nullifies social responsibility on the part of humanity and, especially, Christians. Bennett's analysis calls for an extension of the term, "sin," to cover a variety of social conditions which cry out for positive action in the full awareness that the answers may be difficult. Difficulties should not be used to avoid responsibility, but lead to deeper and more comprehensive solutions. Social evil demands "social salvation."

Social Salvation as Christian Realism in Action

Critics of Niebuhr who charge his later thought was a sell-out to conservatives and the status quo should read John Bennett as if he were Niebuhr in later years.[16] He outlived Niebuhr and other Christian realists and took account of new global developments and the changing consciousness about the "Third World." Christian realism, like liberation theology, is not a school with a fixed point of view, but a style of thinking. For its part, Christian realism tries to be realistic about all the realities confronting us. There is enough in Niebuhr's critical view of the Vietnam War to indicate that his thinking was already evolving when he died in 1971.

One requirement of Christian realism is that it place all relative moral issues in light of an absolute standard, the law of love. While recognizing the finite achievement of relative justice as the goal of realistic thinking and action, there is the absolute demand for love that stands in judgment over all finite achievements of goodness. In speaking to the church, Bennett writes: "Our integrity as Christians depends upon our efforts to overcome the injustice which is the other side of our own privileges."[17] Consequently, there is simply no other option for the Christian than to seek justice as the social expression of love.

It has to be said that many Christians, especially liberal pastors, who were schooled in the "Social Gospel" (of which Christian realists were critics), found it tremendously energizing for a social justice ministry. Christian realists admittedly undercut that enthusiasm. Recognizing that their criticisms took some of the wind out of the sails of Social Gospel Christians, Bennett reassured them of two things: That the gospel is intrinsically social and that real progress in human welfare is possible.

To take the second point first, progress in human welfare takes time and is not achieved overnight. Both Niebuhr and Bennett seemed to think in historical periods of centuries and realized that the Christian ethos was built up over centuries of Christian thinking, experience, and action, which in nominally Christian countries could be taken for granted. Even post-Christian pagans are inheritors of Christian values that they unconsciously witness to. As Garrison Keillor has quipped: "Even the atheists in Minnesota are Lutheran atheists. It is the Lutheran God they don't believe in." A tradition is not so easily shaken off.

It is this Christian ethos, built up over a thousand years, which Bennett fears is dissolving and losing its grip on society. Without it, progress in human welfare is not possible, at least, in Christian terms. He writes:

> We used to live in a world in which people generally realized that Christian standards had a claim upon them, in which minorities could speak freely and keep national life under judgment in the light of those standards, in which those who exercised power were at least inhibited by the scruples of their own or of other peoples' Christian conscience. Europe and America—the so-called West—belonged to that world, and we were conscious of membership in a common moral universe of discourse.[18]

Bennett is not pleading for a "Christian society" that would fly in the face of religious freedom, but he does believe that common values are necessary for social cohesion. Whether these values are the result of Christian ethics, natural law, or a categorical imperative, they still demand instruction that instills their importance and stops evil social processes that erode them.

Churches should not try to influence society by their own political machinations, ignoring the ambiguity in supporting any candidate, platform, or party in the secular political arena. However, by creative thinking and witness, through raising questions about shortsighted policies and programs, by individual Christians motivated by their common faith to involve themselves in the political process, or by the institutional pronouncements on social issues that churches often make, they can have influence that creates social consciousness and conscience.[19]

Bennett's other reaffirmation of Social Gospel thought is that the gospel is intrinsically social. There is no gospel apart from social consequences. He especially singles out churches and Christians in America for preaching a gospel of religious individualism that simply mirrors the economic individualism of our society. "Me and Jesus" is not enough of a religion. It ignores the teachings of Jesus and turns

Christianity into a mere cult of personal salvation.

There are problems to locating the "historical Jesus" in history, because the gospels themselves were not histories but gospels. They were literary witnesses to "The Good News," probably an "emergency literature" written to keep the oral form of witness from disappearing with a dying generation. Over the past two centuries or so, many historians have concluded that we cannot know much about Jesus and moderns who have tried to write such a history tended to read into him their own modern beliefs and assumptions about him. To a progressive Christian at the turn of the twentieth century, Jesus teaches a broad humanitarianism and a social program called "the kingdom of God" free of all apocalyptic excess. This liberalism is now dated due to self-critical liberals like Albert Schweitzer, Karl Barth, and Rudolf Bultmann. Bennett does not try to reconstruct the historical Jesus, but to find in the gospels a clear witness to the moral teachings of Jesus, which characterized his ministry and life.

For Bennett there are six traits that build up a picture of Jesus and his moral example and teaching, which are worth quoting in full:

1. The ethic of Jesus is rooted in his religion. God is the pattern for ethical life. We are to be perfect, merciful, and to love our enemies in order to be like God. Moreover the worth of persons that is a basic assumption of this ethic is known from God's love for them.

2. For Jesus the moral problem is primarily a problem of the inner life. Overt acts are merely expressions of the motives and dispositions of the heart. "But I say unto you that every one who is angry with his brother..."

3. Central and controlling in the ethic of Jesus is love—love without barriers and love to the point of self-sacrifice. The circle of love must include enemies, sinners, publicans, Samaritans, "even these least"—the unnamed victims of society. Love should be absolute not only in its inclusiveness but also in its intensity. It demands singleness of mind. It must forgive seventy times seven. It must be willing to pay the price of the Cross.

4. Jesus maintains a balance between love and aggressive dealing with evil. There is what John McKay calls the "Christ of the whip." He came to cast fire on the earth, to bring not peace but a sword. His denunciations of the Pharisees and his cleansing of the temple, instead of being blemishes to be explained away, reveal the balance of his character.

5. Jesus' scale of values gives first place to the highest spiritual goods but it makes room for the primary needs of health and bread. He saw the evil of wealth and the evil of hunger. He avoided the extremes of ascetic religion and of this-worldly religion, of Hinduism and Communism.

6. Jesus saw the moral and religious importance of humility. One should be as receptive as a child. The poor, the meek, those who know that they

are sinners—they are the folk who are most fit for the Kingdom of God. The parable of the Pharisee and the Publican gives in perfect form this side of Jesus' thought.[20]

Whatever the grounds for skepticism about the historical Jesus, any gospel that neglects his life and teachings threatens to pervert Christianity into a salvation cult only, even if it takes several generations to do it.[21]

Does the Bible Have All the Answers?

From a Christian perspective on the Bible and its central story, Christ redeems fallen Adam. That is usually what Christians mean when they say that the Bible has all the answers. It means that the biblical story is a redemptive story. Christians preach this story, but it can be oversimplified, causing Christians to overstate or distort the Bible's own claims, stoked in large part by notions of its inerrancy and infallibility. There are problems to which the Bible does not speak.

Biblical scholar Victor Furnish, speaking at a ministers conference, told how he heard President Reagan say in a speech, "The Bible has the answer for every question we ask today." About the same time, Walter Cronkite was asked what the three greatest problems facing the world were. He replied, the ecological crisis, the overpopulation of the earth, and nuclear warfare. Furnish then observed that the Bible not only had no answers for these problems, but because they are essentially modern, the writers of the Bible could not even have conceived of them.

Christian realism is an example of Christian thinking trying to be authentic both to the biblical witness to redemption and to the need for creative answers to questions that may never have occurred before. In that sense, Christian tradition is always in a state of creative transformation rather than a deposit of answers for all the questions humanity may ever ask. Christianity, as a movement in history, can only be understood backwards by understanding its historical forms, but history does not dictate what Christianity will be like in the future. All that Christians can hope for in giving serious thought to serious problems is that we bring forward the fire of the tradition and not the ashes.

It is in the tension between past tradition and current issues that Christian realists try to relate the two. For Bennett, this means that the Bible does not offer detailed answers to many modern quandaries and may only offer vague generalities or clues. Arguments about abortion on biblical grounds, for instance, are of this kind. That is the reason that Bennett calls for guiding principles and "middle axioms" to supply more specificity to ethical imperatives without absolutizing relative values or abusing the Bible by reading our own values and ideas into it.

At the 1937 Oxford Conference on Church, Community, and State, the ecumenical church put forth guiding principles or middle axioms for a Christian position on economics, which was as acute then as it is now. There were five of them:

(1) Right fellowship between man and man being a condition of man's fellowship with God, every economic arrangement which frustrates or restricts it must be modified.
(2) Regardless of race or class every child and youth must have opportunities of education suitable for the full development of his particular capacities.
(3) Persons disabled from economic activity, whether by sickness, infirmity, or age, should not be economically penalized on account of their disability, but on the contrary should be the object of particular care.
(4) Labor has intrinsic worth, and dignity, as being designed by God for man's welfare. The duty and the right of men to work should therefore alike be emphasized. In the industrial process labor should never be considered as a mere commodity. In their daily work men should be able to recognize and fulfill a Christian vocation. The workingman, whether in field or factory, is entitled to a living wage, wholesome surroundings and a recognized voice in decisions, which affect his welfare as a worker.
(5) The resources of the earth, such as the soil and mineral wealth, should be recognized as gifts of God to the whole human race and used with due and balanced consideration for the needs of the present and future generations.[22]

In the context of 1937 and the American and European make-up of the conference, it is a set of principles that spoke mainly to the economic misery in the industrial nations and their emerging welfare states. It took account of four conditions common to countries with advanced market economies. Bennett notes: "These principles should be seen against the background of the very drastic criticism of the present economic order in that same report on four counts: that it encourages acquisitiveness, that it creates in some countries 'shocking' and in all countries 'considerable' inequality, that it is characterized by the concentration of irresponsible economic power and that it very generally frustrates the sense of Christian vocation."[23]

The conflict at that time within the industrial countries between those who advocated the value of free markets and those who advocated social planning was particularly sharp in the United States and divided the constituencies of most churches. Without directly challenging the capitalist economic system as such, Bennett proposed two middle axioms that he felt all Christians could agree upon.

> a. That the national community acting through government in cooperation with industry, labor, and agriculture has responsibility to maintain full employment.
> b. That the national community should prevent all private centers of economic power from becoming stronger than the government.[24]

Agreement on these principles may not solve all the problems and disagreements between opposed social policies. They may still cause sharp divisions. Yet, middle axioms do make more specific the issues at stake and take the discussion beyond vague slogans, generalities, and panaceas.

The Church as an Emancipatory Movement

Mainline churches in Bennett's time drew from a broad spectrum of the American society, making agreement on many social issues difficult. Party loyalties often outweighed Christian teaching about social welfare and reform. This is still true today, but some of the most active Christians politically are religious conservatives, not members of the mainline or "oldline" churches.

To speak of one Christian position on any given issue is not only difficult, but Christians often naively assume there is one. Bennett faulted liberal Christians for assuming that only one side of an argument was *the* Christian side. But we have seen in our time the same naive assumption among evangelicals that they alone hold the Christian position on issues that concern them intensely, such as abortion, funding for religious schools, pornography, teaching religion in public schools, and a stronger military defense. The prospects for concerted Christian action on any issue seems dismal and may even be undesirable.

There is another reason for reticence. The Christian is theologically understood as a citizen of two states: in Augustine's terms, the city of heaven and the city of earth. The first judges and guides the second. The implication of that understanding must relativize all political judgments, for political judgments rest upon a God who binds peoples together under a rule of justice. For reasons already given, Christians, like everyone else, have a hard time discovering what justice is in particular situations.

In spite of the difficulties, Bennett sees within the real, concrete churches (not abstractions like the universal church, the body of Christ, or the church invisible) grounds for hope that they might play a positive role in contributing to human welfare and freedom. For instance, the churches are a base of operation for Christians in a world that is often alien to their own values. Time and again, the state has been unable to absorb, neutralize, and crush churches as independent centers of thought and resistance to inhumanity on the part of the state. The very fact of their continuing existence under adverse circumstances makes them notable as alternative institutions calling for a higher loyalty than the state.

Moreover, the public fact of the church also means it should seek to influence the state. The separation of church and state in the U.S. does not prevent this, though keeping religion as a private sphere or concern is often the goal of interests adversely affected by the church's stands. Through its governing bodies, special offices, leading clergy and individuals using the support of the church to speak to government, the religious bodies can have considerable influence. As Bennett says, this should be done openly and after due consideration rather than in any clandestine manner.

> There can be no danger when the Church, after much free discussion, seeks to influence the state, so long as the Church limits itself to those issues concerning which it has competence, and so long as the whole procedure is open and above board. This is quite different from manipulations behind the scenes by ecclesiastics who are assumed to be able to deliver large blocks of votes. The Church should not by high pressure impose upon the whole community a policy that can only be defended on the basis of assumptions that are peculiar to itself.[25]

The church can also have an indirect influence in public life by contributing to the general moral tone of the community. Honesty, hard work, tolerance of others, and sensitivity to human need are constants in the preaching and teaching of the churches. In this regard, Bennett felt it was especially important for churches to overcome within themselves their own racial, social and class segregation.

While churches may be a source of national unity, and tempted to reinforce extreme nationalism, churches also are international in scope with a common allegiance to the same savior. Functionally, this can be, and often is, a source of meeting and understanding that can bring closer peoples of different nations and cultures. Loyalties that transcend the loyalty to the state are significant in building a community of nations.

Nevertheless, whatever the social functions of the churches may be, they cannot appeal to their social benefits as justification for their existence. Religion and the church are *sui generis* and their authority is solely in the nature of the God they worship.

> To regard the Church as a means, in the sense of making these central aspects of its life subordinate to its influence on society, is to turn things around and gradually to undercut that influence. A Church that ceases to be God-centered, that does not mediate the distinctively Christian gospel, that does not meet the deeper levels of human need, that does not have an ultimate faith that transcends all success and failure of social policy—such a Church may be used for a time to promote this or that social cause but it will become secularized. The indirect social effects of what the Church is depend upon its vitality as a worshipping community.[26]

The church as an emancipatory movement depends upon its commitment to that ultimate source of good that transcends and judges it, loves and forgives it, and finally fills and fulfills it with all truth. But in a pluralistic society, the church offers its guidance as one voice among others and there is always the freedom to oppose it both within the church and without.

Conclusion

In sum, Bennett's understanding of salvation is something that happens within the world of our common human experience. Life after death may also be part of that reality, but it is not the sole meaning or even the main meaning. His view, as noted above, fits well with process philosophy, holism, and other forms of "radical empiricism" that inform the liberal and historical trend of Christian theology today.

It must be said that Christian realists take no offense at the scientific study of religion and religious institutions, like churches, from a quantitative point of view. Indeed, much of the self-deception and blindness they decry can be uncovered by such methods. Issues of race, class, anti-Semitism, misogyny and other distortions of Christianity need serious study from a scientific point of view.

In the end, though, Christian faith has to do with meaning, values, quality, and norms. It has to do with the mystery of iniquity and the mystery of grace, mercy, and forgiveness. If not quantitative, these realities are nevertheless empirical and real. John Bennett understood this and with clarity and gentleness brought these realities to bear in his writing to influence both church and society.

Notes

[1] A personal comment to the present author.
[2] Cf. *The Radical Imperative* (Philadelphia: Westminster Press, 1975). The quote is from memory.
[3] "Process Theology, Christian Realism, and Liberation Theology," (October 1982, 3), an unpublished paper available from The Center for Process Studies, Claremont School of Theology, Claremont, CA 91711.
[4] Bennett referred to Schubert Ogden's book, *Faith and Freedom: Toward a Theology of Liberation* (Nashville,Tennessee: Abingdon Press, 1979). Bennett made the remark at the Claremont symposium cited above.
[4] H. Richard Niebuhr, *The Meaning of Revelation* (New York: Macmillan Publishing Co., Inc., 1941).
[5] For a fuller discussion of Bennett's theological method and position, see Daniel Day Williams, "The Theology of John Coleman Bennett," *Theology and Church in Times of Change: Essays in Honor of John Coleman Bennett*, Edward LeRoy Long, Jr. and Robert Handy, eds. (Philadelphia: The Westminster Press, 1970): 239ff.
[6] Bennett, "Process Theology, Christian Realism, and Liberation Theology," 6ff. Bennett expresses strong appreciation not only to Whitehead, but to Henry Nelson Wieman, Daniel Day Williams, John B. Cobb, Jr., and Charles Hartshorne, clearly assimilating his own realism to process theology over neo-orthodoxy.
[7] John C. Bennett, *Social Salvation: A Religious Approach to the Problems of Social Change* (New York: Charles Scribner's Sons, 1935): 213f.
[8] *Social Salvation*, 3.
[9] Nils Ehrenstrom, et al., *Christian Faith and the Common Life* (Chicago: Willett, Clark & Company, 1938): 175.
[10] The "serenity prayer" is usually attributed to Niebuhr and used at meetings of Alcoholics Anonymous. The full version reads: "God, grant me the serenity to accept the things I cannot change; courage to change the things I can; and the wisdom to know the difference. Living one day at a time; enjoying one moment at a time; accepting hardship as the pathway to peace. Taking, as He did, this sinful world as it is, not as I would have it. That I may be reasonably happy in this life, and supremely happy with Him forever in the next."
[11] Ehrenstrom et al., *Christian Faith and the Common Life*, 177f. Bennett acknowledges his indebtedness to F. R. Tennant's discussion in *The Concept of Sin*.
[12] Clyde L. Manschreck, ed., *A History of Christianity: Readings in the History of the Church from the Reformation to the Present* (Englewood Cliffs, NJ: Prentice-Hall, Inc., 1964): 533.
[13] *A History of Christianity*, 530ff.
[14] Bennett, *Social Salvation*, 131.
[15] Ehrenstrom et al., *Christian Faith and the Common Life*, 185.

[16] For a good example of a critic, see Cornel West, "Christian Realism as Religious Insights and Europeanist Ideology: Niebuhr and the Third World," *Prophetic Fragments* (Grand Rapids, MI: Eerdmans Publishing Co., 1988): 144ff.
[17] Bennett, *Social Salvation,* 91.
[18] John C. Bennett, *Christian Realism* (New York: Charles Scribner's Sons, 1952): 2.
[19] Bennett's major writing on church and state issues is *Christians and the State* (New York: Charles Scribner's Sons, 1958).
[20] Bennett, *Social Salvation,* 70ff.
[21] Cf. Bennett, *Christian Realism,* 124.
[22] John C. Bennett, *Christian Ethics and Social Policy* (New York: Charles Scribner's Sons, 1946): 80.
[23] *Christian Ethics and Social Policy,* 81.
[24] Ibid, 81.
[25] Ibid, 94.
[26] Ibid, 104.

Chapter 7

Cups Half Full: John Courtney Murray's Skirmishes with Christian Realism

Leon Hooper, S.J.

As we grasped our expanding economic, cultural and military powers, we older Americans (youngsters in the 1950s) did proclaim at Eisenhower's insistence "In God We Trust." Occasionally even gratitude joined our hope. Often we would sing out, as the King James Bible put it, that our "cup runneth over." The Cold War, as stark as were its possibilities, added a strong sense of mission to our senses of being blessed. Among our abundances, and contrary to the Old World, even our religious voices were multiple and teeming. Yet, only by 1960 did the editors of *Time* magazine turn two of our theologians, namely Reinhold Niebuhr and John Courtney Murray, S.J., into cover stories. To some *Time's* holding our religious icons at arms length betrayed a pervasive secularism within the East Coast establishment. Whether *Time's* limited selections reflected secularism or simply good religious judgment need not detain us here. What is of interest is how each of these two icons viewed that cup that most thought to be overfull to overflowing.

At first sight Niebuhr and Murray seem to be at opposite extremes of American self-understanding. Niebuhr's enshrinement on *Time's* March 2, 1948 cover carried the subtitle: "Man's story is not a success story." This was hardly an endorsement of Manifest Destiny. Following the twists and turns in America's religious culture, Murray's ascendancy took another dozen years. Only on the eve of Roman Catholic John Fitzgerald Kennedy's inauguration to the U.S.

presidency did Murray's uncompromising Roman collar and confident, even mildly triumphant, eyes look out at America from Henry Luce's publication.[1] Murray's achievement, if that is what it was, witnessed to Will Herberg's mid-1950s claim that Catholics and Jews had achieved proximate political and social equality with Protestants.[2] Murray himself was aware of this equality and used it to his advantage. During that same decade, he began an appeal for the increased political involvement of his own religious community with the claim that "we have arrived, we belong,"[3] arguing that Catholics must "resolutely refuse to succumb to what is perhaps the most insidious temptation— the 'temptation of Thabor'"[4]

The iconic magazine covers differed, Niebuhr's bearish and tentative, while Murray's was bullish. Yet I will argue here that each found the American cup to be neither bone dry or overflowing. And the reasons for their convergences were both empirical and theological. A place to begin, though, is Murray's own view of Reinhold Niebuhr, an "attitude" as we might now call it which itself was bearish.

The Skirmish

Murray did not languidly relax into American political and cultural equality. The same year he graced *Time's* cover, in his funniest, if not fairest, discussion of American Protestantism, he took on a group he labeled "the ambiguists." The article began where Murray previously had not been willing to begin, namely, with the admission that the governing spirit of much of America's first century had been Protestant — a public religion he tagged "the old fundamentalism."[4] Here we get Murray's longstanding evaluation of Protestantism's social significance.[5] Its ethic was voluntaristic (an act was good or evil because God commanded it, with reason never able to penetrate to the actual moral quality of the act), subjectivist (the intention was what counted, not the act's moral qualities), and governed by the sole criterion of "altruism."[6] In effect, such a theory was at core individualistic, based on the rather naive presupposition that personal values could be directly imposed on the social order. At best, that ethic, grounded as it was solely on biblical imperatives, could generate only an "interpersonal" ethics, blind to the institutional forces of modern society. This ethic for the most part, Murray in 1960 claimed, has been recognized as a "simplism."

That earlier fundamentalist ethic, he continued, has now been supplanted by an ethics that is out to "reckon with the full complexity of man's nature and of human affairs. Hence against the absolutism of the old morality, in which contingent facts get lost under insistence on absolute precepts, the new morality moves towards a situationalism, in which principles tend to get lost amid the contingencies of fact." Indeed the highest category of this new ethic is the term "ambiguous." Yet, despite its disclaimers, this new religious ethics is based, as was the old, on three premises: (1) a false dichotomizing of the private and public arenas of morality; (2) a faulty concept of "self-interest"; and (3) an abhorrence for, and demonization of, power,[7] which, according to Murray, in combination continue to vitiate the social ethical effectiveness of the "ambiguists" and to seriously endanger the public weal. To venture out into the international field, Murray countered, requires complex notions of society, state and culture, of interests within notions of the common good, of clear notions of the moral possibilities and limits of civic law, of other non-juridical forums for societal development. Complex though they are, these social realities at work can be known. Moreover, they must be known. But, with the ambiguist's views of the public sector, self-interest and power, the only possible response to a difficult international situation is that it

> appears as a "predicament," full of "ironies," sown with "dilemmas," to be stated only in "paradox," and to be dealt with "only at one's hazard," because in the situations "creative and destructive possibilities" are inextricably mixed, and therefore policy and action of whatever kind can only be "morally ambiguous."[8]

If one refuses to use power, then one is "'irresponsible,' and therefore [becomes] more guilty yet."[9] The only responsible alternative to a withdrawal into a "pure" community (Thabor's temptation?) appears to be a commitment to act, sinning bravely, though unavoidably and blindly.

Composed as this article was while Murray and Reinhold Niebuhr met repeatedly at Robert Hutchins' Center for the Study of Democratic Institutions (CSDI) in Santa Barbara for discussions of the Cold War, there could be little doubt at whom these jibes were directed. While Murray and Niebuhr had known each other since 1948, this 1960 article was Murray's first and only attempt to deal directly with Reinhold Niebuhr's Christian realism.

One might concur with Murray when he admitted that he had some difficulty entering into the argument.[10] Here I will begin with four such entries that he himself offered.[11] Then I will correlate these external arguments with the battles he was fighting simultaneously with his church, in-house battles that shaped much of his own views toward that which was American society. I will then suggest that the stances that Niebuhr and Murray adopted toward all human societies ended up in the same ballpark. And I will conclude, however, with what I consider to remain a core methodological and religious difference between them.

Defending the Principle of Consent

So, first of all, Murray's three or four suggested entries into the argument. The first concerns the individual/political dichotomy. One is not less a Christian, Murray contended, for going beyond those personal and familial norms presented in the bible. The political arena is something less than the Kingdom of God; it is a temporal reality with its limited means and limited goals. But these means and these goals, as well as their limited possibilities, derive from the reality of political society itself, as humans have been created for and have a natural drive toward social living, only one aspect of which is political.

Secondly, self-interest as a motive for national action is not in itself wrong or evil. In fact, the norm of self-interest is a good canon for moral as well as political discernment.[12] It becomes evil when self-interest becomes the classical *raison d'etat*, that is, the sole criterion for national action. The "tradition of reason" (Murray's favorite term for Natural Law) situates self-interest within the larger realm of social reasoning, in the international common good. The meshing of national and international interests is a complicated, difficult task ("The casuistry is endlessly difficult"),[13] but the drive toward a national policy which is in line with the international good sustains the moral orientation of national policy, and sets a very real and, although difficult, realizable goal for national action.

And, thirdly, power is an instrument, morally neutral in itself.[14] One can develop criteria, which will distinguish between "force" and "violence." Again, the working out of these criteria, much less their adoption within the international community, are immensely difficult tasks. But without an attempt at those criteria, the entire political field becomes simply barbaric. The criteria, as institutionalized by laws and argued in public debate, establish a thin wall or margin between chaos and public welfare, "but the margin makes the difference."[15]

Now, behind these three criticisms lay the one final issue that anchored most of Murray's secular and ecclesial arguments. Ultimately, he claimed, the "ambiguists" erode the "moral footing from beneath the political principle of consent."[16] As discussed below, Murray had staked much of his argument for religious freedom on the emergence of a Great Act of Faith in the People's ability and right to morally" judge, direct and correct" themselves. He claimed such a development to be a legitimate, Anglo-American realization of the Thomistic authorization principle, namely, that it is the people, not the pope and not the king nor the *studium*, who ultimately authenticate the justice of the law. The ethics of the Christian realist is not really an ethics, but rather a vision of society in which ethical discussion and choice is impossible. "All norms vanish amid the multiplying paradoxes; and all discrimination is swallowed up in the cavernous interior of the constantly recurrent verdict: 'This action is morally ambiguous.'"[17] It contributes to the disintegration of the collective faith in the people as moral agents, in a society that is structurally designed for the workings of such agency. Such an ethics leads to the disappearance of criteria that might guide social, ethical thought; intelligence is replaced by an all-pervasive "fog."

Why Murray's sharp, even *ad hominem*, criticisms of Christian realism? When Murray began writing on religious freedom in 1945, the public state of the discussion was as follows. Pope Leo XIII, in his 1895 *Longingua Aqua* and his 1899 *Testem Benevolentiae*, had insisted, against some American Catholics (who viewed the separation of church and state as divinely providential) that both Roman Catholicism and America would better prosper if Catholicism was declared the religion of the United States and that heretical social voices were suppressed. In fact, however, through the early half of the twentieth century American Catholicism did flourish, as the children of recent immigrants moved up the widening economic ladder. Catholics, reflecting their general working class situation, embraced New Deal politics, and one of their own, Monseigneur John A. Ryan, became a Catholic voice both forming and supporting Franklin Roosevelt's economic policies. Ryan, though, given the weight of Papal teaching, in his otherwise "liberal" study, *Catholic Principles of Politics*[18] had to admit that, all things being equal, Catholics were under an obligation to establish Catholicism as the religion of the state. However, he argued, not all things were equal. Even with the current high Catholic birth rates, he assured Americans and perhaps himself, Catholics would never have sufficient numbers to revoke the religious clauses of the First Amendment.

Looking at the same birth rates, most Protestant Americans were understandably edgy. Murray dismissively deemed their edginess to be based on a "slight misunderstanding" of Catholic First Amendment intentions, an edginess he in fact wanted to quickly dispatch. Simultaneously he was vigorously arguing that Catholics ought to be cooperating directly with all peoples of faith in the task of post-war reconstruction. Protestant edginess got in the way. To clear up this "misunderstanding," several American bishops asked Murray to explore the Catholic groundings for church/state relations. His first attempted clarification, however, collapsed under its own presuppositions and methods. In keeping with Roman Catholic casuistry, Murray began by insisting that any argument concerning religious freedom had to proceed from both natural law and revealed premises, then be applied to the American situation through prudential judgment, this last by the laity, not the clergy. He therefore proposed to write, first, a natural law argument, then a theological argument (both theoretical), and finally an applied argument that would move from the premises of the first two arguments to a justification of Catholic respect for the First Amendment. These three arguments were to appear serially in the Jesuit journal *Theological Studies*. However, only the first saw the light of day, because Murray found that the Catholic manner of argument allowed at best only grudging tolerance of contrary moral and religious practice.[19] The abstraction of the Catholic argument masked over the moral and religious forces that had shaped Western, or at least Anglo-American, notions of the separation of church and state.

He then regrouped and turned to the actual history of church/state dealings, to the particularities of the historical record, after again initially disdaining Protestant moves in that direction.[20] He eventually claimed that a *natural law* understanding of human dignity and human moral agency had developed mostly in non-Catholic countries—a natural law recognition to which the church must be attentive. In effect, by allowing his natural law argument to become historically situated, he recognized that new viewpoints could emerge (truly new, not simply inchoately held in some original insight or revelation) and could correct older viewpoints (which often, especially in educationally and materially developing societies, could become at the least inadequate). That is, by the Second Vatican Council Murray was arguing that sensitivity to the concrete goods and evils embedded in Western political and cultural history obliged the Catholic Church to endorse civic religious freedom. Civic freedom, primarily expressed as immunities from coercive constraint and restraint, is an "intention of Nature," which was Murray's term for the will of God the creator.

So, when Murray and Niebuhr confronted each other in Santa Barbara, the topic of natural law and its legitimate development was dear to Murray's heart; it was this foundation upon which he had based much of his in-church argument pegged (as well as his more public arguments concerning censorship, aid to church schools, *in bello* just war criteria). Given, though, Niebuhr's own fear of natural law formalism, the confrontation appears to have resolved into that "fog" Murray feared. As reported by Dr. George Schuster, an observer of and sometime fatigued participant in their ongoing discussion,

> ...very often our discussions would be sidetracked by Reinie and John into a debate on the merits of natural law theory. They both seemed to have a veritable fetish for this topic. Reinie, especially, used to bring it up. I suppose because he sensed that John better than anyone could help him understand and grasp whatever merit there might be to a natural law perspective. There were times when they just wouldn't put the topic down, which proved very tiring for the rest of us.[21]

The passing of ships in the night tired Murray as well. A decade earlier he had concluded a similarly frustrating attempt at interfaith dialogue with the cries "I seem to be failing to make myself clear...,"[22] "our minds are not meeting—in the sense, I mean, that they are not even clashing."[23]

The Cup's Theological Content

Robin Lovin suggests that Niebuhr (especially in his later development)[24] tried to turn our collective moral attention to the actual mix of goods and evils that we face. This required a turning away from the ideological masking of a fundamentalistic legalism as well as from the liberal, communistic and natural law contractions of reality into preset categories—categories that most often masked one's own individual and/or collective egoism. The tools by which Niebuhr effected those turns were the *theological* doctrines of sin and love. The notion of sin's pervasiveness stripped each and every particular policy recommendation of any absolute certitude that might be conferred by direct appeals to God. And notions of love directed attention to the particular, away from abstracted patterns turned ideological. Murray attempted to reach the same place, or at least a similar non-absolutist social stance, by developing a notion of the historicity of all public knowledge, first, natural knowledge, then, as I will show further on, revealed knowledge as well. This was not simply an insistence that all *applications* are historically embedded products of practical reasoning and therefore changeable as societies grow and decline. Murray found that he had to insist that even the principles, the theoretical grounding insights, of our public reasoning were contingent and emergent, and in constant need of fresh appropriation, correction and development. Yet, in the late 1950s Murray would not allow similar historicity or fluidity to his theological principles.

Given the fact that, since 1954, Rome had silenced Murray's argument on civic religious freedom (save from within an American Constitutional law setting),[25] it is little wonder that he himself did not approach the theological side of the argument until the Second Vatican Council. Yet, more was at play, and had deeper roots in Murray own expectations. As early as 1933 Murray had argued that the break effected by the Reformation had been so severe that the various communities no longer had any common theological languages, that theological dialogue was impossible.[26] Even in the mid-1940s, while arguing for intercredal cooperation, he discounted European attempts to find residual theological terms or symbols around which the post-war pluralistic West could rally reconstruction.[27] And he remained pat on this judgment of the impossibility of public theological discourse. Only natural law, he asserted, could function as a common ground for intercredal cooperation.

Although Murray argued against the possibility of any *theological* grounding for cooperation, however, he did not leave God entirely out of the picture. Quite the contrary: corresponding to and in fact grounding the natural law was a natural theology, that is, a knowledge about God that is open to every person of good will. The crunch point is the notion of a "good will," because it is a small step to the further assertion that no atheist could be of good will, or at least of sound mind. So, while Murray liberally claimed that Pope Pius XII's call for intercredal cooperation "among men of good will" included people of other religious faiths, he could find no principled ground for accepting atheists into the needed substantive collaboration. Even by 1960 all he could supply in defense of the atheist's civic voice was a pragmatic argument that to attempt the suppression of their voices would hurt public appreciation of the faith, or disturb civic peace to the point of anarchy.[28] The general public good required grudging tolerance; no natural or revealed rights adhered to the atheist as such.

Within this context Murray's agonistic response to the Soviet Union becomes fully intelligible — and here he comes close to the political "realists" of his time. From Murray's work with the CSDI, he isolated four elements that guided Soviet foreign policy. The first is the Soviet conviction that power is to be unrestrained by any Western notion of law.[29] The state is to take any available means toward securing its objectives, independently of any notions of justice and human rights. Second, Russia is unique as an *imperium* in that all its moves in the political forum are to be conducted in accordance with Leninist theory.

Thus, "there is no convincing evidence that Mr. Khrushchev represents apostasy or even heresy." Third, there is the Russian imperialistic doctrine, the doctrine of world revolution, which orients the Soviet Union to world domination through whatever means are available. And, fourth, Russia views itself as "inheritors both of Tsarist imperialism and of mystical Panslavist Messianism." It sees its purpose in the scheme of things to be the elimination of that culture which is generally called the "West." Murray then gave several examples of Soviet policy decisions that remain unintelligible to Western politicians, mostly because Westerners cannot imagine policy directed by doctrine rather than by pragmatic and accommodationist concerns.[30]

In tones that echo Murray's 1940s claim that no theological discourse with Protestants was possible (therefore requiring a fallback to natural law and natural theism), Murray now contended that no communication was possible with the current practitioners of Panslavist Messianism. The relationship could be conducted only in terms of power and survival. He further judged that the Russians pursued a policy of minimum risk and maximum security that they would avoid at all cost using force in situations that would endanger their own survival. America on the other hand can think of the use of force only when national survival becomes the dominant issue. Most other times, "We talk too much" and do not consider the use of limited force for limited objectives. Rather, America should pursue a policy of maximum risk and minimum security. America should be able in fact to consider the use of strategic nuclear arms in defense, say, of Korea. But first it must adopt the natural law theory of just war within which such use of force can be rationally controlled, keeping our use of force from devolving either into total annihilation (avoiding such a climate as that "thickening mood of savage violence that made possible the atrocities of Hiroshima and Nagasaki"[31]) on the one hand, or irresponsible absolute pacifism, on the other. Only natural law and just war theory can help us argue rationally in public and can assure that we behave as moral agents in directing and correcting military action.

The God of the Other Half

Given the strength and breadth of Murray's disbelief in any future for East/West discussion, it is striking that his first move toward genuine *theological* discourse arose with atheists, even before he began talking theologically with Protestants. And his way into what became Christian/Marxist dialogue was facilitated by another new understanding of the cognitional core of the human person. In 1963

Murray delivered a series of lectures at Yale University on the "Problem of God."[32] As might be expected, he outlined and defended the development of Nicene and post-Nicene systematic ways of knowing God, of knowing the truth of Christ Jesus in modes of thought that, while remaining compatible with the original common sense, scriptural knowledge of Jesus and the early church, nonetheless required new modes of knowing (theoretical, systematic, dogmatic, historical) if this historically embedded People would remain true to the Spirit that was promised to them until the end of time. Then, though, and not entirely consistent with his earlier appropriation of transcendental Thomism, Murray moved to an understanding of modern atheisms as defined around a permanent dialectic within human consciousness. Twentieth century, "post-modern" forms of atheism have returned to the biblical problematic of whether "God is with us in Power." Contrary to nineteenth-century pretensions about disproving through reason the existence of God, the Marxist and the existentialistic person of the theater admit that God is a beginning point of argument, not a conclusion.[33] The Marxist confronts the evil of human existence; the existentialist the lack of human freedom. Within those historical problematics, they both conceive that they must choose for good and human freedom, on the one hand, or for God, on the other. And their choice lands on human good and freedom. The action following from that choice then is the active suppression of the notion of God in both public and private life. Neither argues from the experience of the absence of God, as do the "death of God" theologians.[34] Both argue that God must not be allowed to exist, God must be killed.

The Christian approach to the post-modern forms of atheism must center on the dialectic, even empirical, question of whether or not human existence is indeed more humane and free within the premise of God's non-existence. Can human life in any sense be human without an awareness of God which includes both *gnosis* and *agnosis*, a knowledge and an ignorance of God, which are both necessary aspects of the human turning toward God. The choice is not between God's existence and nonexistence; it is between existence or nonexistence, on the one hand, and existence and nonexistence, on the other. In such a dynamic way has the Christian God manifested God's self in history?[35] It is in history that this drama is to be played out. Can a temporal political or philosophical system attempt to draw people's openness to the transcendent to itself without creating human tyranny? Or can a human society thrive by destroying the human drive toward that which transcends? The choice is between recognition of ourselves as a people of God or a people of a creature, in Murray's view. As the experience of

God has been situated in history, so the resolution of the contemporary dialectical choice for or against God will have its effects in history.[36] The truth will work, will have real world effect. Error will eventually destroy human society and humanity itself. Truth will advance human dignity and freedom.

Murray, then, attempted to understand two dominant forms of contemporary atheism as outgrowths of the original biblical experience of God as forcefully present but ineffable. (Again, secularist academic atheism is more or less written off as a dull nineteenth century archaism, similar to the death of God theologies.) To opt with the Marxist for the materialistic dialectics of history is to opt for *gnosis*. To choose with the existentialist freedom within a universe which is ultimately absurd is to go with *agnosis*. Christian faith has itself given rise to the choices that threaten to enslave man. Living within these twin poles of human awareness, between *gnosis* and *agnosis*, is the condition for the possibility of our salvation.

For our purposes it is sufficient to note that Murray has once again gone to human reasoning to ground what was previously thought impossible, namely, a conversation with atheism about God's social, historical presence. And this dialectical stance is permanent to human knowing. That is, there can be no absolutist resolving of the form of God's presence (*gnosis*) or for that matter of God's absence (*agnosis*); we cannot tie down God's presence and absence along boundaries set by even our best moral or metaphysical categories. God wills the redemption of all that God has created, sinner and saved alike. God is strangely present (incarnate) and strangely absent (transcendent) to all creation in each and all of its forms.

Murray lived long enough to assure America's unbelievers that the Declaration on Religious Freedom did in principle include the freedom of the atheist to promulgate such commitments,[37] and he himself participated in Christian-Marxist dialogues. Moreover, after the Council he began speaking *theologically* with Protestants.[38] Adopting whole cloth some themes he picked up from Yves Congar and Edward Schillebeeckx, he then argued that because the church is involved in history, it remains open, as does secular society itself, to the possibility of unbelief. "Faith...contains within itself the seeds of its own imperfection; belief itself contains the seeds of unbelief."[39] Both the church and the secular order as engraced fall within the same potential of salvation and damnation. The church must revisualize itself, Murray argued, as a "sacrament" in the more general biblical sense, as "even now" and "not yet" fully a manifestation of the Spirit's action in the world. "Even now the Church is, and is one, and is holy, and yet the

Church is not yet one and not yet holy."⁴⁰ Theological discussions between Catholics and non-Catholics must begin in the historical record, in the mutual recognition that both sides had, at times, violated the principles of Christian constitutionalism or, more generally, of the sacred and secular. That is, given the actual historical record, even the church had to admit that it, as an institution, was *simul justis et pecator*.⁴¹ Out of this attentiveness and honesty in examining concrete historical behavior, new perspectives may arise that might bind back together the sacred and secular, without however obliterating the legitimate, incarnate distinction without excluding any social sector from the possibility of God's grace and revelation.

So, it would appear that Murray, in his own attempt to understand the movement of God in history, was forced, or led, first (1) to add flexibility to his own church's moral theory, then (2) to find at the core of human openness to God a permanent, essentially unresolvable dialectic between what we know of God and the fundamental mystery of God, and finally even (3) to entertain the simultaneous sinfulness and justification of the church as an institution. All of this I contend places the believing actor in a stance similar to that of the later Niebuhr, continually trying to discern, with all the help one can get, the goods and evils, the sin and grace, in the world in which one actually lives.

Knowledge of Goods and Evils

Yet there is a difference between Murray and Niebuhr. Behind Murray's own development was a commitment to the notion that nature and grace are fundamentally compatible, or that reason and revelation in principle are not at war. As he began his own professional life he had argued that the primary task of the priest/theologian was the redemption of human theoretical intelligence, just as the task of the laity was the bringing grace to the social order by means of practical intelligence, redeeming practical intelligence.⁴² As his world became more complex, these tasks exploded beyond the original restrictions according to role and types of reasoning. But Murray's insistence that reason could in principle both be redeemed and redeeming remained with him. Before the Council, when he himself was silenced on the issue of religious freedom, he could write of his own Christian faith that

> Faith, of course, is the fuller and steadier light, and the affirmations of faith have a greater solidity, because the authority of God sustains them.

However, faith could be no light at all, if reason were not also a light. Faith supposes reason as grace supposes nature. If the genuine powers of reason are destroyed or undermined, the true notion of Christian faith suffers the same fate. Faith becomes irrational, unintelligible, indefensible—and unworthy of a man. Thus the destinies of Christian faith are linked with those of human reason.[43]

Or, again,

Not even religion will supply the lack, if reason fails in its functions; for religion cannot form a civilization except as its truths and precepts are mediated to the temporal order through a rational philosophy.[44]

Reasoning in public became for Murray a task intrinsic to the Gospel, much as we are now learning that the practice of social justice is intrinsic to the Gospel, as the transformation of his own society was intrinsic to the faith of Jesus the Christ.

So, is the cup of American social living entirely full or entirely empty? The answer to both is "no." God is at work redeeming America; America is both blessed by God's presence and in need of redemption, as is every other people in human history. Is the cup of America half full or half empty? The answer is "yes," again to both, but the affirmation of both fullness and emptiness is tricky. The manner of breaking away from theoretical frameworks that would mask the other half (empty or full) depends on where one begins. Both affirmation and negation in the hands of believers can mask the real and, as we have recently seen, destroy life with impunity and ignore evil with an invincible surety. Neither our clan's particularity nor that of our enemies is privileged as an exclusive or even ultimate locus of truth, for the simple reason that God can speak out from any and all of creation. God is active in leading the human community toward God's future. It seems to me that Niebuhr and Murray, each coming from distinct religious traditions, tried to highlight the other half of the cup, for the sake of the human and the divine good. Both had to detoxify their own traditions, although the manners in which they did so, while anchored in theological doctrines of grace, nature and sin, differed as they moved each from the traditions that Reinhold's brother H. Richard Niebuhr identified as classic Protestant and Catholic social stances. They each moved toward a transformationalism that looked to God's future for all that God had created, knowing that we do not yet know its full shape.[45]

There is one further way of distinguishing Murray's "Roman Catholic," half-full approach to human societies. Again it deals with where one begins. The beginning suggested by Murray is in the good that one actually confronts, and is followed by a refusal to let go of the good, while at the same time letting go of the limits (tribal or individual or created) of that good. Elsewhere I have argued that this approach to finite good and its relation to God are common both to Murray and to Dorothy Day, the founder of the Catholic Worker movement.[46] And the method shows itself most clearly in an extended study that Day made of the Little Flower, St. Thérèse of Lisieux. Against claims that Thérèse had not a sufficient sense of the awfulness of sin, Day countered that Thérèse knew fully well how awful sin was, because she knew how great true loving can be. That is, those who know the good most fully will know what sin truly is, or is not.[47]

Toward the end of his life Murray's own expectations concerning the social sources of grace and insight shed at least some of their tribal limits. He did this primarily on positive, empirical grounds: "see the good achieved by our enemy." But he also recast the core of the knowing subject into a permanent stance of openness toward the concrete goods and evils that emerge personally and socially, and offered, in a notion of mutual self-correction, a path for grace to operate socially.[48] Murray leaves us with a stance that incorporates notions of divine truth and sin within our social arguments, but sin enters at a different position within Murray's argument than it does within Niebuhr's. Murray's historical societies can indeed still collapse into chaos. History is not necessarily progressive. But it need not collapse, because God never abandons the humanity, and ultimately God will draw all that is good to God's self (whatever that drawing might possibly mean). This affirmation of God's presence is at the core of Murray's search for half-full cups.

Murray once claimed that it was easy to know what Protestants were against, but not what they were for.[49] It might also be claimed that it is often difficult to know what (some) "Catholics" are against. Insofar as either of these claims bear any truth, Niebuhr and Murray each tried to correct limiting expectations of their respective traditions, for the sake of knowing a God who took interest in their mid-century world.

Notes

[1] *Time* (2 December 1960). That Murray was friends with the Henry and Clare Booth Luce, and that his *We Hold These Truths: Catholic Reflections on the American Proposition* (*WHTT*) (New York: Sheed & Ward, 1960) was published the year of the election, of course facilitated *Time*'s recognition. For biographical information, see Donald E. Pelotte, *John Courtney Murray: Theologian in Conflict.* (New York: Paulist Press, 1976), and Leon Hooper, S.J.

1 "Murray, John Courtney," in *American National Biography* 16, ed. John A. Garraty and Mark C Carnes (New York: Oxford University Press: 1999): 158-160.
2 Will Herberg, *Catholic, Protestant, Jew* (New York: Doubleday and Company, 1955).
3 "Catholics in America – a Creative Minority – Yes or No?" *Catholic Mind* (October 1955): 595. See also "Reversing the Secularist Drift," *Thought* 53 (March 1949): 40.
4 The reference is to Jesus' transfiguration, at which Peter, James and John were tempted to build three tents, one each for Jesus, Moses and Elijah, and stay there forever (Mt 17; Mk 9). Jesus and the disciples of course had to descend from Mount Tabor and advance toward Jerusalem and the crucifixion. Murray has the phrase in quotation marks, without reference, with that peculiar spelling, i.e., Thabor.
5 Murray, *WHTT*, 276. The article, new for *WHTT*, was Chapter 12: "The Doctrine is Dead: The Problem of a Moral Vacuum," 275-94. Murray's use of the term "fundamentalism" was not exact. It often covered both contemporary forms of uncritical biblical positivism and also the entire evangelical tradition. Previously he had insisted that that which was true about the foundations and development of the Republic was anchored in natural law philosophy, not any forms of Protestant theology.
6 For an earlier, even less civil image of American Protestantism, see "The Construction of a Christian Culture: I. Portrait of a Christian; II. Personality and the Community; III. The Humanism of God," in *Bridging the Sacred and the Secular: Selected Writings of John Courtney Murray*, ed. Hooper (Washington, DC: Georgetown University Press, 1994 [1940]): 101-23.
7 *WHTT*, 276-77.
8 Ibid., 279-81.
9 Ibid., 283.
10 Ibid., 282.
11 It has been suggested that Murray was playing off Niebuhr's technical term "ambiguity," without really understanding it. Perhaps so. But Murray appeared most uneasy with the moral contrast implicit in the formula "moral man and immoral society," the title of Niebuhr's 1932 book which Murray quotes in the present article (p. 285). Such a biasing toward individual perfection has been criticized by others (Ronald H. Stone, *Reinhold Niebuhr: Prophet to Politicians* (Washington, D.C.: Abingdon Press, 1981): 84) and by Niebuhr himself (*The Responsible Self* (New York, Harper and Row, 1965): 15). Keeping with the (rough) playfulness of Murray's tone, Catholic Michael Novak entitled an article as follows: "Moral Society and Immoral Man" in *Church-State Relations in Ecumenical Perspective*, ed. Elwyn A. Smith (Pittsburgh: Duquesne University, 1966): 92-112.
12 *WHTT*, 285-86.
13 Ibid., 286-87.

¹⁴ I have not here spelled out how Murray thought human knowing could and did arrive at true and correct moral and factual judgments. All of this was anchored, during his last few years, in the cognitional theory of fellow Jesuit, Bernard Lonergan, S.J. In the 1940s Murray had published sections of Lonergan's dissertation and in 1958 ran a seminar at the Catholic Theological Society of America conference on the impact of Lonergan's *Insight: A Study of Human Understanding* (New York: Philosophical Library, 1958) on systematic theology, and worked himself during the council with an early draft of Lonergan's "The Transition from a Classicist World-View to Historical-Mindedness" in *A Second Collection*, ed. William, F.K. Ryan and Bernard J. Tyrrell (Philadelphia: Westminster, 1974): 1-10, a paper on historical modes of knowing. See also note 48.
¹⁵ *WHTT*, 288-89.
¹⁶ Ibid, 189.
¹⁷ Ibid, 293.
¹⁸ Ibid., 292.
¹⁹ *WHTT*, 288-89.
²¹ That article appeared as "Freedom of Religion, I: The Ethical Problem," *Theological Studies* (June 1945): 229-86. We have an outline that Murray presented to Archbishop Joseph Mooney of that, and the promised theological and application argument ("Notes on the Theory of Religious Liberty," an April 1945 Memo to Archbishop Mooney, Lauenger Library, Georgetown University, Special Collections, Murray Archives, file 7-555). Again, he turned from the methods and cognitional framework that grounded this first argument, and found that he had to think of even theory as open to real development and decline, as historically embedded as are practical applications.
²² "Current Theology: Freedom of Religion," *Theological Studies* (March 1945): 85-113.
²³ From page 45, note 1 of Edward Charles Krause's dissertation, "Democratic Process in the thought of John Courtney Murray and Reinhold Niebuhr," (Boston: Boston University, 1975).
²⁴ "Correspondence with Robert MacIver," dating from 1952 through 1954, Murray archives, # 3. The discussion was with Protestant Robert M. MacIver. The issue was the grounds on which the academic freedom of Marxists could be curtailed in state colleges. Out of these discussions Murray wrote what would later end up as the concluding chapter of *WHTT*, "The Doctrine Lives: The Eternal Return of Natural Law." That article first appeared in collection edited by MacIver as "The Natural Law," in *Great Expressions of Human Rights*, edited by Robert M. MacIver (New York: Harper, 1950), 69-104.
²⁵ "Correspondence with Robert MacIver," # 10.
²⁶ Robin W. Lovin, *Reinhold Niebuhr and Christian Realism* (Cambridge: Cambridge University, 1995).
²⁷ The silencing was delivered indirectly through Murray's religious superior, the Jesuit General (actually one of the General assistants). Murray was reported to have dramatically returned all his church/state books to the Woodstock

Library. On the silencing, see Pelotte, *Theologian in Conflict*, 51-54, and Joseph A. Komonchak, "The Silencing of John Courtney Murray," in *Cristianesimo Nella Storia: Saggi in onore di Giuseppe*, ed. A. Melloni (Milano: Alberigo, 1998): 657-702.

[28] Murray, "Crisis in the History of Trent," *Thought* (December 1932): 463-73.

[29] Murray, "Co-operation: Further Views," 100-111.

[30] This claim that truth would not prevail until the eschaton entered his last, suppressed argument for religious freedom and two articles he submitted to Rome for the censor's approval while still under the ban. See "Leo XIII and Pius XII: Government and the Order of Religion" in *Religious Liberty: Catholic Struggles with Pluralism*, ed. Leon Hooper S.J. (Louisville, KY: Westminster/John Knox, 1955c): 49-125, and "Unica Status Religio," Murray Archives, file 7-558.

[31] *WHTT*, 222f. First published as "Confusion of U.S. Foreign Policy," in *Foreign Policy and the Free Society*, ed. John Courtney Murray and Walter Millis (New York, NY: Oceana Publications, 1958): 21-42.

[32] *WHTT*, 227. First published as "Morality and Foreign Policy, Part I & II," *America* (19 March 1960): 729-32; (26 March 1960): 764-67.

[33] *WHTT*, 265. First published as *Morality and the Modern War* (New York: The Church Peace Union, 1959).

[34] *The Problem of God, Yesterday and Today* (New Haven: Yale University Press, 1964).

[35] Ibid., 105-6.

[36] In a 1967 address given at the University of Connecticut, Murray discussed the current "death of God" movement in America. He argued that the death of God theologians argued from "an experience of the absence of God" or from an "absence of experience of God" to the conclusion that God is dead. For Murray this was in line with the nineteenth century attempt to argue from reason or action to the nonexistence of God. They are the "soft radicals" who have been transcended by the contemporary "hard radicals" of Marxism and existentialist atheism ("The Death of God," 10 January 1967, address at the University of Connecticut. Murray Archives, file 6-462).

[37] Murray, *Problem of God*, 120-21.

[38] Murray, "The Unbelief of the Christian," in *The Presence and the Absence of God*, ed. Christopher Mooney (New York: Fordham University Press, 1969): 69.

[39] Murray, "Acceptance Speech" (New York: Unitarian-Universalist Association, 1965), and in most of his post-conciliar commentaries of *Dignitatis humanae*.

[40] On reading his "The Status of the Nicene Creed as Dogma," (*Chicago Studies*, Spring 1966): 65-80, with its heavy Lonergan vocabulary and a bit of an in-your-face tone, one might suspect that Murray's attempts to talk Trinitarian theology with the Lutherans was not whole hearted. His 1967 "Our Response to the Ecumenical Revolution," *Religious Education* (March-April):

91-92, 119, delivered to Episcopalians calls for all future theology to emerge out of ecumenical dialogue.
[41] Murray, "Unbelief of the Christian," 74.
[42] Ibid., 72.
[43] Ibid., 78-79.
[44] See Murray, "The Problem of its Finality," 43-75.
[45] "The Liberal Arts College and the Contemporary Climate of Opinion," in *Bridging the Sacred and the Secular*, 144.
[46] Ibid., 146.
[47] H. Richard Niebuhr, *Christ and Culture* (New York: Harper and Row, 1951).
[48] A manuscript submitted for publication under the title: "Affirmation and Negation in the Theological Writings of John Courtney Murray and Dorothy Day."
[49] Dorothy Day, *Therese* (Springfield, IL; Templegate, 1979): 81ff.
[50] I have not taken up Murray's eventual adoption of the notion of "virtually unconditioned judgment" with which he was certain that he could guarantee most judgments of truth and falsity. He adopted the notion from Bernard Lonergan. Murray's own notions of public discourse can add to Lonergan's original idea of mutual correction the suggestion that all our knowing is embedded in societies as ongoing (corrective) conversations. With the notion of virtually unconditioned judgment and society as ongoing conversation, he and his tradition have a plausible scenario for arriving at true claims without collapsing into an ideological absolutism.
[51] "The Catholic Position: A Reply" *American Mercury* (September 1949): 274-83; (November 1949): 637-39. The former is Murray's harshest slam at a Protestant. The latter included a backhanded apology for some of the first.

Chapter 8

Christian Realism in a Pluralistic Society: Interactions between Niebuhr and Morgenthau, Kennan, and Schlesinger

Roger L. Shinn

Historical changes since the rise of the Christian realists of the twentieth century have heightened a problem that lurks in the terminology: *Christian realism*. How do Christian faith and a Christian ethic address a pluralistic society? The problem is not brand new. It has existed from biblical times. In American history the Declaration of Independence could talk of "Nature and Nature's God," of rights endowed by the "Creator," of the "Supreme Judge of the World," of "firm reliance on the Protection of Divine Providence"—while carefully avoiding any specifically Christian language. The Constitution, a far more secular document, avoids any mention of God, but (unlike the Declaration) dates itself "in the Year of our Lord one thousand seven hundred and Eighty seven." Such language, though conventional, becomes jarring in the increasingly pluralistic American society. On a world scale the Universal Declaration of Human Rights (1948) echoes some exact phrases of the American Declaration of Independence, while carefully excising the religious references.

The age of Christendom, everybody knows, is long gone. Yet as late as 1912 Walter Rauschenbusch, the foremost theologian of the Social Gospel, could entitle a book *Christianizing the Social Order*, an exceedingly unlikely label for a book today. In 1940 T.S. Eliot, far more the traditionalist than Rauschenbusch, published *The Idea of a Christian Society*. More surprising, Emil Brunner still later wrote that "in the course of some fifteen centuries something like a Christian civilisation has been created."[1] All these references seem oddly dated in a present world more aware of the diversity of human cultures and faiths.

In this context the Christian realism of our time aims to address both the Christian churches and wider publics. In doing so it faces two questions. (1) What is Christian about Christian realism? Does it, in seeking to be persuasive to pluralistic societies, lose its distinctive Christian character? (2) How does it enter into conversation with a wider public? Does its Christian particularism isolate it from interaction with those who do not share its faith?

This chapter addresses these issues by focusing on the most influential of the Christian realists in the United States, Reinhold Niebuhr, and investigates his interactions with three realists prominent in public life: Hans J. Morgenthau, George F. Kennan, and Arthur Schlesinger Jr.[2]

Contexts, Traditional and Contemporary

As Hans Morgenthau has pointed out, realism as a theory of international relations is at least as old as Thucydides (471-401 B.C.): "Of the gods we believe, and of men we know, that by a necessary law of their nature they rule wherever they can." Thucydides is here quoting (or imaginatively reconstructing) the statement of the Athenians in negotiation with the Melians. Christians can easily dismiss the Athenians' belief about the gods; it is harder to disregard what they asserted "of men." Reinhold Niebuhr defines Augustine's (and his own) moral and political realism as "the disposition to take all factors in a social and political situation, which offer resistance to established norms, into account, particularly the factors of self-interest and power."[3]

Historians through the centuries have assumed that political units (tribes, nations, or empires) generally act in their own interests, struggling to survive and often to dominate in a world of competing societies. That competition may be cultural, technological, economic, charismatic, or ideological; often it is, not solely but unmistakably, military, whether in defense or aggression. To recognize that fact is not to endorse it, but it is to take account of the context and the tortuous ethical problems of international relations.

From biblical times Christians, as individuals or as communities of faith, have often refused to participate in war. Usually they had no expectation that nations would adopt this policy. Once Christians became a major force in the world of nations—a situation inconceivable to the churches of the New Testament—they had to consider their responsibility in national and international relations. Sometimes, in acts of spiritual effrontery, they claimed to fight crusades for the cause of Christ, an undeniable fact of their history, which they now almost unanimously regret. Often they developed doctrines of just war or, or as Paul Ramsey called it, "justifiable" war, since he recognized that no war is purely just. That is to say they believed that war might in some definable circumstances be less evil than giving in to unchecked military power. Sometimes they extended the doctrine to include just revolution against tyranny.[4]

All these doctrines have been abused; they have been co-opted to support wicked practices. A common sin among all people, obviously including Christians, is to use respectable language and beliefs to justify unrespectable conflict. But the fact that slogans of just war and just revolution can be expressions of aggressive hostility does not mean that the doctrines are inherently wicked, just as the fact that pacifism can be an expression of cowardice does not mean that pacifism is inherently cowardly.

The new modern note was the union of Christian motivation with the doctrine of progress arising in the Enlightenment. A conspicuous example is Charles C. Morrison in the weekly journal, *The Christian Century,* which he edited from 1908-1947. Later editors have wryly noted that, at the start of the twentieth century, the obscure publication, *The Christian Oracle*, changed its name to *The Christian Century,* with expectations that now seem oddly humorous. Morrison, with great energy and editorial skill, soon transformed the journal into the most influential magazine of non-denominational Protestant America.

Morrison's book *The Outlawry of War* (1927) was written during the negotiations of the Kellogg-Briand Peace Pact signed in Paris on August 27, 1928, then ratified by the United States Senate on January 15, 1929. In this treaty sixty-three nations agreed to "renounce" war as "an instrument of national policy." Morrison saw history as a progress in which institutions once respected, like slavery and dueling, were overcome. The Peace Pact, he believed, would inaugurate "the most stirring and glorious chapter in the upward progress of man," an age in which the voice of the people "would indeed be the voice of God." He deliberately used eschatological language to describe what was happening: "It is the emergence of the social sciences that is now quickening a revival of the pristine social vision which the early Christians conceived under eschatological and supernatural categories." Morrison's friend, John Dewey, America's most influential philosopher at that time, wrote a foreword, describing the outlawry of war as a completion of the historic experience of mankind. It was not, said Dewey, a simple step-by-step process but involved a right-about-face, typical of "all social progress."[5]

Morrison, although often regarded as a pacifist, even by some later writers in *The Christian Century,* said himself that he was not a pacifist. He combined a craving for peace, characteristic of all authentic Christianity, with a confidence in progress and a strong tinge of isolationism, as represented in Senator William Borah—whom he hailed enthusiastically. Borah had opposed United States participation in the League of Nations and the World Court, but as chair of the Senate Foreign Relations Committee strongly advocated the Kellogg-Briand Peace Pact. Some of Morrison's critics thought they detected in *The Christian Century,* published in Chicago, shadows of the *Chicago Tribune,* the self-styled world's greatest newspaper, with its combination of isolationism and Anglophobia.

But it was not Anglophobia that inspired the Oxford Peace Pledge of 1933. Originating in Oxford University, then spreading far and wide through England, the movement enlisted youth to pledge that they would "in no circumstances fight for its [England's] King and Country." By 1936 some 130,000 men and women had signed the pledge. A slightly revised version won many signers in America.

In that era a widespread quasi-pacifism, not always Christian but often tinged with Christian belief, swept the Anglo-American world. As a high school and college student in those days, I shared that mood. I never quite became a pacifist; I was too conscious of the role of military power, even when not overtly used, in resisting aggression, and I was alarmed by the growing Nazi-Fascist threat. But I came close.

Reinhold Niebuhr, twenty-five years older than I, grew up in that atmosphere of quasi-pacifism. He reluctantly supported World War I. Then, visiting the economically devastated Ruhr after the war, he decided to have done with war. Beginning in 1922 he wrote frequently, sometimes unsigned editorials and sometimes articles under his own name, in Morrison's *Christian Century.* There was tension between the two, and Niebuhr in 1924 turned down Morrison's offer of a job on the *Century.* In 1929 Niebuhr joined the Fellowship of Reconciliation, a presumably pacifist organization, although there was considerable disagreement within it. In 1931 he became chair of its executive council, but resigned from that position in 1933. He was experiencing the transformation that he later described as "Ten Years that Shook My World."[6] He had already published the groundbreaking *Moral Man and Immoral Society,* in which he turned away from his pacifism or quasi-pacifism. On February 10, 1941, with a few friends, he launched the bi-weekly *Christianity and Crisis*, to urge support of the allied nations resisting Nazism.

The shaking of his world he attributed primarily to "the pressure of world events." That pressure led him to a rediscovery of elements of traditional Christianity that, he charged, had been lost in modern liberalism. He acclaimed "the new orthodoxy," although he soon came to dislike the classification of "neo-orthodox," partly because of his disagreements with the Swiss Karl Barth, the most eminent of neo-orthodox theologians. His "Christian realism," a term that he chose, came to be the dominant position of American Protestantism throughout Word War II: a position that rejected any concept of a "holy war," while supporting the war as a tragic necessity. It was not a fixed theology or ethic, and the present re-thinking of it is consistent with its own inner dynamic.

Addressing Both Church and World

Niebuhr's turn toward realism came with an intensification of his theological commitments. From the very sparse theology of *Moral Man and Immoral Society* (sub-titled *A Study in Ethics and Politics),* he went on to his Gifford Lectures, *The Nature and Destiny of Man,* his most sustained theological work.[7] From then on he concentrated on the relation between theological and social-political concerns.

Addressing Christians, he wrote *Why the Christian Church is Not Pacifist.* Here his reasoning is clearly theological, with its reliance on the Christian doctrine of Atonement and its insistence that "political controversies are always conflicts between sinners and not between righteous men and sinners." His theological influence is evident in two famous addresses: one to the Oxford Conference on Church, Community and State (1937), "The Christian Church in a Secular Age," and another to the First Assembly of the World Council of Churches in Amsterdam (1948), "The Christian Witness in the Social and National Order."[8]

Simultaneously, Niebuhr was addressing a pluralistic society in which many people did not share his Christian commitments. *Christianity and Crisis,* although not at all bashful about its Christian purpose, was read by at least one justice of the Supreme Court, at least two senators, a vice-president of the United States, and numerous people in public life. Niebuhr wrote frequently for diverse publications: *The Nation, The New Statesman and Nation, The New Republic, The New Leader, The Yale Review, The Harvard Business Review, Foreign Affairs, Journal of International Affairs, The American Scholar, The New York Times Book Review, The New York Herald Tribune Books, The Saturday Review of Literature, Harper's, Scribner's, The Atlantic, The Bulletin of the Atomic Scientists, Life, Fortune, the Saturday Evening Post,* and others too numerous to mention. No Christian writer today comes close to reaching so diverse an audience—a fact that says something about the eminence of

Niebuhr and something about the changed cultural situation since his time.

How was a leader, so open about his Christian commitments, able to communicate with so many people who did not share his faith? Part of the answer is that Christian realists, trying to influence public policy, deliberately aim for bi-lingual discourse. They believe that some—certainly not all—Christian beliefs can be stated in secular terms. Their critics sometimes charge that this means a compromising of Christian belief. Christian realists answer that a faith confessing that "the Word became flesh," a faith that celebrates sacraments of such common stuff as water, bread, and wine, has some opportunities to communicate in everyday language.

One of the traditional ways in which Christians have sought to share their ethic with people who did not share their faith has been the doctrine of natural law. It holds that significant parts—certainly not all—of the Christian ethic are known to the world at large and are available to human reason. Natural law is firmly established in Roman Catholicism, but Luther and Calvin also endorsed it, though with serious reservations. For example, some of the Ten Commandments—"Thou shalt not murder" and "Thou shalt not steal"—belong to natural law. Many religions endorse them and many societies attempt to enforce them. Others of the Ten Commandments—"Thou shalt have no other gods before me" and "Remember the Sabbath Day to keep it holy"—are known through biblical faith. Christians have often co-operated with people of many faiths in supporting and legislating the natural law. But they have known that parts of their ethic are unpersuasive apart from Christian belief.

Niebuhr distrusted the ethic of natural law for two reasons. First, he had learned from Ernst Troeltsch that many beliefs and practices, often assumed to be ethical absolutes, are historically and culturally shaped. As times change, they change. Most of the traditional formulations of natural law turn out to be historically conditioned, often unpersuasive in the contemporary world. So Niebuhr believed that "reason is not capable of defining any standard of justice that is universally valid or acceptable."[9]

Second, Niebuhr, far more than Troeltsch, pointed to the way in which sin enters into human ethical standards and practice. Natural law has, from time to time, endorsed subordination of women, acceptance of class structures, even slavery. These undeniable facts are a warning to all of us, including Christian realists.

Unwilling to find security in the ethics of natural law, Niebuhr nevertheless cooperated enthusiastically with people who did not share his faith or his theology. As John C. Bennett put it, "He continually emphasizes what Christians have in common with secularists who have a passion for justice and who combine dedication to the public welfare with great astuteness concerning policy."[10] Niebuhr frequently commented that he found a greater sensitivity to issues of justice among Jews, by and large, than among Christian church people, by and large.

What, then, was the basis for Niebuhr's hope and practice of communicating and cooperating with diverse people who did not share the theological basis of his own ethics? All people, he said, "have, in some fashion, the experience of a reality beyond themselves." There is "the testimony in the consciousness of every person that his life touches a reality beyond himself, a reality deeper and higher than the system of nature in which he stands." There is "a universal human experience, the sense of being commanded, placed under an obligation and judged."[11]

Again, he wrote: "... any rigorous analysis of the moral life of man will partially disclose the tangents towards the eternal in all morality." But "it is not possible without faith to follow these implications through to their final logical conclusion."[12] In his published sermons, prayers, and theological writings, Niebuhr did "follow through these implications," to the extent that a fallible human mind can do so. But he also worked closely, day in and day out, with diverse people and groups, without that follow-through. Any of us who enter into political activity, even in the politics of a parent-teacher association or of a church, maybe even in family politics, know that if, in such associations, we always try to "follow through" the theological implications of our actions, we may never get around to doing anything. That does not lesson the importance of the theological implications, but it does mean that we have some responsibilities for immediate decisions, day in and day out.

Thus Niebuhr found a workaday basis for cooperation and communication in a pluralistic world, less formal and less ambitious than natural law, in "the common-sense of mankind, embodied in the judgments which men and nations make of each other."[13] Did it always work? Of course not. Nothing always works in human relations. It was a way, often effective, of living out, in a pluralistic world, Christian faith, with appreciation for others of different faiths, who sometimes support and sometimes shame Christians in their actions.

Three Dialogues

For a further understanding of the relation of Christian realism to diverse worlds of discourse, it is helpful to look at three dialogues that helped to define Niebuhr's realism: those with Hans Morgenthau, George Kennan, and Arthur Schlesinger Jr. All were prominent public figures who interacted with Niebuhr. Here I am here looking at them in chronological order, starting with the most senior.

Hans J. Morgenthau (1904-80)

Morgenthau was probably the most conspicuous political scientist defining and advocating political realism. He was a younger contemporary of Niebuhr; his years were 1904-1980 and Niebuhr's were 1892-1971. In some ways the two were very different characters: the highly educated transplanted German scholar and the Midwestern American pastor who did his most serious scholarly work after his appointment to the faculty of Union Theological Seminary in New York. Yet each acknowledged the stimulus of the other.

Morgenthau's first major American publication was *Scientific Man Versus Power Politics*, comparable to Niebuhr's *Moral Man and Immoral Society* in its assaults on the reigning liberal rationalism of its time. Niebuhr hailed it as an "authoritative" refutation of the vain "hope for the gradual elimination of the moral ambiguity of politics through historic development." Morgenthau's central declaration in this book was: "... power politics, rooted in the lust for power which is common to all men, is ... inseparable from social life itself." Often in later writings he pursued this theme, occasionally using Augustine's phrase, *animus dominandi*. Other political scientists sometimes criticized Morgenthau for the virtual equivalence of this with the Christian doctrine of sin. Morgenthau, unbothered by that criticism, acknowledged his appreciation of Niebuhr's *The Nature and Destiny of Man*. Years later he dedicated one of his books "To the Memory of Reinhold Niebuhr."[14]

At a colloquium on Niebuhr at the Cathedral of St. John the Divine in New York on October 20, 1961, Morgenthau was one of the three principal speakers—the other two were Paul Tillich and John Bennett (Niebuhr regrettably could not be present because of his failing health.). Morgenthau startled his audience with his concluding words:

> I have always considered Reinhold Niebuhr the greatest living political philosopher of America.... It is indicative of the very nature of American politics and of our thinking about matters political that it is not a statesman, not a practical politician, let alone a professor of political science or of philosophy, but a theologian who can claim this distinction of being the greatest living political philosopher of America.... It needed a man who could look at American society, as it were, from the outside—*sub specie aeternitatis*—to develop such a political philosophy: and that man, I think, is Reinhold Niebuhr.[15]

The surprising element in this tribute is its pointed reference to Niebuhr's theology. Niebuhr's admirers in the secular world included those whom Harvard philosopher Morton White playfully called "Atheists for Niebuhr." They took Niebuhr seriously in spite of his theological commitments. Morgenthau, by contrast, saw the theological insights as the source of Niebuhr's creativity. Morgenthau's phrase (taken from Spinoza), *sub specie aeternitatis,* corresponds to Niebuhr's "tangents toward the eternal."

Some hasty readers of Morgenthau assumed that his polemics against sentimental moralism meant a rejection of any place for ethics in international relations. They failed to notice his insistence: "The Decalogue is a code of ethical norms which cannot be derived from premises of natural utility." So they were unprepared for his later book, *The Purpose of American Politics,* in which he argued that "a great nation" must "pursue its interests for the sake of a transcendent purpose that gives meaning to the day-by-day operations of its foreign policy." Many of them were even more startled when Morgenthau became a severe critic of the American involvement in Vietnam, endorsed by his friend Henry Kissinger. Morgenthau went on to write *A New Foreign Policy for the United States of America,* in which he affirmed a vital place for ethics in politics and international affairs. Is this a dramatic change of direction in his realism? There are fundamental continuities in his developing thought; there are also changes in accent.[16]

One difference between Morgenthau and Niebuhr is their attitudes toward pacifism. Both think that a commitment to pacifism is an impossible foreign policy for a nation. Both recognize the covert violence that lurks in every established order. Both see that pacifism may be the ideology of the privileged, who oppose any violence that may overthrow their comfort. But then they differ. Morgenthau holds that the pacifist is not only ineffectual but also irresponsible. The pacifist "embodies a particular kind of personal selfishness which cultivates the peace of one's own conscience bought by abstention from meaningful political action." Niebuhr, even in his powerful argument against political pacifism, affirms: "It is a terrible thing to take human life.... We who allow ourselves to become engaged in war need its testimony of the absolutist against us, lest we accept the warfare of the world as normative, lest we become callous to the horror of war, and lest we forget the ambiguity of our own actions and motives and the risk we run of achieving no permanent good from this momentary anarchy in which we are involved."[17] The differences are subtle, yet important. The two men reject equally—and polemically—what I have earlier described as the quasi-pacifism that lurks in our culture.

I am not affirming that either Morgenthau or Niebuhr derived their thought from the other. I am saying that their relationship enriched the insights of both men and showed the possibility of communication between worlds of discourse that are too often kept separate.

George F. Kennan (1904-)

George Frost Kennan differs in two ways from the others I am considering here. First, they are professional teachers and scholars, but he spent most of his career in the United States Foreign Service, meeting in practice the issues that Niebuhr, Morgenthau, and Schlesinger investigated from different perspectives. His government service included three tours of duty in Moscow, and he probably knew more about the Soviet Union than anybody else in this country. In the late 1940s he joined the Institute for Advanced Studies in Princeton, continuing there with interruptions as Ambassador to the Soviet Union and to Yugoslavia. His later scholarly writings show evidence of his practical experience.

Second, unlike Morgenthau and Schlesinger, he was an acknowledged Christian. Very rarely did he say so in his writings. Mostly he ignored any such reference for the good reason that he considered it his responsibility, as a public officer, "to invoke those values which, as it seemed to me, had attained the quality of accepted ideals of our society as a whole."[18] In conversation he has said that some policies, which he would personally endorse, he would not advocate as a public official, because they were too far from any possible public acceptance.

Kennan is known as a political realist. His attacks on moralism and legalism in politics are quite similar to those of Morgenthau and Niebuhr. Like them, he thinks it wiser (and therefore morally better) to base foreign policy on national interest than on "the tyranny of slogans" with their "grandiose and unrealistic, or even meaningless phrases designed simply to make us feel better about the bloody and terrible business in which we are engaged."[19] Like them, he also believed that differing national interests are more negotiable than conflicts between our side's claimed virtue and an opponent's evil.

Thirty-five years after his early attacks on political moralism, he said that they may have been too cryptic. He saw little harm and little good in "high-minded but innocuous professions," but he still objected to letting self-interest "masquerade under the mantle of moral principle," at "the histrionics of moralism at the expense of substance," and at the judgments that condemn the faults of other nations and claim exaggerated virtue for ourselves. And he advocated "the effort to distinguish at all times between the true substance and the mere appearance of moral behavior."[20]

But, again like the realists with whom I am comparing him, he insisted that national interest is not primarily military conquest or annihilation of an enemy. In our competition with Russia, he wrote (in 1951, when that was a more inflammatory issue than now), we cannot ignore issues of armaments, but the real question is "the spirit and purpose of American national life itself," and the influence this may have on "a world which, despite all its material difficulties, is still more ready to recognize and respect spiritual distinction than material opulence."[21]

In the years following World War II, Niebuhr accepted several missions for the Department of State, which was less interested in his theological eminence than in his political and cultural insights. Kennan invited him to a two-day meeting of the State Department's Policy and Planning Committee, which Kennan chaired. It is often said that Kennan referred to Niebuhr as "the father of us all." Here "us" apparently refers to those professionals who shared Kennan's realism. One biographer of Niebuhr, Charles C. Brown, reports that Kenneth Thompson heard the words from Kennan in a telephone conversation. Another biographer, Richard C. Fox, says that nine years later Kennan did not remember saying that. Plainly verifiable is Kennan's appreciation of Niebuhr. For example, he quotes Niebuhr's *The Irony of History* with agreement: "... collective man always tends to be morally complacent, self-righteous and lacking a sense of humor." Again, he writes: "... there is, as Reinhold Niebuhr so brilliantly and persuasively argued, no power, individual or collective, without some associated guilt." The two had frequent conversations when Niebuhr much later spent a year (1958) at the Princeton Institute for Advanced Studies, writing *The Structure of Nations and Empires.*[22]

Kennan and Niebuhr share, in part, their beliefs about human nature. Kennan, unlike Niebuhr, attributes human aggressiveness to the inheritance from animals and contrasts it with the soul, which "has an existence wholly separate from that of the body." That approaches the Platonic dualism that Niebuhr rejects; he sees sin as an attribute of the human spirit. Kennan sounds more like Niebuhr when he writes: "The more the ego is allowed to expand, the more powerful the temptation to reach for even larger expansion." Because of the human "lust for authority" (cf. Morgenthau) he warns against "any and every sort of utopian purpose or expectation. Man is not perfectible. These fissures in the human psyche are profound and elemental." Yet he closes his most personal book with the warning: hopelessness is "the unpardonable sin." And he offers his book "with a view to encouraging others to take heart" and "to act." That is close to Niebuhr's dialectical understanding of human nature and destiny.[23]

Kennan's most explosive impact on American public awareness came with his article, "The Sources of Soviet Conduct." It was originally written as a private memorandum to Secretary of Defense James Forrestal.

Although later published anonymously, over the name of "X," in *Foreign Affairs*,[24] its authorship soon became widely known, and it made "containment" a familiar word in discussions of American foreign policy.

Its argument is complex and subtle. Given the controversies about the article, any quick summary is bound to be inadequate. But the point of this essay requires me to try. Kennan says that the Stalinist Soviet Union is a severe dictatorship that, to maintain its "iron discipline" and its "principle of infallibility," must keep alive "the concept of Russia as in a state of siege." The issue is no longer communism versus capitalism, but perpetuation of the dictatorship. Therefore, "the main element of any United States policy toward the Soviet Union must be that of a long-term, patient but firm and vigilant containment of Russian expansive tendencies." This must be done in ways "not too detrimental to Russian prestige." Since Soviet power "bears within itself the seeds of its own decay," such a policy may lead to "either the break-up or the gradual mellowing of Soviet power."[25]

Critics, including the respected Walter Lippmann, accused Kennan of inciting Soviet hostility; they urged a more conciliatory approach. Others understood Kennan to be softening the American militance that had urged a "roll-back" of the Soviet Union. In subsequent writings Kennan explained repeatedly that we had made militarization "a national addiction," that in our "anti-Communist hysteria" we had demonized Soviet leadership and exaggerated its ambitions, that our intervention in Vietnam was a radical misappropriation of his doctrine of containment, that we needed greater restraint in military involvements far from home. Years later, looking back on that article, he reflected that he may have used the language of containment too "lightheartedly." He intended it as a contribution to "provisional stabilization in Western Europe" that might make possible "negotiation of a general European political settlement." And he often reaffirmed his warnings against lust for power and his belief that national interest was not primarily military power.[26]

Kennan and Niebuhr may have differed in details, but they agreed in (1) their opposition to Soviet ideology and expansion, (2) their desire to avoid unnecessary provocation of the Soviets, and (3) their affirmation of a national interest that was not predominately military.

Arthur Schlesinger Jr. (1917-)

Whereas Morgenthau believed that Niebuhr's theological vocation contributed to his greatness and Kennan shared Niebuhr's Christian belief, Schlesinger first approached Niebuhr as an outsider, who confessed "disrespect for organized religion." When a recent Harvard graduate and current member of the "Harvard Society of Fellows," he went, "under protest," at his wife's insistence, to hear Niebuhr preach in the university Memorial Church. To his surprise, he found himself captivated by Niebuhr's "jagged eloquence," combined with his "cool, rigorous and powerful argument." He could not then guess that future decades would see a long, friendly, and stimulating relationship between the two.[27]

As a writer-researcher for the Office of War Information, where he occasionally wrote "low-level messages" for President Roosevelt, then later as a special assistant to President Kennedy with an office in the White House, Schlesinger worked with many of the high and mighty; and as America's most widely-read historian and a professor at Harvard and at the City University of New York, he knew his way around among the great and those who esteemed themselves great. Yet he told Charles Brown, biographer of Niebuhr: "He was the greatest man I knew."[28]

Schlesinger, Niebuhr's junior by twenty-five years, never shared the socialism and radicalism of Niebuhr at the time of the Great Depression. But soon they found themselves allied in support of Roosevelt's New Deal and the liberal left of later years. Niebuhr chaired the Union for Democratic Action (UDA), founded in May 1941, primarily by intellectuals, journalists, and trade union leaders, to support the progressive efforts of the New Deal and oppose communism. Later, during the Truman administration, Republicans won both houses of Congress and Henry Wallace, formerly Roosevelt's vice president, ran for president on the Progressive ticket, protesting Truman's opposition to communism. The UDA saw the need for a larger organization of firmly non-communist liberals. A meeting in Washington in January 1947 organized Americans for Democratic Action (ADA). Among the 130 participating were Niebuhr, Schlesinger, Eleanor Roosevelt, Hubert Humphrey, John Kenneth Galbraith, Walter Reuther, David Dubinksy, Leon Henderson, and other notables. From this distinguished crowd, Niebuhr's speech won a standing ovation. (A curious note is that one of the early members of ADA was a Hollywood actor known as Ronnie Reagan, a fact sometimes noted by the realists with their accent on the ironies of history.) At the center of the planning was James Loeb, executive secretary of UDA, who became executive director of ADA. It was here that Schlesinger first actually met Niebuhr and found him impressive for his combination of "unforced humility" and "polemical vigor." Years later Schlesinger identified Niebuhr as "ADA's intellectual leader."[29]

Politically both were, in the American spectrum, left of center, but totally untainted by Soviet Communism. There were differences between the two. Schlesinger, picking up Niebuhr's self-description in the phrase,

"The Triumph of Experience over Dogma," a chapter title in Niebuhr's *The Irony of American History,* gently chided Niebuhr for his slowness in moving from socialism to Roosevelt's New Deal, and Niebuhr accepted the criticism. Schlesinger liked the term, "the vital center," and was perhaps less fond of Niebuhr's "jagged" style than he had been as a Harvard student. Schlesinger was a little more comfortable than Niebuhr with Kennedy-style politics, although it is easy to exaggerate the differences.[30]

As Niebuhr's later writings gave more attention to American culture (*The Irony of American History* and *Pious and Secular America*), he welcomed the knowledge of Schlesinger, the professional historian of America. Schlesinger, in turn, found Niebuhr's insights impressive. He dedicated the first volume of *The Age of Roosevelt* "For Reinhold Niebuhr." Kennan, in a favorable review of Schlesinger's *The Cycles of American History* (1986), said: "Schlesinger leans heavily on the brilliant insights of Reinhold Niebuhr's *Irony of American History* to challenge directly the validity of this messianic approach." Like Morgenthau and Niebuhr, Schlesinger insists on the importance of national interest in foreign policy, but with them he asks for a recognition of the importance of an ethical component in national interest and for the recognition of an understanding of the importance of national interests of other nations, including our antagonists. In a biting attack on the dogmatism of Noam Chomsky, he writes: "...as one supposed Reinhold Niebuhr had demonstrated long since, most secular questions intermingle good and evil in problematic proportions and are more usefully handled in other than moralistic categories."[31]

As Schlesinger put it in his review of Niebuhr's *Faith and History,* "...the distinction of his analysis is his success in restating Christian insights with such irresistible relevance to contemporary experience that even those who have no decisive faith in the supernatural find their own reading of experience and of history given new and significant experience."[32] Schlesinger probably should not have used the term "supernatural." Aware of the slogan, "Never say never," I cannot say that Niebuhr never used the term. I can say that he normally did not. It has too many echoes of dualistic ontologies, and Niebuhr was suspicious of ontology. He often spoke of transcendence.

The point of the comparisons of Niebuhr with the trio of Morgenthau, Kennan, and Schlesinger has been to illustrate Niebuhr's own belief that Christian realism, while intentionally Christian and theological, can be communicated in significant measure to those who do not share its theological assumptions. The transcendence of God was utterly important to Niebuhr, and his secular admirers sensed this. As Schlesinger wrote:

"One felt the irony—did Reinie also?—that unbelievers, appropriating so much of this thought, left off when the part that meant most to him—the ineffable mystery and grace of God—came in."[33]

Toward Some General Insights

This inquiry into Christian realism cannot end in a set of conclusions. As Schlesinger puts it, "History has a marvelous capacity to outwit all our certitudes."[34] Realism recognizes that solutions to political problems—above all, international problems—usually generate new problems. But I can conclude with a few general insights, persistent in Christian realism and likely to guide its future.

First, the euphoria that provoked the response of American Christian realists in the decades leading to World War II is gone. History betrayed the cheerful optimism over the Peace Pact that renounced war. It shattered the expectations that sprang from the liberal rationalism of the enlightenment with its confidence that scientific method would lead to progress in social and international conflicts comparable to its achievements in the physical sciences. The twentieth century, one hailed as the "Christian" century turned out to be the bloodiest century of history. It was not the realists who refuted the messianic expectations of those bygone times; it was historical events. The realists pointed out what was happening. Hazardous conflict is part of the human story. It can be creative or destructive. There are better and worse ways, both in effectiveness and in ethics, of dealing with conflict. There is no point in pretending that it does not exist.

Second, Christian faith is constantly relevant to politics. The church has lived in many political systems, sometimes enduring their persecution, sometimes accepting their patronage, often trying to change them. The present church has a heritage which moves it sometimes to gratitude, sometimes to shame and repentance. There have been versions of Christian faith—the lives of hermits, some (not all) mystics, and persecuted minorities—that shunned political activity. But Christians for the most part have believed that Christian love requires enactment in justice. Avoidance of political activity is a tacit acceptance of the status quo. There is no Christian faith—perhaps no faith of any religion—without political consequences. Perhaps Kennan is right in suggesting that there is no "morality that does not rest, consciously or otherwise, on some foundation of religious faith."[35] But the faith that actually motivates people sometimes has little relation to the conventional faith that they confess or reject. One responsibility of Christian realism is to remind Christians of the political implications of the faith they claim to hold.

Third, the distance between religion and politics is as important as the connection. To identify religion and politics—to assert that the territorial claims of Jews and Muslims in the Middle East can be determined by texts in the Bible or the Qur'an, or that the response to AIDS can be discovered in proof-texts of Scripture or papal encyclicals—is destructive of both religion and politics. Political decisions come out of an interaction between basic commitments and empirical investigations of an ever-changing world. Christian realists often find themselves allied with secularists in resisting the dogmatism of religionists who claim officiously that their politics is endorsed by God. At present, Christians in India want to preserve a secular constitution in the face of those Muslims and Hindu nationalists who want a religious state.

Fourth, the recognition of Christian realists of national interest has its wisdom and its dangers. William Temple, Archbishop of Canterbury during part of World War II, wrote: "... a statesman who supposes that a mass of citizens can be governed without appeal to their self-interest is living in a dreamland and is a public menace." That was his political realism. He combined it with vigorous efforts to enhance social justice in Great Britain and the international order. That, too, he believed was realism. The recognition of national interest can dull the sharpness of Christian ethical demands that are offensive to society. In our time liberation theologians have criticized Christian realists for too easy accommodation to sinful social structures. They have shared the realists' alertness to the realities of self-interest and power. As harsh realities dimmed the utopianism of the early liberation theologians, the kinship became more obvious. Gustavo Gutierrez, the eminent liberation theologian, in his "Introduction to the Revised Edition" of his powerful book, *A Theology of Liberation,* is a realist in his warnings against "facile enthusiasms" and his awareness of "how very complex" the world is. Liberation theologies can be seen as a version of Christian realism, as the doctrine of just revolution is a version of the doctrine of just war. The liberation theologians still make the indispensable contribution of seeing history from the underside. We can hope that the chastening of utopianism will not mean the dulling of the sensitivity to injustice.[36]

Christian realism, even when it makes its peace, more or less, with national interest, has insisted on the rejection of any idolatry of the state. One reason that Niebuhr liked Morgenthau was Morgenthau's awareness: "The state has become indeed a 'mortal God,' and for an age that believes no longer in an immortal God, the state becomes the only God there is."[37] Christian realists actually believe that the nation, in a conventionally meaningless phrase of the American Declaration of Allegiance, lives "under God."

Fifth, Christian realism asks of the nation a union of courage and modesty in foreign policy. It has most often, in the United States, warned against excessive ventures of power and national messianism. Arrogance is the great temptation of a nation with immense power. History has humbled us—somewhat. "The American Century" turned out to be the century in which America first lost a war. But the collapse of the Soviet Union meant that America was left as the sole "superpower" on earth—with all the temptations of such a role. One of the curious ironies of our time is that a President, who campaigned on an appeal for greater "humility" in foreign policy went on to locate in three nations the world's "axis of evil" and then to mass a huge army thousands of miles from American soil, ready to accept the endorsement of the United Nations, if that should be forthcoming, but equally ready to go it alone, if the UN should refuse endorsement.

Modesty, while not our greatest temptation, has its problems, too. It easily becomes the pretext for ignoring human pain and misery on a vast scale. The true fact that we cannot solve all the problems of the world—of starvation, AIDS, slavery, exploitation of the poor—does not mean that we can do nothing. It does not entitle us to enjoy vast wealth and exploit the world's resources for our complacent comfort.

Christian realism—and the overwhelming problems of the past century—has reminded us of the reality of sin. Both arrogance and modesty can be instruments of sin. Christian realism now faces the challenge of reminding us constantly of the perils of both.

Sixth, Christian realism has, for good reasons, made much of the reality of national interest. Yet there is a curious strangeness in the concept of national interest. To anybody living through the ordeals of our present generation, the notion that national interest actually determines the policies of nations is transparently fallacious. Did such tyrants as Hitler and Stalin really advance the national interests of their countries? Did the Japanese military forces serve their national interest in their attack on Pearl Harbor? Was it truly national interest that prompted the United States in its military actions in Vietnam, or in its long-term development of an oil-dependent economy, or—to reach back farther into history—in its original constitutional acceptance of slavery and its continuing racism? Could it be that guidance by national interest is the exception more often than the rule? The Christian realists recognize that the operative national interest is very often the interest of some faction within the nation or of some deep misperception of the real interests of the nation. Why do nations so often misperceive their national interests? Partly the answer is simply human fallibility and short-sightedness. Partly it is moral failure, what Senator Fulbright called "the arrogance of power."[38] Christian realists will be wise, whenever they acknowledge national interest, to give equal accent to the importance of continually reconceiving national interest and recognizing, as we have seen Niebuhr, Morgenthau, Kennan, and Schlesinger do, that it has an ethical component.

Seventh, Christian realism must now face a world vastly different from that of the days prior to World War II, when the 20th century version of Christian realism took shape. It is not Hitlerism and Stalinism that are our problems. We must deal with legacies of the Cold War, widely dispersed nuclear weapons, the proliferation of other weapons of mass destruction, the facts and potentialities of terrorism and ecological destructiveness, the perplexities of technological and economic globalism. Christian realism has no easy answers for this strange new world. Neither does any other political philosophy.

The Cold War, with the development of the massive American and Soviet nuclear arsenals, brought the fear of a nuclear holocaust—most dramatically at the time of the Cuban missile crisis, which President Kennedy and Chairman Khruschev, with a combination of wisdom, restraint, and luck, stopped short of disaster. Most of the realists yearned for an end to the cold war. It came sooner than they expected. What did not come was a relaxation of anxiety. True, we no longer wonder whether, tomorrow or next day, we or the Russians may in a rash or accidental act release a few intercontinental ballistic missiles and provoke a counter-attack from weapons already targeted and supposed to be a deterrent. But we have discovered that a few men, armed with box-cutters, can seize airliners and destroy a World Trade Center and part of the Pentagon. We know that several countries are capable of loading a nuclear bomb on a ship and exploding it the harbor of New York or San Francisco. We know about deadly bacteriological and chemical weapons. We know of desperate dictators who are more likely than Kennedy or Khruschev to act rashly and unpredictably, because they have less to lose. We know of reckless religious fanatics for whom the desire for survival—a motive that we used to think we could count on—does not inhibit the desire to destroy. This is an anxious world.

All this may mean a change in the mission of Christian realists. Once they saw a responsibility to awaken a too-complacent world to the reality of evil. Complacency is still a problem. But now there is an equal responsibility to arouse an anxious world to hope.

Once Reinhold Niebuhr jarred people into recognition of the universality of sin. That is a persistent need, especially in the face of the self-righteousness so obvious in public life. He did it well. But he saw also the need to maintain hope. "For the freedom of man," he wrote, "makes it impossible to set any limits of race, sex, or social condition upon the brotherhood which may be achieved in history." Characteristically he accompanied that with the warning: "...each new development of life, whether in individual or social terms, presents us with new possibilities of realizing the good in history;... [but] we also face new hazards on each new level, and ... the new level of historic achievement offers us no emancipation from contradictions and ambiguities to which all life in history is subject."[39]

How do we turn that theological insight into policy—in a realistic way? The "search for a higher and wider integration of the world community," though arduous and precarious, is "not vain." "That task must and will engage the conscience of mankind for ages to come." It is possible that "the degree of mutual danger will overcome the constant inclination of nations to fear each other more than they fear the danger which their enmity has caused for each and both."

"Were this to happen a really novel factor would have emerged in history. We cannot rule out the possibility that it will emerge, but we cannot have any confidence in its emergence."[40]

Realism urges that, for the time being, we engage in holding actions, seeking by every device of diplomacy and power to avoid the destructive explosion and grasping for every opportunity to build on the common interests shared by all who value civilization. During this interim, which may lead to a "really novel" era of history, we have no assurance of security. Christian faith here offers some support to the efforts that realism endorses. It is, in Niebuhr's words, "a faith which understands the fragmentary and broken character of all historic achievements and yet has confidence in their meaning because it knows their completion to be in the hands of a Divine Power, whose resources are greater than those of men, and whose suffering love can overcome the corruptions of man's achievements, without negating the significance of our striving."[41]

That expresses the most distinctive Christian contribution to political realism. It is clearly an expression of faith. Christians can pray, hope, and act for the realization of that faith in works.

Notes

[1] Walter Rauschenbusch, *Christianizing the Social Order* (New York: Macmillan, 1912). T.S. Eliot, *The Idea of a Christian Society* (New York: Harcourt, Brace, 1940). Emil Brunner, *Christianity and Civilisation*, Vol. I (New York: Charles Scribner's Sons, 1949): 4-5, i.

[2] For a discussion of Christian realism in a wider context see Normunds Kamergrauzis, *The Persistence of Christian Realism* (Uppsala, Sweden: Uppsala

University Library, 2002). Although this book focuses on the British economist-theologian Ronald H. Preston, its scope is international, including the World Council of Churches.

[3] Hans Morgenthau, *Politics among Nations: The Struggle for Power and Peace*, Third ed. (New York: Alfred A. Knopf, 1966): 35. Thucydides, *The History of the Peloponessian War*, tr. Richard Crawley (New York: E.P. Dutton, 1950), Book V, Ch. 17, 406; standard pagination, 103. Reinhold Niebuhr, "Augustine's Political Realism," Ch. 9 of *Christian Realism and Political Problems* (New York: Charles Scribner's Sons, 1953): 119.

[4] In 1978 the editors of *The Ecumenical Review*, quarterly publication of the World Council of Churches, asked me to do an article on "just revolution." They were responding to the liberation theologians, primarily in Latin America, who sometimes justified revolution. My guess it that they thought I might propose such a doctrine. Instead, I found evidence that it had existed, although not with that precise name, since the third century. To take a single conspicuous example, St. Thomas Aquinas, immediately following his discussion of "just war," takes up the case of rebellion against a tyrant and affirms that it is the tyrant, not the rebels, who is "more guilty of sedition." Centuries later, Lord Acton attributed to St. Thomas "the earliest exposition of the Whig theory of revolution." Roger L. Shinn, "Liberation, Reconciliation, and 'Just Revolution,'" *The Ecumenical Review*, 30: 4 (October 1978): 319-32. Thomas Aquinas, *Summa Theologiae*, II-II, Question 42, Art. 2 (London: Blackfriars, 1972): vol. 35, 106-107. John E.D.D.Acton, *Essays on Freedom and Power*, ed. Gertrude Himmelfarb (New York: Meridian Books, 1955): 88.

[5] Charles Clayton Morrison, *The Outlawry of War* (Chicago: Willett, Clark and Colby, 1927): 97-98, 280-81. Morrison, *The Social Gospel and the Christian Cultus* (New York: Harpers, 1933): 151. John Dewey, Foreword to Morrison, *The Outlawry of War*, xx-xxi.

[6] Niebuhr, "Ten Years That Shook My World," *The Christian Century* (April 26, 1939): 542-46.

[7] Niebuhr, *The Nature and Destiny of Man*, Vol. I, Human Nature, Vol. 2, Human Destiny (New York: Charles Scribner's Sons, 1941 and 1943)

[8] Niebuhr, *Why the Christian Church is Not Pacifist*, published as a 47-page booklet by the Student Christian Movement Press of London in 1940, then as Ch. 1 of *Christianity and Power Politics* (New York: Charles Scribner's Sons, 1940). My citations are from the latter edition, 21, 23. The Oxford Conference address is published in *Christianity and Power Politics*. The World Council of Churches address is in *Christian Realism and Political Problems* (New York: Charles Scribner's Sons, 1953).

[9] Niebuhr, "Christian Faith and Natural Law," *Love and Justice: Selections from the Shorter Writings of Reinhold Niebuhr*, ed. D.B. Robertson (Gloucester, MA: Peter Smith, 1976; first published in *Theology* (February 1940)): 48.

[10] John C. Bennett, "Reinhold Niebuhr's Contribution to Christian Social Ethics," in *Reinhold Niebuhr: A Prophetic Voice in Our Time*, ed. Harold R. Landon (Greenwich, CT: Seabury Press, 1962): 74.

[11] Niebuhr, *The Nature and Destiny of Man*, Vol. I, Human Nature, 127, 129.
[12] Niebuhr, *The Nature and Destiny of Man*, Vol. II, Human Destiny, 75-76.
[13] Niebuhr, *Faith and History: A Comparison of Christian and Modern Views of History* (New York: Charles Scribner's Sons, 1949): 96.
[14] Niebuhr, book review in *Christianity and Society* 12 (Spring 1947), 33-34. Morgenthau, *Scientific Man Versus Power Politics* (Chicago: University of Chicago Press, Phoenix Books, 1965; first published, 1946): 9. The book that Morgenthau dedicated to Niebuhr was *Science: Servant or Master?* (New York: World Publishing Co., Meridian Books, 1972).
[15] Morgenthau, "The Influence of Reinhold Niebuhr in American Political Thought and Life," in *Reinhold Niebuhr: A Prophetic Voice in Our Time*, 109. Niebuhr regrettably could not be present because of his failing health, but his comments on the recorded transcript of the occasion are included in this book.
[16] Morgenthau, *Scientific Man and Power Politics*, 209; *The Purpose of American Politics* (New York: Alfred A Knopf and Random House Vintage Books, 1963; first published, 1960): 8; *A New Foreign Policy for the United States* (New York: Frederick A. Praeger, for the Council on Foreign Relations, 1969).
[17] Morgenthau, *Scientific Man Versus Power Politics*, 174. Niebuhr, *Christianity and Power Politics*, 31.
[18] George F. Kennan, *The Nuclear Delusion: Soviet-American Relations in the Atomic Age*, Expanded, Updated Edition (New York: Pantheon Books, 1983), 201. This one chapter was originally a lecture at Princeton Theological Seminary (27 April 1982).
[19] George F. Kennan, *American Diplomacy*, Expanded Edition (Chicago: University of Chicago Press, 1984): 144. The quotation is from his chapter on "America and the Russian Future," reprinted from *Foreign Affairs* 29:3(April 1951): 351-70.
[20] Kennan, "Morality and Foreign Policy," in *A Century's Ending: Reflections 1982-1995* (New York: W.W. Norton, 1996): 269, 271, 275, 277. This chapter was originally published in *Foreign Affairs* (Winter 1985-86).
[21] Ibid., 154.
[22] Charles C. Brown, *Niebuhr and His Age: Reinhold Niebuhr's Prophetic Role and Legacy*, New Edition (Harrisburg, PA: Trinity Press International, 2002): 243. Richard Wightman Fox, *Reinhold Niebuhr: A Biography* (New York: Pantheon Books, 1985): 238. Brown summarizes the evidence on 302, n. 49. Kennan, *A Century's Ending*, 211; *Around the Cragged Hill: A Personal and Political Philosophy* (New York: W.W. Norton, 1993): 82n, 183.
[23] Kennan, *Around the Cragged Hill* (New York: W.W. Norton, 1993): 28, 259.
[24] X [George Kennan], "The Sources of Soviet Conduct," *Foreign Affairs* XXV, no. 4 (July 1947:, 566-82. Reprinted over the name of Kennan in *American Diplomacy*. My page references are to this later printing.
[25] Ibid, 116, 110, 119, 125, 127,
[26] Kennan, *American Diplomacy*, 172; *A Century's Ending*, 99, 150.
[27] Arthur M. Schlesinger Jr., *A Life in the 20th Century: Innocent Beginnings, 1917-1950* (New York: Houghton Mifflin, 2000): 268, 249.

[28] Brown, *Niebuhr and His Age*, 1.
[29] Ibid, 460.
[30] Schlesinger, "Reinhold Niebuhr's Role in American Political Thought and Life," in *Reinhold Niebuhr: His Religious, Social, and Political Thought*, ed. Charles W. Kegley and Robert W. Bretall (New York: Macmillan, 1956): 125-150. Niebuhr, "Reply," 436. Schlesinger, *The Vital Center* (Boston: Houghton Mifflin, 1962).
[31] Niebuhr, *The Irony of American History* (New York: Charles Scribner's Sons, 1952); *Pious and Secular America* (New York: Charles Scribner's Sons, 1959). Kennan, "In the American Mirror," *A Century's Ending*, 211. This review of Schlesinger's *The Cycles of American History* (Boston: Houghton Mifflin, 1986) appeared originally in the *New York Times Review of Books* (6 November 1986). Schlesinger, *The Crisis of Confidence* (Boston: Houghton Mifflin, 1969): 89.
[32] Schlesinger, book review in *Christianity and Society* 14: 3 (Summer 1949): 27.
[33] Schlesinger, *A Life in the 20th Century: Innocent Beginnings, 1917-1950*, 513.
[34] Ibid, 523.
[35] Kennan, *A Century's Ending*, 281.
[36] William Temple, *Christianity and Social Order* (New York: Seabury Press, 1977; first published, 1942): 65. Gustavo Gutierrez, *A Theology of Liberation: History, Politics, and Salvation*, 15th Anniversary Edition, tr. and ed. by Sister Caridad Inda and John Eagleson (Maryknoll, NY: Orbis, 1988): xviii, xvi.
[37] Morgenthau, *Scientific Man Versus Power Politics*, 197.
[38] J. William Fulbright, *The Arrogance of Power* (New York: Random House, 1966).
[39] Niebuhr, *The Nature and Destiny of Man*, Vol. II, Human Destiny, 85, 206.
[40] Niebuhr, *Christian Realism and Political Problems*, 29; *The Structure of Nations and Empires* (New York: Charles Scribner's Sons, 1959): 272.
[41] Niebuhr, *The Children of Light and the Children of Darkness* (New York: Charles Scribner's Sons, 1944): 189-90.

Chapter 9

The Ironies of Christian Realism: The End of an Augustinian Tradition in International Politics

Roger Epp

The account of the ascent–even the ascendancy–of Christian realism with its Augustinian language of human and international affairs, and then of its virtual disappearance by the 1960s, engages several plot lines.[1] One involves the revival of religion in intellectual circles, to which vigorous responses would be summoned in the name of humanism during the early 1950s. Another is the development of an aspirant academic field of international relations in a political context of Cold War, U.S. predominance and British decline, and an intellectual context marked by the enormous gravitational pull–at least on the American side–of more rigorously scientific modes of inquiry. But the stage of the discipline was far from determined at the outset of the post-war period. The foremost names that became associated with Christian realism, including Niebuhr, Butterfield and Wight, were engaged in a wider conversation with historians, theologians, philosophers, and even the occasional political scientist about the perspective appropriate to a tumultuous era of recent history from which there seemed no immediate prospect of relief. Much of this conversation, moreover, was pitched at an educated lay audience and conducted in public: on the BBC, in sponsored lectures, in newspaper columns, and in books characterized by brevity and scarcity of footnotes. It took place at some remove from the expansion or creation of new programs in international relations at universities on either side of the

Atlantic, and from the work of study groups especially in the U.S. on appropriate approaches and curriculum.[2]

In this wider conversation, Augustinian themes did find a prominent if short-lived place. More specifically, those associated with Christian realism–Wight, for example, never identified himself as such–tended to appropriate four important concepts or themes from Augustine having to do with the nature of human beings, history, and the relationship between order, justice, and *caritas*, or the "law of love."[3] First, in contrast to Enlightenment and liberal optimism, Christian realists took up Augustine's conception of sin and pride, though not without also stressing humanity's free will and capacity for reason. Niebuhr's anthropology of free human essence and sinful existence was mediated through Kierkegaard's account of the inescapable anxiety of finite beings. It could be deployed legitimately, though perhaps unconventionally, in the context of the Cold War against any tendency towards self-righteous moralism. Second, Christian realists understood secular history as the realm of human moral freedom, as indeterminate rather than either cyclical or progressive, but as governed ultimately by the purposes of divine providence. Thus, at least some Christian realists could achieve a kind of critical separation from the fate of any particular regime, including their own, even amid the serious international conflicts of their time. Third, Christian realists understood from Augustine the importance of social and political order–the consequence of the sinful corruption of human community. But they also understood, as Niebuhr put it, that order had to be balanced with justice to endure, and that both were to be held subject to the higher law of love: a transcendent ideal, an "impossible possibility," and a buffer against realist cynicism even if it could not constitute a practical political program on its own. As with Augustine, political violence might sometimes be necessary for the sake of order and justice, but, unlike the Weberian ethic of responsibility, its exercise was never beyond either outside ethical scrutiny or deep personal regret.

The Augustinian language of Christian realism was prominent throughout the 1940s and 1950s, in large part due to the contributions from Protestant theologians and Protestant-dominated ecumenical forums organized after the war, whose activities attracted considerable interest on the part of the mainstream press. However, by the end of the 1950s such activity took place increasingly at the margins of intellectual life generally and academic international relations in particular, for the reasons to be considered in this chapter. For the moment, it might be pointed out that the claim of marginalization made about a tradition of thought implies an earlier prominence. Likewise, the claim of atrophy, which will be argued later, implies a former vitality and critical thrust. In the postwar decade at least, Augustinian themes did enjoy a relative prominence and vitality, most notably from the writings of Niebuhr and Butterfield. This was the period in which Arthur Schlesinger, Jr., in one such review, could presume a knowing readership for his anachronistic boast that, "[w]hatever you say about Augustine, at least he would not have been much surprised by the outcome of the Russian Revolution." Perhaps the most fervent of Niebuhr's secular disciplines, Schlesinger added the claim that many others would reaffirm: that it was possible to "derive rewarding insights from the Christian conception of man without accepting the Christian drama of sin and salvation as true."[4]

The story of the Augustinian tradition's ascent and decline, then, is at once much broader than the development of international relations in the universities, but nonetheless intimately interconnected with it. The general post-war phenomenon of what Russell Jacoby has described as the disappearance of "public intellectuals" into the academy, and into professionalized, increasingly segmented realms of discourse, is borne out here.[5] But beyond it lies a particular and very real struggle for an aspirant discipline of international relations fought in the 1950s, chiefly in the U.S., which must be located in turn within wider trends in the social sciences. In that struggle, it will be argued, the claim for a scientifically-respectable, autonomous academic specialization of international relations in which research could be conducted and grants solicited on the basis of a demarcated expertise, necessarily came into conflict with resistant elements of the Christian realism tradition. In other words, a specialization could only develop to the exclusion of explicit theological categories and of theological-philosophical considerations; these were among the "antiquarian relics" that, as David Ricci has said of the study of politics, seemed to clutter the field and "dismay those who aspired to scientific status."[6]

The Struggle for a Discipline

It is an irony worthy of Niebuhr that essentially the same context of crisis that gave conceptual space for Augustinian theological themes also propelled the social sciences to a position of unprecedented power in the U.S. Already in wartime, the hope of reconstructing society on scientific lines arising out of the New Deal received a powerful boost. Social scientists were recruited, as available, as an essential part of the war effort; economists, above all, proved invaluable in planning and supervising production and rationing schemes. After the war, the institutional infrastructure for social scientific research expanded exponentially with the creation or reinforcement of both government and private-foundation funding programs. By 1947, Carl Friedrich observed that "the work of political scientists is now...intimately connected with the work of governmental agencies in the United States," though he added that there remained a place in this peculiarly American discipline–unlike in economics–for reasoned judgement.[7]

Against the imperatives of the Cold War and the new self-conscious sense of the status of world power, it was not surprising that the still-uncongealed study of international relations should share in this bonanza. The thirst for expert policy advice and the sudden increase in demand for trained foreign service personnel served as a stimulus to the definition and development of a distinct domain of study, albeit most often with an institutional linkage with political science. Thus, as Stanley Hoffman and others have suggested, international relations did grow up as an American social science, propelled by the problems confronting U.S. foreign policy and the need to rationalize global involvements and the accumulation of military power.[8] The growing corpus of critical literature on the extent to which international relations theory has constituted a justification of American power cannot be canvassed here. In broadest strokes, it can be said that if the recently-arrived *emigre* realists offered a "crash course in statecraft, ... a convenient crib of European diplomatic wisdom"–more convincing on campus with a German accent"–the home-grown contribution was the scientific impulse, the preference for exactitude and technical problem-solving.[9] In precisely this spirit Quincy Wright's 1949 presidential address to the American Political Science Association called the study of international relations to the task of "understanding, developing, and *regulating*" a "dynamic, complex, stable, and peaceful world."[10]

These broad strokes, however, and the critical narratives of the discipline's development present too retrospective, too neat a story. They obscure the contested character of that development, even if the sides were unevenly matched (and not always readily distinguishable). In that contest, the rival poles–to borrow a term that was to become indispensable to analyses of power in the "international system"–might be centred geographically at Yale-Columbia and Notre Dame. The case can be made, alternatively, for the corridors of the University of Chicago, where Morgenthau's critique of "scientism" was issued just after he was granted tenure and where pitched battles were waged over methodological matters. But it was from the other locales and the journals attached to them that the loudest opening volleys, to extend the military metaphor, were launched.

In 1946, the year in which Grayson Kirk of Columbia was engaged in a countrywide series of consultative conferences under the auspices of the Council on Foreign Relations toward what became *The Study of International Relations in American Colleges and Universities*, a perhaps pre-emptive proposal regarding the nature of that study appeared in the *Review of Politics*. Written by editor Waldemar Gurian, an emigre whom Bernard Crick later celebrated among the brave critics of American scientism, the article doubted that international relations constituted a separate subject; at most, it brought together other subjects under a distinct and, in light of the times, defensible perspective. He argued nonetheless that the subject could only be studied by a combination of historical and philosophical approaches:

> Without a knowledge of history, comparative government and geography, the student of international relations would be lost. It would be tragic if he would receive the impression that some mechanistic schemes of power relations could replace concrete factual knowledge and an understanding of the particular perspectives of historical situations.

Later, citing Pascal, he added:

> Man is neither beast nor angel; rather he is being faced by a task of making life as human as possible in a changing world of time and history, and, even though he belongs to some particular group, he must never forget that he participates always in the unity of mankind.[11]

This conception of the subject, with its strong echoes of elements of the Augustinian tradition, was equally at odds with that declared by Frederick Dunn in the inaugural issue of *World Politics*: that the scope of subject was limited to "questions that arise in relations between autonomous groups in a world system in which power is not centered at one point."[12] Dunn, who had been director of Yale's Institute of International Studies since the early 1930s, was in 1948 also chairman of the government-funded Social Science Research Council's committee on international relations research. The committee's secretary was William Fox, a former student of Dunn, who proposed a similar definition in a paper on interwar research written for the committee and published in *World Politics* in 1949. It looked ahead towards a "body of political theory dealing with a system characterized by an absence of central authority [which] has yet to be developed." The paper was no less significant in terms of its unflattering depiction of interwar research in the U.S. The first paragraph described much of that work as "irrelevant,... even trivial." The second, to illustrate the "disesteem" in which that work was held in the wider scholarly community, quoted a which was said to have "passed unchallenged" in a discussion among leading social scientists in 1930: "The emotional drive is so highly developed in the kind of person who goes into the international relations field that it often leads to unclear thinking." The third paragraph described the "desire for legitimacy" as a powerful "spur to soul-searching activity" of the sort necessary to know why the academic expectations of the 1920s were shattered by events of the next decade, and therefore to be "taken seriously in the 1950s."[13]

Within these two poles, then, the nature of academic international relations was contested. *World Politics* was the flagship journal of the more delimited, more rigorous, definition of international relations as a distinct academic enterprise covetous of scientific legitimacy. The *Review* was a favourite outlet in the early 1950s for critics of what Voegelin called the "new science of politics." The latter journal, characteristically, was the first to publish Butterfield's work in the U.S., in this case "The Tragic Element in Modern International Conflict," first presented as a lecture at Notre Dame. It also published the core of Morgenthau's soon-to-be-released *Politics Among Nations* and, later, his critique of political science's retreat from the commitment to telling the "truth about power" to "the formal, ...the pure theoretical."[14] It would be an exaggeration to suggest a division between two mutually exclusive camps, represented by different journals. Some individuals, indeed, did attempt to straddle the line that others had drawn. *World Politics* included in its second volume Niebuhr's protest against both "idealist" and "realist" strategies vis-a-vis the Soviet Union ("Communism must be contained; but the strategy of containment cannot be primarily military."[15]). But *World Politics* also published, within three years, the first sustained criticism of Niebuhr's thought, by Robert Tucker, to appear in a journal of politics. Tucker's conclusion, that Niebuhr ascribed too little freedom to the conduct of foreign policy, may not have been warranted by a closer reading of the relevant texts. The complementary claim that he seemed to "condemn the social sciences to the status of an irrelevant futility in their attempts to clarify the problems of the contemporary social world," struck closer to the issue at hand, and echoed Fox's own views.[16]

The differences that did exist were sharpened in the setting of a committee organized by the Rockefeller Foundation, under the direction of Thompson, for the advance of international relations theory. In his report in the *American Political Science Review* on the initial meeting, which included Fox, Morgenthau, Niebuhr, Wolfers, Walter Lippmann, Paul Nitze and Dean Rusk (also with the Foundation), Thompson suggested that its inspiration had been the request of a former Secretary of State–no doubt Dean Acheson–for an "applicable body of theory in foreign policy." The report observed almost in passing that those present were divided as to whether theory meant predictability and the construction of abstract models. Thompson urged a spirit of mutual respect between "philosophical" and "behavioural" approaches and proposed that closer union was possible; for, as he put it: "Theory without vindication is metaphysics."[17] That metaphysics was a term of derision needing no further explanation may attest to the pragmatic character of the age. But Thompson's somewhat terse summary and appeal on this point of the discussions betray little of the deep divisions within the group that contributed to its premature demise.[18]

In the end, the project generated only one volume, published under the title *Theoretical Aspects of International Relations* in 1959. Fox was its editor and had organized the additional seminars at Columbia to which the seven eventual contributors presented papers. The volume itself fell short of the status of a classic, though it marked Kenneth Waltz's debut on the utility of traditional political theory for ordering and comprehending the data of international relations, and contained, appropriately next to it, economist Charles Kindleberger's suggestion of a market analogy for explaining the balance of power. Fox, in his preface, noted the lack of an agreed theoretical framework but also shared concern that international relations be more than contemporary history, "if it is to evolve as a legitimate academic speciality or is to yield results relevant to the major choices which governments and opinion leaders must make in world politics." The compromise solution was to create categories of theory: rational, empirical/scientific and normative. About the contribution on power and ideology by Niebuhr–who doubtless fit the normative label– Fox wrote, almost apologetically, that it was perhaps the only one "in which the preferences of the author... are at least implicitly suggested."[19] In his own contribution, he eschewed any idea that the social scientist should "tell men what they ought to want"; instead, invoking Weber, he proposed that the purpose of theory was to "heighten the rationality of choice," to show the most efficient path towards whatever ends were desired, and to minimize ignorance.[20]

A more enduring impression on the study of international relations was made by a book released later in the year: Waltz's *Man, the State, and War*. The book originated as a Ph.D. dissertation written under Fox and should be read as a continuation of his own agenda. Its canvassing of political philosophers from across the centuries for representative positions on the cause of war was, from the perspective of the history of ideas, unsophisticated and given to anachronisms; it could not have occurred to Augustine, for example, to attribute war to a state-system that did not exist in his own time. Perhaps this was not an impediment to success, as had been demonstrated previously with Karl Popper's *The Open Society and Its Enemies*. What was more important, in any case, was the book's introduction of three categories or levels of analysis, into which it filed Spinoza, Kant, and Rousseau alongside Lasswell and Lenin. Classical political thought, as Fox wrote in his foreword, constituted "one of the storehouses least systematically inventoried" for its "usefulness" in understanding international relations.[21] Decades later, it is difficult to imagine the theoretical literature in the field without Waltz's categories.

Beneath those categories, however, lies a more subtle subtext that is easily overlooked from a generation's distance. Waltz's treatment of Niebuhr as a "first-image pessimist" has been commented on elsewhere and is not at issue here. More fundamental is the manner in which his categories operate as means of exclusion. While particular wars occur for reasons related to the first and second images–the nature of individuals (or decision-makers) and states–wars ultimately are the result of an anarchical system in which "there is nothing to prevent them."[22] The individual personalities and the social and ideological complexion of states are idiosyncratic elements; the international system is the source of recurrent patterns of behaviour, hence the stuff of generalization and theory. The logic of this argument has been drawn out most fully in Waltz's later *Theory of International Politics*. But it is already embedded in the former book, whose implications might be summarized as follows. The theory of international relations and the "explanation" of its central problem–the phenomenon of war–can be set apart analytically from the first and second images, from theological or philosophical speculation on the human condition, from psychology and even from comparative politics. The road to academic specialization in the field of international politics passes through the third image.

There is no suggestion here that Waltz wrote a treatise precisely to excise theology and theologians from the subject. That excision had already become a reality, in a sense, in the profusion of textbooks issued by American publishers for classroom use in the 1950s. Waltz's book reinforced a powerful shift away from any meaningful encounter with the problems of human, historical existence–Augustine's *saeculum*, if you will–raised by the philosophers and theologians whose storehouse it "inventoried." The considerable attention given to Augustine and Niebuhr is another indication of their relative standing at the time, but the effect is their domestication and marginalization for the study of international relations. In his conclusion Waltz proposed that a third-image account of war could be the basis for a "realistic approach,"

> That avoids the tendency of some realists to attribute the necessary amorality, or even immorality, of world politics to the inherently bad character of man... No matter how good their intentions, policy makers must bear in mind the implications of the third image, which can be states in summary form as follows: Each state pursues its own interests, however defined, in ways it judges best. Force is a means of achieving the external ends of states because there exists no consistent, reliable process of reconciling the conflicts of interest that inevitably arise among similar units in a condition of anarchy. A foreign policy based on this image of international relations is *neither moral nor immoral, but embodies merely a reasoned response to the world about us.*[23]

This conclusion does not merely misrepresent the Augustinian conception of human beings. It also exalts a purely instrumental reason freed of moral considerations, one that assumes too much by way of self-interested calculation and too little, if any, of conscience. Even Butterfield, for all his concerns with moralism, had insisted that international politics could not be abstracted from an underlying moral order. But the Augustinian tradition, with its "normative" dilemmas and its search for perspective on the contemporary world, was no serious rival as a source of research agendas in the social scientific bloom of the latter 1950s. Its academic heart in the U.S. was a theological seminary–Union in New York–which, whatever prominence it attained in the postwar decade, did not educate doctoral candidates to teach international relations in the universities. In the major universities with such graduate programs, it claimed few strategic footholds; and, as often as not, as with John Hallowell at Duke, these involved individuals identified with other branches of political science. Niebuhr continued to present papers, for instance, at American Political Science Association annual conferences. As important a thinker as John Herz would indicate in his *International Politics in the Atomic Age* (1959) that Niebuhr's essays in *Christianity in Crisis* were still required reading and that there was a fundamental affinity between his description of the security dilemma and that first suggested by Butterfield in *Christianity and History*.[24] But a narrower, more consciously scientific definition of the study of international relations than that which Gurian proposed, and which would have been more hospitable to the Augustinian tradition, had won out. Niebuhr's own protests against the pretensions of the social sciences belonged to what had become a minority chorus.[25]

The British Experience: The Riches of Poverty

The existence of a distinctive British–perhaps English–"school" in the study of international relations emanating from the teaching of Wight and Charles Manning at the London School of Economics (LSE) in the 1950s is well known. [26] British scholarship has been, and is still, strikingly different in tone from mainstream American scholarship in the subject: more firmly anchored in the humanities; more suspicious of generalization, scientific technique and social engineering; less given to research that is "policy relevant" in a direct sense. Explanations of this divergence tend to emphasize the peculiar legacy of British academic inclinations toward the classics, history, and philosophy. A strong case, however, might be made for an alternative emphasis: that the decisive break between British and American idioms of inquiry comes about as a result of the shift in the latter case toward social science on the model of its most prestigious discipline, economics. Between the wars, the literature in the field of international relations betrays no profound differences of national style of the kind that were entrenched later. Indeed, only in the 1950s does it become problematic to refer to a single "Anglo-American" theoretical enterprise.

Any discussion of why the British did not follow the American lead cannot, of course, neglect material considerations. If the expansion of the social sciences in the U.S. was propelled by relative prosperity, a new global role, and a thirst for expert policy advice, such conditions did not exist in Britain, where political and economic decline resulted in a dearth of institutional support for research, at least outside of Chatham House. For this and other reasons, the period from 1946 and 1960 has been characterized as one of "darkness and stagnation" for the study of international relations in Britain, following the brief creative period that generated Carr's *Twenty Years' Crisis*, George Schwarzenberger's *Power Politics*, and Wight's treatise of the same name. Outside of occasional "striking" essays or monographs by Butterfield, Beloff, and Denis Brogan, the literature through which the subject was taught was, according to the same survey, mostly American–notably, Morgenthau's *Politics Among Nations*. This overall imbalance may have reflected a junior-partner status in academic as well as diplomatic realms, and was said to prevail at least until the early 1960s, when books published by Manning, F. H. Hinsley, Joseph Frankel, and Hugh Seton-Watson marked an intellectual renewal. On the U.S. side, though, an overall estrangement from the British literature was, if anything, exacerbated in subsequent years. By one count of citations in American journals from 1958 through 1973, merely three foreign authors–Raymond Aron, Carr, and the British mathematician

Lewis Richardson–ranked among the top 50 names.[27]

It was against this backdrop of stagnation, or perhaps dependence, that in 1958 Butterfield accepted a long-standing offer from Thompson on behalf of the Rockefeller Foundation to underwrite a British committee similar to the American one for the theory of international relations. Butterfield, too, had been skeptical of making the subject an academic specialization, to the point of writing a paper in 1949 opposing Manning's efforts to promote it, which provoked a challenge on his next trip to the U.S. from Dunn and others. But by 1958 Butterfield had become, as he recalled, "bitten by the idea that England needed... some more structural thinking in international politics." His immediate response was to bring Wight and Desmond Williams on side; his "great ambition" as the Committee's first chairman was to "meet the ideals and desires of Martin Wight in particular."[28] It was Wight who, in turn, insisted on the inclusion of a philosopher, in particular the theologian-philosopher Donald MacKinnon, whose interests ranged from Kant to Kierkegaard and Marx to Collingwood, and from Greek tragedy to Christian social ethics. MacKinnon was a dissenting member of the 1946 British Council of Churches commission that produced *The Era of Atomic Power*, and was thereafter a sharp critic of Western reliance upon–and Christian assent to– nuclear weapons.[29] Wight also was instrumental in enlisting Hedley Bull, a younger colleague at the LSE.

From the start, the Committee's work was self-consciously outside the methodological mould of American social science. Butterfield would later claim Bull's famous argument for a "classical approach," against Kaplan and others of that perspective, as "the English way," and "the method of our Committee" in contrast to "extravagant scientism."[30] *Diplomatic Investigations*, a distillation of papers prepared for the Committee since its inaugural meeting in January 1959, was published in 1966, the same year that Bull's broadside appeared in *World Politics*. In the preface to the book, Butterfield and Wight signalled a discomfort with the banner, "theory of international politics," given to the Committee by its sponsor. The phrase, they explained, was "without wide currency or clear meaning in this country. The group took it to cover enquiry into the nature of the international states-system, the assumptions and ideas of diplomacy, the principles of foreign policy, the ethics of international relations and war."[31] The book proposed no neat division of normative and other theory. It encompassed Wight on Western values, Bull on the "Grotian conception of international society," MacKinnon on natural law, Butterfield on the emergence of the *idea* of the balance of power by extension of the Newtonian physics of equilibrium. The editors noted modestly that the "connoisseur of national styles may notice" the contrasts between *Diplomatic Investigations* and the book generated by their U.S. colleagues, which itself was "in some respects traditional compared with the flourishing contemporary school... of systems analysis." The Committee had been concerned more with the historical and philosophical that with the scientific, the methodological, and the contemporary. In their discussions members were unable "to forget that foreign affairs and international relations, however they may be studied or analysed, are in themselves *not a closed theoretical system*. They are the political region pre-eminently of the contingent and the unforeseen."[32] There are echoes here of Wight's earlier argument over free will, determinism, and the social sciences. In an important way, there exists in this branch of the British school the assumption that the so-called great issues of political theory–order and justice, power and authority–are increasingly played out at the international level.[33] In the U.S., *Diplomatic Investigations* found easily its most enthusiastic reviewer in Morgenthau who, in a rearguard action, urged teachers of international relations to set the insights contained in Wight's two major essays alone "against the theoretical propositions of any number of volumes on behaviourism, systems analysis, game theory, decision-making, and so forth."[34]

There is no simple and necessary correlation, however, between the Augustinian tradition and the British school or any one methodological position. Individuals such as the Australian Arthur Lee Burns, indeed, could combine a commitment to scientific method as practiced by Kaplan with a rootedness in similar theological assumptions and vocabulary. Conversely, critics of narrow scientific conceptions of the subject or proponents of alternatives including the British school were not, by definition, Augustinians. What can be said is that the fate of the Augustinian tradition applied to international relations was bound up in the methodological crossfire of the 1950s and early 1960s. And those who have tended to minimize this contention as an in-house quarrel within a uniform "realist" paradigm should take into account the stakes involved: namely, the survival or the strength of specific traditions or languages; and, in a Kuhnian sense, the sort of questions posed by those working within an academic specialization. In the U.S., the case for an autonomous and scientifically-respectable field of international relations in the circumstances of the 1950s did have to be made against the not-so-ancient "relics" of the Augustinian tradition. In Britain, for the complex of reasons suggested above, the climate remained more congenial to perspectives and questions grounded in the same tradition–that climate having been shaped, in part, by a Committee initially organized by

Butterfield in Wight's image. Beyond this, there are elements of Augustinian thought that appear resistant to some expressions of international relations as social science: the emphasis on the will; the idea of political structures as historical artefacts rather than as given in nature; the refusal to reduce war ("so horrible, so ruthless") to a quantifiable abstraction.

For the present, recognition should be given to those remnants of the Augustinian tradition that persisted near the core of the subject in Britain, more so than in the U.S., through the junior members of the Rockefeller Committee–Bull and Michael Howard–or others influenced by its founders. Bull, who borrowed heavily from Wight's categories, despite a public confession of unease about the extent to which the latter's view of international relations derived from his religious beliefs, made the tension between order and justice the central issue of his main work, *The Anarchical Society*. And if that book, as its critics have argued, leans too much to the side of order, the fact is often overlooked that it begins explicitly from Augustine's definition of "purposive order"–as more than merely the absence of strife.[35] Bull, too, once reminded an International Institute of Strategic Studies (IISS) symposium on the future of strategic deterrence that whereas the West may have reason to persist with such policies, it should not lose sight of their "true moral character," their "wickedness," or become "fully reconciled to them."[36] Howard, meanwhile, spars occasionally with Augustine in *The Causes of War* but echoes the Bishop of Hippo, almost verbatim, in his conviction that the only legitimate object of war is a better peace.[37] Similarly, Geoffrey Goodwin has located himself within the Christian realism of Niebuhr and Butterfield in treating the moral dimensions of international relations and nuclear deterrence in particular. In the later respect his contribution to an edited volume produced from a church-sponsored study group in 1982 made the case for "cosmic humility" as a Christian virtue:

> There is a major responsibility on Christian churches to face up to the dilemmas posed, more acutely perhaps in a nuclear age that ever before, by the often competing claims of peace, order and justice and to the complexities of the management of power in international society. A responsible attitude is not helped by indulging in idealistic prescriptions that ignore the realities of power in favour of simplistic notions of international right and wrong. What is needed is a vision of the ideal, of the reconciling act of God in Christ and that the world is indeed one in the sense that it is 'God's world,' coupled with a grasp of the parameters of the possible; an awareness of the wonder of God's redemptive love and of the workings of Divine Providence in history with a realisation of the necessarily fallen

character of a quasi-anarchical international society... Above all, conflict in international society needs to be seen, not so much in terms of the conflict of good with evil (though at times it is that), but more as an inescapable part of the human predicament.[38]

Christianity and Power Politics

What is perhaps most noteworthy in Goodwin's synthetic statement of what he identifies as Christian realism is the audience at whom it is pitched primarily: that is, the churches rather than teachers of international relations or practitioners of foreign policy. But the process of staged retreat from wider domains of academic and public engagement was already under way by the late 1950s, notwithstanding Ernest Lefever's claim in *Survival* that the conversation between those "literate" in the worlds of theology and international politics was on the increase.[39] As observed, theological categories were excluded from the mainstream of academic international relations as it had congealed in the U.S., and certainly were muted in Britain (not least in Wight's own writing). Beyond the academy, the postwar religious revival which enabled Niebuhr and Butterfield to speak powerfully from Augustinian themes was waning; and both of them, having done much to sustain that revival and give it intellectual respectability, were beyond their most creative and energetic publishing years. Thus by the mid-1960s, Niebuhr would admit to the "unpardonable pedagogical error" of opposing "modern optimism with the theological doctrine [of sin] which was anathema to modern culture." [40] Butterfield would advise Christians to disguise as common sense whatever wisdom their religion had to contribute to contemporary politics, for reasons that included the justifiable suspicion of a secular society over ecclesiastical accommodation with power.

The conversation to which Lefever referred nonetheless did exist for a time, especially in the pages of *Worldview*. Lefever himself was an important participant in it, following the 1957 publication of his *Ethics and United States Foreign Policy*. The book took international politics to be "an intense, unending and universal struggle of power and purpose among nations," rooted in human sinfulness, and sided with Morgenthau's pursuit of the national interest as the appropriate moral course for foreign affairs. Lefever, who lectured at the American University's School of International Service and elsewhere in the 1950s, had been brought up in the pacifist Church of the Brethren only to embrace "realism" along Niebuhrian lines during the war. His book's argument proceeded from a distinction between "realist" and "idealist" assumptions about human nature–the latter leading to infatuation with the United Nations, the former to the State Department, to pragmatic policies and limited objectives, and, in immediate policy terms, the necessity of "regional defense alliances in the face of the Soviet threat and military and economic aid to our allies of the non-Soviet world."[41]

Lefever helped set the prevailing tone for *Worldview* when, in a review of Niebuhr's collection of short essays, *Love and Justice*, he both hailed the author as a true prophet and assured readers that if he had "clung emotionally to the shreds of Marxist dogma" for too long, he was now no softer on communism than was Winston Churchill.[42] In echo of Niebuhr, his subsequent articles presented the moral question within the recognition "that for finite and sinful man there will always be an unbridgeable gulf between his highest aspirations and their temporal fulfilment"; the requisite "art" was to relate "ethics to political necessity without slipping into moral pretension on the one side or cynicism on the other." In the "tragic realm of world politics," Judeo-Christian wisdom gave statesmen the "courage" to act. The reader may be excused, however, for detecting in Lefever's argument an unsubtle slide from Niebuhr to something reflective of a simple reading of Max Weber's account of the political vocation. Lefever did, in fact, call his position an ethic of responsibility, with the proviso that God be added to the list of those to whom it was owed.[43] The love that stands beyond all temporal social achievements as a measure of criticism, even as the "impossible possibility," is scarcely to be found. In a later article critical of Kennan's Princeton speech for its moralistic judgement on nuclear defenses, he argued that *calculation* was "the heart of ethics." And, whereas he recognized the limits of calculation in response to the trenchant criticisms that ensued, he affirmed his essential position in dispatching the just-war doctrine as morally irrelevant to the nuclear (or any other) age: "If the statesman has moral reservations about the justice of his cause or serious inhibitions about the use of coercion, his acknowledged or unacknowledged feelings of guilt may restrict the effective use of force and thus invite failure...If the cause is just ...it has a moral right to succeed."[44]

Lefever's uncomplicated conflation of justice and necessity in the name of calculation appears to contain the seeds of the crusading spirit that he and many others eschewed. As counsel to Americans in a global competition with Soviet communism, experiencing the first pangs of mutual assured destruction, it evinces no anguish, no criticism of U.S. policy from a more transcendent vantage point, unless admonitions against squeamishness and in favour of tough-mindedness can be counted as such. There is no hint of Augustine's equation of empires with great robberies–

whatever good may come of them–or of the Augustinian notion that political power is the source of human suffering as well as order. Likewise, Niebuhr's tension of love, justice and order is collapsed so as to strip it of much of its critical potential.

Lefever's appropriation of the Augustinian tradition of or Niebuhr specifically may well have been one-sided–Niebuhr did endorse his book nonetheless–but others revealed similar tendencies in *Worldview* and in monographs written at the time. In two earlier essays for the *Review of Politics* Thompson had associated himself with the "moral dignity of the national interest" as the political wisdom that lay between moralism and cynicism, and argued that even Niebuhr confused abstract principles with what was possible in a given political context; principles, as for Morgenthau in *Politics Among Nations*, had to be "filtered through circumstances of time and place."[45] In a later two-part series in *Worldview* on "moral choice" in foreign affairs, Thompson asserted that, since "nations in the present anarchic world society tend to be repositories of their own morality," and even "create their own morality," the concern for rational calculation of means in relation to ends had prevailed as an answer to the "dilemma." Rather than leave the relativist implications of this argument unqualified, Thompson appealed to the judgement of "elementary ethical standards," although the sources of these standards and their relation to "morality" was not made clear. His sympathy, in any case, lay in the "lonely path of the responsible official" who "must place first the safety of his nation–its defense against destruction and attack." In other words, "political morality" in 1958 demanded the "courage and wisdom to pursue an intelligent, accelerated arms program," to rally U.S. military strength, alongside the search for limited diplomatic solutions in Central Europe.[46]

Thompson's argument, again, is not framed in Augustinian language. He came the closest in his *Christian Ethics and the Dilemmas of Foreign Policy* (1959), the product of lectures given at Duke and published in a series under the auspices of an endowment for research in "Christianity and Politics" directed by Hallowell. The book appealed to a tradition of Christian realism from Augustine to Niebuhr that was "richer, more authentic and...free of all the illusions and confusions of the presently fashionable revivalist trend," and that grappled "patiently with the perplexities and limitations of the day." This tradition, he argued, was directly relevant to the search for "applicable norms" in the Cold War. It resisted the inherent Christian temptation to shrink from "Caesar's world"; it rooted the human predicament in a view of man "at war with himself" that had suffered "blatant attacks" from Nazi and Communist doctrines but was also anathema to American optimism; and, it appreciated the difficulties of "relating Christian standards for human conduct"–above all, the renunciation of force–"to the ambiguous associations of states." As a result, "most Christian experts" in international relation, from theologian Niebuhr to layman Kennan, gave only a "very modest role" to religion in the conduct of foreign policy. If anything, they saw the danger of justifying interests in Christian terms and thereby raising the stakes in conflict.[47] Thompson suggested that this preferred interpretation of Christianity could contribute to "the world of *realpolitik*" by pointing to the marks of a common humanity, inculcating public patience vis-a-vis foreign policy, humanizing U.S. aid to new nations, refusing to sanctify American life and institutions, and supplanting self-righteousness with the sense of "cosmic humility" under divine judgement. Still, the Christian ethicist throughout history had lived in tension with the surrounding society:

> [S]tandards of love, justice, and forgiveness place him forever at odds with cruelty, injustice, and a politics of revenge. Yet he has never been completely free to practice the law of love or the doctrine of reverence of life. These pure truths must pass through the filter of circumstances which he can work to improve but can never perfect.[48]

There is a time-bound quality to the peculiar genre of writing of which Thompson's book is a leading example. Its survey of a melange of recent thinkers from Niebuhr and Butterfield to Churchill and Acheson–Christian or otherwise–is apparently meant not to introduce "Christian principles" to policy-makers, so much as to introduce the realities and dilemmas of international politics to a certain stratum of the American public. The book identified its target as the deeply-entrenched "spirit of utopianism," moral superiority, and abstract legalism that left the U.S. unable to come to terms with the "facts of power, armaments, and force," as they impinged on the dilemmas posed by atomic defenses and anti-colonialist agitation.[49]

A striking feature of Thompson's book and others of the genre is a relatively limited engagement with concrete contemporary policy issues. A beginning point in Christian realism evidently could yield an elastic range of political judgements: one man's calculated interest was another's legalistic hypocrisy. Thompson's main objective was to articulate something of the proper disposition for international relations, through which policy problems appear less amenable to permanent solutions, more as enduring "dilemmas" of statecraft to which public expectations, or intrusions, must conform. His *Political Realism and the Crisis of World*

Politics (1960), which again originated with an invitation to give lectures on foreign affairs at New York's prestigious Riverside Church, made much the same point against American naivete and "lack of realism" by reference to a slightly different cast of thinkers and practitioners. The book appealed less to theological themes. Its criticisms of the "American mind" were explicated more in terms of a *political* realism indebted to Morgenthau, Niebuhr, and Kennan, but also to Carr and Nicholas Spykman, among others. It was this wider tradition that remained unpopular and that required careful presentation in light of the problems of American foreign policy. It was "a framework and not a doctrine"–one which did not assume the inevitability of war, which looked to the "ancient tradition" of diplomatic accommodation for the "instrument by which mutual annihilation must be forestalled."[50]

Thompson's *Political Realism* brought a stinging review by William Fox that was reprinted in *Worldview* after first appearing in the *Union Seminary Quarterly Review*–one of several signs by the early 1960s that the tide was turning in theological circles. Fox asked, first, how one could know a realist on seeing one (why did Carr count and not Neville Chamberlain?); and, second, to what extent did the "strictures against salvationary utopianism develop criteria by which we can judge a pragmatic meliorism" or clarify the "perplexing choices" of statesmen: "How, paraphrasing Reinhold Niebuhr, can we as realists save ourselves from cynicism?"[51]

By then, *Worldview* had also published the Jesuit John C. Murray's castigation of those he called the moral "ambiguists," who followed Niebuhr along the path of irony, predicaments and dilemmas, and who pushed pragmatism to the point of relativism. The ambiguists' dilemmas, he suggested, existed not in fact, but in the eye of the beholder; they represented a construction of situations in terms of an antecedent moral theory, laden with Protestant moral anxieties over power and self-interest. The ambiguist position, moreover, while it usefully criticized utopianism, was hard-pressed to specify those ends to which policy should be directed: "It can throw rocks after the event, but it can lay no cornerstones. It points out all the moral hazards and takes none."[52]

Even among self-described Christian realists, however, differences of political judgement had become more pronounced. Kennan's position on nuclear weapons articulated at Princeton Theological Seminary in 1959– and essentially seconded by Butterfield–was perhaps a lightning rod in this respect. It earned an editorial denunciation in *Worldview* in the condescending, if coolly respectful, tone otherwise saved for Barth's "theologically unassailable" by politically naive neutralism.[53] Lefever's own criticisms followed. In between, one correspondent reproached *Worldview* for its fondness for the word ambiguity, "which seems to afford for you a moral blank check as an alternative to the too rigorous absolutes of the Christian Gospel."[54] The argument over ethical approach and political judgement extended for several months in articles and letters.

The text of Kennan's Princeton speech was excerpted not only in the *Atlantic* monthly, but also *Survival* and various other places. Its wide reverberations attest to the anxieties of a time extending roughly from 1957 to the early 1960s, encompassing the Soviet demonstration of ballistic missile technology, NATO's introduction of tactical nuclear weapons into Europe amid a new strategic interest in limited war, Britain's acquisition of its own hydrogen bombs and the corresponding emergence of the Campaign for Nuclear Disarmament, the Berlin and Cuban crises, even Herman Kahn's admonition to "think the unthinkable." As an editorial in *Survival* put it, questions that historically had troubled the "consciences of Christians"–which presumably meant the lapsed as well as the faithful–had become more urgent. In that same issue, which included the Kennan excerpt, there also appeared part of a recent pamphlet prepared for study under the auspices of the British Council of Churches (BCC), which helps to show how thoroughly Augustinian themes had permeated theological contributions to several sides of the nuclear debate.

The pamphlet, "Christians and Atomic War," gave a reluctant justification for the possession of atomic weapons solely for the purpose of deterring the adversary from using them, at the level of sufficiency instead of superiority, until the relationship of mutual terror could be alleviated, even overcome. The supporting argumentation has a familiar ring. Christian hope was precisely not the expectation of an earthly millennium: "there is no final solution in history," which was not a closed system and which would find its fulfilment and judgement outside of time. The principal controversy was between all humanity and God, a stance that challenged self-righteous claims surrounding the East-West conflict. Communism did "attempt to imprison the free spirit of man," but Christians must look beyond the conflict to reconciliation, love enemy and neighbour alike, and promote policies of restraint. Peace was "not simply the absence of armed conflict, but the state of human affairs in which men are enabled to be true men in their relationship with one another." Although the Church could not defend itself by the sword, its members as citizens were responsible for justice and order–the task of governments–for which the proportionate use of force was justifiable. Still, because nuclear weapons could, if used, cause devastation out of proportion to any gain, they had called into doubt the role of force in international politics. The pamphlet at minimum proposed a transition to conventional defenses, implied that Britain did not need an independent arsenal, and called for the cessation of atmospheric nuclear tests.[55]

The BCC study's rather cautious conclusions reflected something of Niebuhr's own uneasy middle position and cited his authority at places. Some, however, were more comfortable in their discomfort than others. While Kennan and Butterfield inclined towards nuclear renunciation, a view which was echoed from another theological-ethical perspective by the mainly Catholic contributors to a British volume, *Nuclear Weapons and Christian Conscience* (1961), Thompson and Lefever were more sympathetic to limited-war strategies and civil defense planning. In his essay for *Nuclear Weapons and the Conflict of Conscience* (1962), Thompson argued that the Western tradition of "political ethics" repudiated both cynicism and unilateral renunciation. His realism was willing to accept the statement that if 90 million Americans died in a nuclear attack, another 90 million would still survive even in the absence of civil defense measures that could increase that number.[56]

Bennett, for his part, described such thinking emanating from Kahn and the RAND Corporation as "facile" and reflective of a "basic lack of wisdom," despite "all the show of technical knowledge of weaponry and strategy."[57] Bennett agreed, in any case, that the U.S. could not then take the risk of nuclear renunciation for fear of inviting aggression; Americans had to face the "responsibility that goes with power" and thus were not as predisposed to nuclear pacifism as the British, Germans, or Japanese. But Bennett also confessed to having lived with the nuclear dilemma for a decade, without "too great inner disturbance," assured that communism was the only threat to peace. He urged readers to confront the ultimate moral issue involved in any proposed use of nuclear weapons, not least the "monstrous guilt"–Niebuhr's phrase–and the "moral destruction of a civilization" that would be incurred.[58] In the foreword to the book, Bennett echoed the suspicion about instrumental rationality associated with Niebuhr and Butterfield:

> The confidence that a war in which tactical nuclear weapons are used can be kept limited seems to be waning. In much of this discussion of strategy the most hard-boiled 'realists' have often assumed an optimism about human rationality under stress that is not much more credible than the optimism about human morality among the 'idealists.'[59]

Any lingering optimism, he suggested, would disappear as the arms race accelerated and new nuclear weapons induced greater degrees of fear.

This revulsion against tactical nuclear weapons and the preference for a declared no-first-use policy that Niebuhr and Bennett shared had already been denounced in a 1961 symposium in *Christianity and Crisis*. Thompson insisted that if nuclear weapons were held only in reserve as the "ultimate defense, we have assisted the Soviet Union in plotting a campaign of expansion and imperialism." It was at this point in the debate that Carl Mayer, a sociologist with the New School for Social Research, proclaimed the end of "what came to be known as Christian realism"– partly at Niebuhr's own hand.[60]

The Niebuhr/Bennett position, however, received a powerful backing from Alan Booth's *Christianity and Power Politics* (1961). Booth, staff secretary of the WCC's Commission of the Churches on International Affairs, built his argument on the familiar foundations. The basic solidarity of humanity was "solidarity in sin"; but this understanding was a means of mitigating the self-righteousness that exacerbated international conflict. The social order created by men was "never final, never unconditionally just, always tending to favour the strong over the defenseless." If government was necessary to give coherence to the "multitude of conflicting wills," it also acted on its own behalf. The great powers, in particular, were driven by both pride and fear to the pretension that each represented the welfare of all humanity. But, in the last analysis, every political system is "provisional and imperfect and cannot demand the final loyalty of a human being." From this point of view–significantly, perhaps, from Britain rather than the U.S.–the Christian voice "could not be heard too loudly" in its proclamation that "defense is made for man, not man for defense."[61] Booth suggested that the Christian could not be content with a policy that involved threats of massive retaliation, but accepted possession of nuclear weapons for the sole purpose of deterrence, combined with a public declaration of no-first-use and greater resort to conventional forces. If that meant a risk of defeat, he added, then it must be said that "victory can be bought at too high a price."[62]

Perhaps the other important branch of argument explicitly rooted in Augustinian themes, if not strictly Christian realism, and engaged in the nuclear polemics of monographs and *Worldview* articles was that of Paul Ramsey. A Protestant ethicist and theologian who had been the executive-secretary of the *Duodecim* society, devoted to Augustine, in 1945-47, and who had welcomed effusively Butterfield's *Christianity and History* in *The New York Times Book Review*, Ramsey's project was to save something of natural law and the just-war tradition against those who reduced ethics to means-ends calculation. But his appeal to natural law owed more to Augustine than to Aquinas or the early modern jurists. His ethics derived from charity, his just war from the duty to love one's neighbour and protect the innocent, in a world in which the force of sin persisted. As for Niebuhr, charity is approximated in justice, of which "higher" forms are possible in human history, through the transformative role of charity. Ramsey's stress on *jus in bello* criteria–proportionality and discrimination between combatants and non-combatants–was the source of his criticism of massive-retaliation strategies and his openness to tactical, counter-force nuclear weapons first exposed in *War and the Christian Conscience* (1961).[63] Ramsey's overall concern was to articulate moral limits to the use of force, but equally to rebut the pacifist idea that politics could be conducted and the highest values preserved without force or the threat of force. Love did not rule out absolutely all possible forms of nuclear deterrence or of counter-insurgency warfare.

By the mid-1960s, it was U.S. military involvement in Vietnam more than nuclear deterrence that preoccupied, and accentuated the divisions among, those who could be identified with the labels of Christian realist or Augustinian. Again, the eschewal of readily applicable principles could yield a range of political judgements. The major impulse, however, was one of opposition to American policy beginning as early as the 1965 escalation under the Johnson Administration. It would not be an exaggeration to accord *Christianity and Crisis* a primary role in articulating mainline Protestant dissent over the war. Its editorial board– with Thompson's conspicuous abstention–signed a joint statement in June 1965, questioning the Munich analogy that was said to underlie American intervention, opposing the bombing of North Vietnamese cities, arguing that U.S. policy was counter-productive of stated aims and hurt chances of reconciliation with China, and urging direct negotiations.[64]

The board took a stronger collective position in March 1966, with Thompson's signature again absent. The circumstances were propitious: a dinner to celebrate *Christianity and Crisis*' twenty-fifth anniversary, at which the guest speaker was to be Vice-President Hubert Humphrey, a long-time associate of Niebuhr in liberal anti-communist groups such as Americans for Democratic Action. Humphrey was preceded to the platform by Morgenthau, who praised Niebuhr and criticized Administration policy in Southeast Asia; and by Bennett, who recounted the positions the journal had taken over the years and ended by reading parts of the just drafted editorial, "We Protest the National Policy in Vietnam." It began with a passage from Butterfield's *Christianity and History*:

The hardest strokes of heaven fall in history upon those who imagine that they can control things in a sovereign manner, as though they were kings of the earth, playing Providence not only for themselves but for the far future–reaching out into the future with the wrong kind of farsightedness, and gambling on a lot of risky calculations in which there must never be a single mistake.[65]

The editorial then proposed that U.S. involvement in Southeast Asia had become a case study in that thesis. The war, it argued, was destructive of the people "we claim to be defending"– the burning of villages, the bombing of populated areas, and the use of napalm were all mentioned–as well as harmful to global peace and American interests alike. Those members of the board who signed the editorial were not necessarily of a single mind on the question. Some apparently accepted that the U.S. had some responsibility to assist the South Vietnamese in the fight against communism, but that its tactics were self-defeating. (Niebuhr, too, had tended to this view as late as 1965.)[66] But there was sufficient consensus in opposition at this relatively early stage of the war, such that the editorial board could broach the subject of "neo-colonialism."

Humphrey, in turn, found little support for his attempt to justify U.S. involvement on Niebuhrian grounds. The deeper irony nonetheless in the pervasiveness of themes traced to Niebuhr in the 1940s and 1950s is that his success may have helped till the ground for the sort of toughminded foreign policy that he and his colleagues came to oppose when it was practiced in Vietnam. Richard Barnet has argued in *Roots of War* that many of the "national security managers" of the Kennedy-Johnson era were profoundly influenced by the dichotomy derived from *Moral Man and Immoral Society*. Individuals could be altruistic, states could not:

Thus, men who were on the whole scrupulous in their private lives came to believe that when they stepped into their public role, everything was permitted. Impressed by the philosophical tension between moralism and pragmatism in public policy, they confused the two in the making of it. What was expedient also became right.[67]

Schlesinger was not alone among White House advisers in attesting to Niebuhr's guidance. McGeorge Bundy, for example, at that time called the theologian "probably the most influential single mind in the development of American attitudes which combine moral purpose with a sense of political reality."[68]

This appropriation of Niebuhr and Christian realism was an embarrassment or perhaps a disappointment to those who opposed the war from within the same general framework. Richard Neuhaus, then involved with the Committee of Clergy and Laymen Concerned about Vietnam (CCLAV), felt compelled to tell *Worldview* readers that Bennett and his associates were "saddened to see their position of ethical realism exploited in support of ethical cynicism and enlisted in the service of what seems politically expedient to the present Administration." This experience, he added, showed "how readily susceptible to distortion" this position, with all its ambiguity, could be. Neuhaus, however, also made it clear that the CCLAV position had been influenced "enormously" by Niebuhr and Bennett, who at Union had helped shape a new theological generation, and also by Butterfield. That position, as reflected in the book of essays sponsored by CCLAV, *Vietnam: Crisis of Conscience* (1967), emphasized both "realistic" policy and the need for greater humility, for a more modest evaluation of (American) man's ability to reconstruct the world in a preferred image. What explained the U.S. "stumbling into war," unable to "stumble out," was not a failure of nerve, but rather a failure of humility in Washington's "web of arrogance."[69] Butterfield's authority was cited often in this respect. Not since he aroused the ire of Henry Luce in *Life* magazine, indeed, had his words played so central a role in public controversy over U.S. foreign policy.

Niebuhr, who had been appalled that Humphrey had appropriated his "anti-Nazi stance" for the Vietnam War, strengthened over time the vocabulary of his opposition. In the *New Republic* in 1967, he proposed that Americans were the victims of an ideological self-deception which veiled imperial interests behind worthier aims. The U.S. was a "democratic nation whose power"–ironically–"has grown to imperial proportions"; in truth, it had become every bit as imperialistic as its rival, the Soviet Union, the other professedly anti-colonialist great power of the age.[70] His criticism of American policy, and of the willingness of religious figures, like Billy Graham, to bless it as "court prophets" of the White House, intensified after the election of Richard Nixon. The dislike was mutual: Nixon at one point requested an FBI report on the aging theologian.[71]

Niebuhr's opposition to the war did present difficulties for those Niebuhrians or Christian realists who either continued to support it or preferred a less clear-cut position. Thompson, for example, seemed more comfortable with setting out a rather wide swath of moral ambiguity and complexity, between unacceptable extremes, that allowed policy-makers a greater freedom. Thus, in 1967, he called attention in *Christianity and Crisis* to both the "promise" and "peril" of halting the bombing of the North (the issue being not so simple as moralists proposed); and, in 1971, he argued against the alternatives of "simple-minded militarism" and its pacifist inversion. Thompson's essay tended to avoid engagement with the positions that lay between his extremes, particularly the non-pacifist but categorical "no" to the war that prevailed in the pages of *Christianity and Crisis* and that characterized his mentors, Niebuhr and Morgenthau.[72] By comparison, the stark cover of the subsequent issue of *Christianity and Crisis* spoke without ambiguity: "STOP THE KILLINGS."

While Thompson retreated into an abstract middle ground–doubtless neither idealistic nor cynical–Lefever lashed out in *Worldview* at what he described as the "reckless rhetoric" of opponents of the war. A contributing editor of the magazine, he took particular offence at Martin Luther King's attempt, before his assassination, to conjoin civil rights with peace in Southeast Asia; it had, he claimed, violated the "moral limits of public debate and advocacy."[73] That King, too, had acknowledged his indebtedness to Niebuhr's Christian realism and to the radical analysis of *Moral Man and Immoral Society* again indicates the extent to which those themes permeated American theological and popular argument.[74] Lefever's position evoked strong criticism from *Worldview*'s eclectic array of contributors and at least a partial defense from Ramsey, whose *The Just War* (1968) advanced a moral as well as political justification for military involvement in Vietnam. Ramsey would testify on Lefever's behalf in 1981 before the Senate confirmation hearings that derailed the latter's nomination by President Ronald Reagan as assistant secretary of state for human rights and humanitarian concerns. The hearings reprised in public the old debate among claimants to Niebuhr's legacy for the conduct of foreign policy. Ramsey argued that, while others had left Niebuhrian realism, "by going left," Lefever "stood steadfast . . . on the need for an ordered peace as well as justice, the need to use power responsibly." Ramsey had directed the same frustration at Niebuhr himself during the Vietnam War, identifying Bennett's influence as the key: Niebuhr, he complained, was now signing petitions and editorials as if the earlier Niebuhr had never existed.[75]

"Up to Our Steeples in Realism"

There is a long path, tortuous, overgrown, and difficult to follow in places, but a path nonetheless that unites Augustine's majestic *City of God* to the postwar reclamation of Augustinian themes for international politics–providence, will, sin, charity, order–and then to the Christian realism that divided on U.S. foreign policy questions. Whether Augustine would have recognized his own ideas in what congealed as the latter in the 1950s is both unanswerable and perhaps immaterial. Of those who employed derivatives of those themes, or otherwise claimed the influence of those who did, on behalf of increasingly divergent political causes, it can be assumed that not all had read Augustine himself and that fewer were immersed in the complexity of his theology. Traditions or languages may indeed evolve, lapse, or be revived through countless historical mediations, by the activity of individuals engaged in changing circumstances and concerned to interpret or transform them. The question of why some traditions persist while others retreat to the margins–the focus of this chapter–does not admit a definitive answer, though it is possible to describe how a conceptual space was opened for the Augustinian tradition specifically and what uses were made of it in relation to the issues of the day.

The marginalization of that same tradition, in turn, would seem to have proceeded according to the two stages outlined above. In the first place, the construction of a social-scientific academic specialization of international politics almost unavoidably involved the exclusion of theological categories, even where the motivation was not hostility to an Augustinian perspective so much as the aspiration for an autonomous branch of certifiable expertise. In the second place, the Augustinian tradition became increasingly the preserve of theologians and churchmen, isolated from mainstream academic international politics, though still in conversation with a broader spectrum of political scientists, historians, and ethicists. To imply that Augustinian categories met their demise in this realm mainly because of internal disagreements over nuclear deterrence and Vietnam, however, would be misleading. The cultural opportunity, Auden's "age of anxiety," that had sustained the conversation by granting intellectual standing to theological language and arguments was past. By the mid-1960s, even theologians–or perhaps only theologians–were grappling with the death of God and the virtues of the "secular society." The latest waves of European theology had washed over many of the next generation who took their places on the editorial board of *Christianity and Crisis*: among them Harvey Cox, Tom Driver, the liberationist Richard Shaull. On the rebound from Vietnam, too, it was widely argued, and not without reason, that Christian realism had helped prepare the way for U.S. involvement and needed to be either redirected or replaced as a paradigm for social theology. As one critic lamented in *Worldview*: "We are up to our steeples in . . . Realism."[76]

The surest sign that Christian realism had run its course was the appearance of self-searching autopsies in both *Christianity and Crisis* and *Worldview*. The former published a symposium on the subject in 1968 in which Bennett affirmed the traditional analysis of evil and tragedy but called for Christian realism to come to terms with the threat of nuclear war, diversity in the communist world, the need to encourage revolution in the Third World, and the danger of U.S. foreign policy in its counter-revolutionary orientation. He reminded readers that Christian realism had begun in the 1930s with socialist commitments distorted by the war and Stalinism, and suggested it was time to move back in this direction.[77] In a 1972 reflective essay in *Worldview*, on "Realism and Hope after Niebuhr," he declared his desire to be free of the term Christian realist and the "static stereotype" associated with it–no doubt, in the names of Ramsey and Lefever. He also argued for a reading of Niebuhr's overall outlook as "fluid and dialectical" rather than one of "fatalism or dogmatic pessimism," as open to possibilities in history and as suitably critical of American messianic illusions.[78]

Other critiques ensued in *Worldview*, from theologians and churchmen at least. Christian realism, in one case, was said to have come to grips with the centrality of interest over universal principle–this stripped politics of idolatrous tendencies and left it to its proper secular function–but needed to stand in greater tension with any state or movement that understood its interests without a concern for others. In another case it was proposed that realism as the natural ideology of the powerful had to be integrated, to save itself, with new Third World theologies of liberation. In a third case Christian realism was accused of providing the moral space for a *realpolitik* that knew only power and not ideals; of entering the political debate on the politicians' terms, "with the mystical power of religion as sanction," and choosing "lesser evils" from within that limited perspective for fear of appearing weak, soft or morally ineffectual.[79] What might also have been said was that, at its worst, Christian realism appealed to a generic "religion" as the source of moral ideals for society, in much the same way as nineteenth-century liberal Protestantism. The effect was again to limit "religion" to the role of flatterer–this time to a more disillusioned age. If the complacent expectation of gradual evolution towards those ideals was supplanted by arguments as to why they would remain out of reach in the tragic realm of politics and international relations, the temptation of cultural accommodation and the suspension of critical judgement (except against the faint of heart) was strikingly similar.

As Lefever once argued, the churches were "custodians and interpreters of our basic values," giving statesman the courage to act. Christianity, or Judeo-Christianity, in short, became a political resource in a framework that could not envision a more critical stance with respect of the state and its foreign policy. Words of judgement against the pride and pretension of the powerful were silenced.

It has been suggested that Christian realism developed from the polemical situation of the 1930s and has maintained its creative edge when it functions as a corrective to the specific complacencies of its age, instead of solidifying into a doctrinaire position. In this spirit, the pages of *Christianity and Crisis* were awash in the early 1970s with the problem of whether Christian realism could be radicalized and redirected to the political left, and whether it was compatible with liberation theology.[80] This theological debate nonetheless occurred at a greater distance from the centre of American public life. Christian realism did resurface in the presidency of Jimmy Carter, who in the 1976 campaign routinely spoke of Niebuhr's influence–perhaps to allay fears of an unsophisticated fundamentalist piety–and recited Niebuhr's words almost as a personal credo: "The sad duty of politics is to establish justice in a sinful world."[81] Whether he manifested in practice the Christian realism with which he associated himself is a matter for its contending branches to decide. Carter, in any case, was defeated in 1980 by a candidate who showed himself less inclined to see ambiguity in politics, more inclined to identify good and evil as contending forces in a renewed Cold War. In the bellicose atmosphere that surrounded the early years of the Reagan presidency, the Niebuhrian legacy was again contested in public, to some extent, by neo-conservatives like Michael Novak, "centrists" like Bennett, and theological left-liberals like Robert McAfee Brown, in relation to the issues of nuclear deterrence and U.S. policy in Central America.[82] If nothing else, the contest showed that Niebuhrian remnants continued to exist on the periphery of American political debate.

Notes

[1] This essay is excerpted from a chapter in "Power politics and the *civitas terrena*: The Augustinian sources of Anglo-American thought in international relations," PhD dissertation, Queen's University, 1990. Some of these ideas have been developed, for example, in *The 'Augustinian Moment' in International Politics: Niebuhr, Butterfield, Wight, and the Reclaiming of a Tradition*, International Politics Research Paper, No. 10. (Aberystwyth, UK: University of Wales, Department of International Politics, 1991); and, "Martin Wight: International Relations as Realm of Persuasion," in Francis Beer and Robert Hariman, eds., *Post-Realism: The Rhetorical Turn in International Relations* (East Lansing: Michigan State University Press, 1996).

[2] Neither Niebuhr nor Butterfield, it might be recalled, actually taught international relations; and Wight, who did, was sceptical of the claim that it constituted a distinct academic specialization.

[3] Epp, *The 'Augustinian Moment' in International Politics*.

⁴ Arthur Schlesinger, Jr., "Niebuhr's Vision of Our Time," review of *Discerning the Signs of the Times*, in *New Republic* 162 (22 June 1946): 745. Schlesinger voted for Niebuhr's *The Nature and Destiny of Man* in a generational survey, "Outstanding Books, 1931-1961," *American Scholar* 30 (Autumn 1961): 624. In a recent reflection on this era Carl Schorske recalls typically that in the social science faculty at Wesleyan University several non-religious liberal activists turned to Niebuhr in the late 1940s for political groundings. See "A Life of Learning," in *Recasting America: Culture and Politics in the Age of the Cold War*, ed. Larry May (Chicago: University of Chicago Press, 1989): 101.
⁵ See Russell Jacoby, *The Last Intellectuals: American Culture in the Age of Academe* (New York : Basic Books, 1987).
⁶ David M. Ricci, *The Tragedy of Political Science: Politics, Scholarship, and Democracy* (New Haven: Yale University Press, 1984): 143.
⁷ Carl J. Friedrich, "Instruction and Research: Political Science in the United States in Wartime," *The American Political Science Review*, 41: 5 (October 1947): 983.
⁸ Stanley Hoffman, "An American Social Science: International Relations," *Daedalus* 106 (Summer 1977): 41-60. See also, Steve Smith, "Paradigm Dominance in International Relations: The Development of International Relations as a Social Science," in *The Study of International Relations*, 3-27; and Ekkart Krippendorf, "The Dominance of American Approaches in International Relations," in ibid., 28-39. A more detailed study that pays special attention to the role of private foundations is Robert A. McCaughey, *International Studies and Academic Enterprise: A Chapter in the Enclosure of American Learning* (New York: Columbia University Press, 1984), esp. chs. 5-9.
⁹ Hedley Bull, "The Theory of International Politics, 1919-1969" reprinted in James Der Derian, ed., *International Theory: Critical Investigations* (New York: New York University Press, 1995): 117.
¹⁰ Quincy Wright, "Political Science and World Stabilization," *American Political Science Review* 44 (March 1950): 13.
¹¹ Waldemar Gurian, "On the Study of International Relations," *Review of Politics* 8 (1946): 279, 282. Gurian was among those present – as were Morgenthau and Wright – at Kirk's regional conference in Chicago. Crick's view is from *American Science*, 232-233. The connection between Gurian, the *Review*, and the Committee on Social Thought at the University of Chicago is described by John U. Nef, "The Significance of the *Review*," *Review of Politics* 17 (1955): 24-32.
¹² Frederick S. Dunn, "The Scope of International Relations" *World Politics* 1 (October 1948): 144.
¹³ William T.R. Fox, "Interwar International Relations Research," *World Politics* 5 (October 1949):1-2, 12.
¹⁴ Hans J. Morgenthau, "World Politics in the Mid-Twentieth Century," *Review of Politics* 10 (1948): 154-173; and, "Reflections on the State of Political Science," *Review of Politics* 17 (1955): 431-460.
¹⁵ Reinhold Niebuhr, "A Protest Against a Dilemma's Two Horns," *World Politics*

2 (January 1950): 338-344

[16] Robert W. Tucker, "Faith, Reason, and Power Politics" *World Politics* 5 (April 1953): 392-413.

[17] Kenneth W. Thompson, "Toward a Theory of International Politics," *American Political Science Review* 49 (1955): 733, 746.

[18] Interview with Kenneth Thompson, August 1989.

[19] William T.R. Fox, ed. *Theoretical Aspects of International Relations* (Notre Dame: University of Notre Dame Press, 1959): ix, xi.

[20] Ibid, 49.

[21] William T.R. Fox, foreword to Kenneth Waltz, *Man, the State, and War* (New York: Columbia University Press, 1959).

[22] Waltz, 232.

[23] Ibid, 282.

[24] John Herz, *International Politics in the Atomic* Age (New York: Columbia University Press, 1959): e.g. 18, 188, 234-35. This book was also written with the support of the Rockefeller Foundation in 1954.

[25] See, e.g., Niebuhr's "Ideology and the Scientific Method," in *Christian Realism and Political Problems*, 75-94. Here his argument rests on the status of observers as more than detached minds, and on the contingent elements of history that qualify any supposed cycles, recurrences, and analogies.

[26] On the English school in particular see, e.g., Tim Dunne, *Inventing International Society* (London: Macmillan, 1998); and my own "The English school on the frontiers of international society: a hermeneutic recollection," *Review of International Studies* 24 (1998), special issue. Some of these differences are explored in the essays in Steve Smith, ed., *International Relations: British and American Perspectives* (Oxford: Basil Blackwell, 1986).

[27] Richard B. Finnegan and John J. Giles, "A Citation Analysis of Patterns of Influence in the International Relations Research" *International Studies Notes* 1 (Winter 1975): 11-21. Confirmation of an enormous Anglo-American gap is found in the autobiographies of some 34 scholars, most of whom were educated in the 1950s and early 1960s, in *Journeys Through World Politics*, ed. Joseph Kruzel and James Rosenau (Lexington, Mass.: Lexington Books, 1989). Coral Bell, one of the few non-Americans included, recounts an education under Wight at LSE that bears no relation to that of the others. Her chapter is suitably entitled, "Journey with Alternative Maps," 339-350. Niebuhr, meanwhile, is cited only by Bell and two older scholars: Herz and Fox.

[28] Herbert Butterfield, "Raison d'Etat: The Relations between Morality and Government," The First Martin Wight Memorial Lecture, University of Sussex, 23 April 1975: 5-6.

[29] MacKinnon's BBC Third Programme commentary on *The Church and The Atom*, the Anglican follow-up to British Council report, is found reprinted as "An Approach to the Moral and Spiritual Problems of the Nuclear Age" (1948), in his *Borderlands of Theology and Other Essays* (London: Lutterworth Press, 1968): 175-183. See, in the same volume, a second BBC commentary, "Reflections on

the Hydrogen Bomb" (1954), 184-192. Wight, too, had criticized the Anglican study for its faith in the manufacture of the atomic bomb as a "powerful deterrent, which all history shows to be nonsense," in *International Affairs* 25 (1949): 74. MacKinnon, meanwhile, reviewed Butterfield's *Christianity and History* and Niebuhr's *Faith and History*, along with John Baillie's *The Belief in Progress*, in the *Scottish Journal of Theology* 4 (1951): 415-20.

[30] Butterfield, "Raison d'etat," 6; Hedley Bull, "International Theory: The Case for a Classical Approach," *World Politics* 18 (1966): 361-377.

[31] Butterfield and Wight, eds. preface to *Diplomatic Investigations* (Cambridge: Harvard University Press, 1966): 11-13. As Bull's chapter put it, the book was intended to "warm the coals of an older tradition during the long dark winter of the 'social scientific' ascendancy" ("The Theory of International Politics," 48).

[32] Ibid, 12-13.

[33] This insightful point is registered in Christopher Hill, "The Study of International Relations in the United Kingdom," in *The Study of International Relations: The State of the Art*, 271.

[32] Hans J. Morgenthau, review of *Diplomatic Investigations* in *Political Studies Quarterly* 82 (1967): 462.

[35] Hedley Bull, *The Anarchical Society*. (London: Macmillan, 1977): 115.

[36] Hedley Bull, "Future Conditions of Strategic Deterrence," *Adelphi Papers* no. 160 (London: International Institute of Strategic Studies, 1980): 16.

[37] Michael Howard, "Temperamenta Belli: Can War be Controlled?" in *Restraints on War*, Michael Howard, ed. (Oxford: Oxford University Press, 1979): 14. Howard's inclination towards Wight's theological position is suggested in his turn at the Memorial Lecture, 1977, "Ethics and Power in International Policy," esp. 54-55, 63-64. The annual lecture in Wight's name has been a significant means of keeping alive some of his preoccupations. See, e.g., Elie Kedourie, "Religion and Politics: Arnold Toynbee and Martin Wight," *British Journal of International Studies* 5 (1979), 6-14; and, Donald MacKinnon, "Power Politics and Religious Faith," *British Journal of International Studies* 6 (1980): 1-15.

[38] Geoffrey Goodwin, "Deterrence and Détente: The Political Environment," in *Ethics and Nuclear Deterrence*, Geoffrey Goodwin, ed. (London: Croom Helm, 1982): 36.

[39] Ernest Lefever, review of *Christians and Power Politics* by Alan Booth, *Survival* 3 (September-October 1961): 248-249.

[40] Reinhold Niebuhr, *Man's Nature and his Communities* (New York: Charles Scribner's Sons, 1965): 23.

[41] Ernest Lefever, *Ethics and United States Foreign Policy* (New York: Living Age Books, 1957): 5-6, 14-17, 23-24, passim.

[42] Ernest Lefever, "The Meeting of Religion and Politics," book review in *Worldview* (February 1958): 10-11.

[43] Ernest Lefever, "Patriotism and Religious Value," *Worldview* (May 1958): 3-5.

[44] Ernest Lefever, "The Ethics of Calculation" *Worldview* (October 1959): 6-8; "The Just War Doctrine: Is it Relevant to the Nuclear Age?" *Worldview* (October

1961): 9-10.

[45] Kenneth W. Thompson "The Study of International Politics: A Survey of Trends and Developments," *Review of Politics* 14 (1952): 453-54. See also Thompson's defense of Niebuhr against later so-called revisionist interpreters in "The Ethics of Major American Foreign Policies," *British Journal of International Studies* 6 (1980): 111-24.

[46] Kenneth W. Thompson, "Moral Choices in Foreign Affairs," *Worldview* (September 1958): 4-7; "American Approaches to Moral Choice," *Worldview* (October, 1958): 3-5.

[47] Kenneth W. Thompson, *Christian Ethics and the Dilemmas of Foreign Policy* (Durham, NC: Duke University Press, 1959): 114-125, passim.

[48] Ibid, 144.

[49] Ibid. Ch. 2, esp. 57, 60-61

[50] Kenneth W. Thompson, *Political Realism and the Crisis of World Politics*, especially preface, 104-110, 248-251.

[51] William T.R. Fox, "Queries for Contemporary Political Theorists," *Worldview* (July-August 1962):15-16.

[52] John C. Murray, "Morality and Foreign Policy," *Worldview* (May 1960): 2-9.

[53] "On 'Absolute' Morality," editorial in *Worldview* (June 1959): 1-2.

[54] William Robert Miller, letter to *Worldview* (June 1959): 9.

[55] "Christians and Atomic War," *Survival* (July-August 1959): 75-83; editorial, 74.

[56] Kenneth W. Thompson, "Ethical Aspects of the Nuclear Dilemma," in *Nuclear Weapons and the Conflict of* Conscience, John C. Bennett, ed. (New York: Charles Scribner's Sons, 1962): 67-89. Lefever wrote earlier in *Worldview* that, "according to the calculations of those in the best position to know," even the worst nuclear war possible would still leave 80 percent of the earth's population alive and healthy ("The Ethics of Calculation," 8). Cf. Kennan's plea in his *Russia, the Atom, and the West*: "Are we to flee like haunted creatures from one defensive device to another each more costly and humiliating that the one before, cowering underground one day, breaking up our cities the next, attempting to surround ourselves with elaborate shields on the third, concerned only to prolong the length of our lives while sacrificing all the values for which it might be worth while to live at all?" (54).

[57] John C. Bennett, "Moral Urgencies in the Nuclear Context," in *Nuclear Weapons and the Conflict of* Conscience: 99, 105. Against Kahn, he cited the "mature realism" of Morgenthau's *Commentary* essay, "Death in the Nuclear Age."

[58] Ibid, 95-96, 106.

[59] Bennett, foreword to *Nuclear Weapons and the Conflict of Conscience*, 9-10.

[60] "The Nuclear Dilemma—A Discussion," *Christianity and Crisis* 21 (13 November 1961): 200-204; Carl Mayer, "Moral Issues in the Nuclear Dilemma," *Christianity and Crisis* 22 (19 March 1962): 38.

[61] Alan Booth, *Christians and Power Politics* (London: SCM Press, 1961): 29-31, 35, 45-46, 51-52, 69, 73-74, *passim*.

⁶² Ibid, 75-76. Of interest too is his *Not Only Peace: Christian Realism and the Conflicts of the Twentieth Century* (London: SCM Press, 1967). The later book makes an extended case for history as a drama or process moving toward a fulfilment still to be disclosed, and for the provisional character of social structures. It displays a considerable openness to Marxist insight (e.g. 93, 132-135) and accepts the need to abandon "theological shorthand" when much of mankind–even in the West–could not find meaning in it (8).

⁶³ Paul Ramsey, *War and the Christian Conscience* (Durham, NC: Duke University Press, 1961): esp. ch. 2 and 3 for the Augustinian foundation of his position. See also Ramsey's contribution to *Nuclear Weapons and the Conflict of Conscience*, and his leaning towards Kennan in response to Lefever, "Right and Wrong Calculation," *Worldview* (December 1959): 6-9. His review of Butterfield, meanwhile, is found in the *New York Times Book Review* (30 April 1950): 58-60.

⁶⁴ "U.S. Policy in Vietnam: A Statement", *Christianity and Crisis* (14 June 1965): 125-26. Thompson was one of three members–of 19 in total–who did not sign; the other two had just been selected and both signed the later document cited below.

⁶⁵ "We Protest the National Policy in Vietnam," *Christianity and Crisis* 26 (7 March 1966): 33-34. The quotation is taken from Butterfield, *Christianity and History*, 104. An excerpt of Humphrey's speech is reprinted as "A Tribute to Reinhold Niebuhr," *Christianity and Crisis* 26 (30 May 1966): 120-23.

⁶⁶ See, e.g., Reinhold Niebuhr, "The Problem of South Vietnam," *Christianity and Crisis* 23 (5 August 1963): 143. A more enthusiastic statement of American responsibility to check communism in Asia was his "American Hegemony and the Prospects for Peace," *Annals of the American Academy of Political and Social Science* 342 (July 1962): 154-60.

⁶⁷ Richard Barnet, *Roots of War: The Men and Institutions Behind U.S. Foreign Policy* (Harmondsworth: Penguin, 1972): 64-65.

⁶⁸ McGeorge Bundy, "Foreign Policy: From Innocence to Engagement," in *Paths of American Thought*, Arthur Schlesinger, Jr. and Morton White, eds. (Boston: Houghton Mifflin, 1963): 306.

⁶⁹ Richard John Neuhaus, "American Religion and the War," *Worldview* (October 1967): 10.

⁷⁰ Reinhold Niebuhr, "Vietnam: Study in Ironies," *New Republic* 156 (24 June 1967): 11-12.

⁷¹ Reinhold Niebuhr, "The King's Chapel and the King's Court," *Christianity and Crisis* 29 (4 April 1969): 211-212. See the valuable description of Niebuhr in relation to the public controversies over Vietnam in Fox, *Reinhold Niebuhr*, ch. 12.

⁷² Kenneth W. Thompson, "Stopping the Bombing: Promise and Peril," *Christianity and Crisis* 27 (27 November 1967): 269; and, "Tides and Traumas," *Christianity and Crisis* 31 (5 April 1971): 62-63. Thompson contributed an essay to the magazine's twenty-fifth anniversary issue on the subject of "Christian Realism and Foreign Policy" (21 February 1966) which studiously skirted

Vietnam.

[73] Ernest Lefever, "Reckless Rhetoric and Foreign Policy," *Worldview* (November 1970): 9-12.

[74] See Stephen B. Oates, *Let the Trumpet Sound* (New York: 1982), 34-35, 40. Niebuhr wrote the foreword to one edition of King's 1967 speech at New York's Riverside Church to which Lefever referred.

[75] Paul Ramsey, "The Betrayal of Language," *Worldview* (May 1972): 7-10; and *The Just War: Force and Political Responsibility* (New York: Charles Scribner's Sons, 1968), esp. ch. 20. Ramsey's testimony on Lefever's behalf is in U.S. Congress, Senate, Foreign Relations Committee, *Nomination of Ernest Lefever*, 18-19 May, 4-5 June 1981.

[76] Charles McCullough, "Up to Our Steeples in Realism: Ethics After Vietnam," *Worldview* (June 1973): 24.

[77] John C. Bennett and others, "Christian Realism: A Symposium," *Christianity and Crisis* 28 (5 August 1968): 175-76, 182.

[78] John C. Bennett, "Realism and Hope After Niebuhr," *Worldview* (May 1972): 8-11.

[79] Charles C. West, "A Theology of National Security," *Worldview* (April 1972): 44. Ronald Stone, "The Realists and their Critics," *Worldview* (June 1973). McCullough, "Up to Our Steeples in Realism," 24-27.

[80] See, e.g., Dale Patrick, "Opening Niebuhrian Thought to the Left: Radicalizing Christian Realism," *Christianity and Crisis* 30 (19 October 1970): 212-15; Thomas Sanders, "The Theology of Liberation: Christian Utopianism," and Rubem Alves, "Christian Realism: Ideology of the Establishment," *Christianity and Crisis* 33 (17 September 1973): 167-73, 173-76; John C. Bennett and others, "Liberation Theology and Christian Realism," *Christianity and Crisis* 33 (15 October 1973): 196-206.

[81] Jimmy Carter, *Why Not the Best?* (New York: Bantam, 1976).

[82] See, e.g., Michael Novak, "Not Yet: Biblical Realism and Power Politics," *Catholicism in Crisis* (July 1984): 22-29; *The Spirit of Democratic Capitalism* (New York: Simon & Schuster, 1982): 316-32. John C. Bennett, "Niebuhr's Ethic: The Later Years," *Christianity and Crisis* 42 (12 April 1982): 91-95. Robert McAfee Brown, "Reinhold Niebuhr: His Theology in the 1980s," *Christian Century* 103 (22 January 1986): 66-68. See also Ronald Preston's effective refutation of the neo-conservative claim in "Reinhold Niebuhr and the New Right," in *Reinhold Niebuhr and the Issues of Our Time*, ed. Richard Harries (Oxford: A. W. Mowbray, 1986): 88-104.

Select Bibliography

Bennett, John C. *Christian Ethics and Social Policy* (New York: Charles Scribner's Sons, 1946).
Bennett, John C. *Christian Realism* (New York: Charles Scribner's Sons, 1952).
Bennett, John C. *Christians and the State* (New York: Charles Scribner's Sons, 1958).
Bennett, John C. *Social Salvation: A Religious Approach to the Problems of Social Change* (New York: Charles Scribner's Sons, 1935).
Butterfield, Herbert. *Christianity, Diplomacy, and War* (London: Epworth, 1953).
Butterfield, Herbert. *Christianity and History* (New York: Charles Scribner's Sons, 1950).
Butterfield, Herbert. *Discontinuities Between the Generations of History*. Rede Lecture, 1971 (London: Cambridge University Press, 1972).
Butterfield, Herbert. "God in History," in C. T. McIntyre, ed. *Herbert Butterfield Writings on Christianity and History* (New York: Oxford University Press, 1979).
Butterfield, Herbert. *Human Nature and the Dominion of Fear*, Christian CND pamphlet no. 3 (London: CND, 1962).
Butterfield, Herbert. *International Conflict in the Twentieth Century: A Christian View* (London: Routledge and Kegan Paul, 1960).
Butterfield, Herbert. "Raison d'Etat: The Relations between Morality and Government," The First Martin Wight Memorial Lecture, University of Sussex (23 April 1975).
Carr, E.H. *The Twenty Years Crisis*. (London: Macmillan and Co., 1940).

Coll, Alberto. *The Wisdom of Statecraft: Sir Herbert Butterfield and the Philosophy of International Politics* (Durham: Duke University Press, 1985).

Dunne, Timothy. *Inventing International Society: A History of the English School* (New York: St. Martin's, 1998).

Dulles, John Foster. *War, Peace, and Change* (New York: Harper and Brothers, 1939).

Epp, Roger. "The 'Augustinian Moment' in International Politics: Niebuhr, Butterfield, Wight and the Reclaiming of a Tradition," International Politics Research Papers, no. 10 (Aberystwyth, UK: Department of International Politics, University College of Wales, 1991).

Epp, Roger. "Martin Wight: International Relations as a Realm of Persuasion." In Francis A. Beer and Robert Harriman, eds. *Post-Realism: The Rhetorical Turn in International Relations* (East Lansing, MI: Michigan State University Press, 1996).

Fox, Richard. *Reinhold Niebuhr: A Biography* (New York: Pantheon, 1985).

Fox, Richard. "Reinhold Niebuhr and the Emergence of the Liberal-Realist Faith 1930-1945" in *Review of Politics* 38 (July 1976).

Gilpin, Robert G. "The Richness of the Tradition of Political Realism" in Robert O. Keohane, ed., *Neorealism and its Critics* (New York: Columbia University Press, 1986).

Goodwin, Geoffrey, ed. *Ethics and Nuclear Deterrence* (London: Croom Helm, 1982).

Hooper, Leon, S.J., ed. *Bridging the Sacred and the Secular: Selected Writings of John Courtney Murray* (Washington, DC: Georgetown University Press, 1994).

Hooper, Leon, S.J., ed. *The Ethics of Discourse: The Social Philosophy of John Courtney Murray* (Washington, D.C.: Georgetown University, 1986).

Hooper, Leon, S.J., ed. *Religious Liberty: Catholic Struggles with Pluralism* (Louisville, KY: Westminster/John Knox, 1955).

Jacoby, Russell. *The Last Intellectuals: American Culture in the Age of Academe* (New York : Basic Books, 1987).

Krause, Charles Edward. "Democratic Process in the thought of John Courtney Murray and Reinhold Niebuhr," doctoral dissertation (Boston: Boston University, 1975).

Lefever, Ernest. *Ethics and United States Foreign Policy* (New York: Living Age Books, 1957).

Lefever, Ernest. "The Just War Doctrine: Is it Relevant to the Nuclear Age?" *Worldview* (October 1961).

Long Jr., Edward LeRoy and Robert Handy, eds. *Theology and Church in Times of Change: Essays in Honor of John Coleman Bennett* (Philadelphia: The Westminster Press, 1970).
Lovin, Robin W. *Reinhold Niebuhr and Christian Realism* (Cambridge: Cambridge University, 1995).
Kedourie, Elie. "Religion and Politics: Arnold Toynbee and Martin Wight," *British Journal of International Studies* 5 (1979).
Kegley, Charles & Robert W. Bretall, eds. *Reinhold Niebuhr: His Religious, Social and Political Thought* (New York: Macmillan, 1961).
MacKinnon, Donald. "Power Politics and Religious Faith," *British Journal of International Studies* 6 (1980).
Mulder, John. "The Moral World of John Foster Dulles," *Journal of Presbyterian History* 49 (Summer 1971).
Murray, John Courtney, S.J. *Morality and the Modern War* (New York: The Church Peace Union, 1959).
Murray, John Courtney, S.J. *The Problem of God, Yesterday and Today* (New Haven: Yale University Press, 1964).
Murray, John Courtney. *We Hold These Truths: Catholic Reflections on the American Proposition* (New York: Sheed & Ward, 1960).
Niebuhr, Reinhold. *The Children of Light and the Children of Darkness* (New York: Charles Scribner's Sons, 1972).
Niebuhr, Reinhold. *Christianity and Power Politics* (New York: Charles Scribner's Sons, 1953).
Niebuhr, Reinhold. *Christian Realism and Political Problems* (New York: Charles Scribner's Sons, 1953).
Niebuhr, Reinhold. *The Irony of American History* (London: Nesbit & Co. Ltd., 1952).
Niebuhr, Reinhold. *Man's Nature and his Communities* (New York: Charles Scribner's Sons, 1965).
Niebuhr, Reinhold. *Moral Man and Immoral Society* (New York: Charles Scribner's Sons, 1932).
Niebuhr, Reinhold. *The Nature and Destiny of Man* (New York: Charles Scribner's Sons, 1964).
Niebuhr, Reinhold. *The Responsible Self* (New York, Harper and Row, 1965).
Pelotte, Donald E. *John Courtney Murray: Theologian in Conflict* (New York: Paulist Press, 1976).
Rasmussen, Larry, ed. *Reinhold Niebuhr: Theologian of Public Life* (London: Collins, 1989).
Rice, Daniel F. *Reinhold Niebuhr and John Dewey: An American Odyssey* (Albany, NY: State University of New York Press, 1993).

Smith, Michael Joseph. *Realist Thought from Weber to Kissinger* (Baton Rouge: Louisiana State University Press, 1986).

Stone, Ronald H. *Reinhold Niebuhr: Prophet to Politicians* (Washington, D.C.: Abingdon Press, 1981).

Thomas, Scott M. "Faith, History, and Martin Wight: The Role of Religion in the Historical Sociology of the English School of International Relations," *International Affairs* 77:4 (October 2001).

Thompson, Kenneth W. *Christian Ethics and the Dilemmas of Foreign Policy* (Durham, NC: Duke University Press, 1959).

Thompson, Kenneth W. *Ethics, Functionalism, and Power in International Politics: The Crisis in Values* (Baton Rouge: Louisiana State University Press, 1979).

Thompson, Kenneth W. *Herbert Butterfield: the Ethics of History and Politics* (Washington, D.C.: University Press of America, 1980).

Thorp, Malcolm R. *Herbert Butterfield and the Reinterpretation of the Christian Historical Perspective*, Studies in Religion and Society, vol. 40 (Lampeter: Edwin Mellon Press, 1997).

Thorp, Malcolm R. "The Inescapable Predicament: Sir Herbert Butterfield's Views on the Human Dilemma," *Fides et Historia*, 16 (Fall, 1983).

Tillich, Paul. *The Protestant Era*, abr. ed. (Chicago: The University of Chicago Press, Phoenix Books, 1957).

Toulouse, Mark. *The Transformation of John Foster Dulles: From Prophet of Realism to Priest of Nationalism* (Macon, GA: Mercer University Press, 1985).

West, Cornel "Christian Realism as Religious Insights and Europeanist Ideology: Niebuhr and the Third World" *Prophetic Fragments* (Grand Rapids, MI: Eerdmans Publishing Co., 1988).

Wight, Martin "Christian Pacifism," *Theology* 33:163 (July 1941).

Wight, Martin. *International Theory: The Three Traditions*, Gabriele Wight and Brian Porter, eds. (New York: Holmes and Meier, 1992).

Wight, Martin. *Power Politics*, Hedley Bull and Carsten Holbraad, eds. (Leicester: Leicester University Press, 1978; reprint, Leicester: Leicester University Press, 1995).

Wight, Martin. "War and the Christian Conscience," *The Haileyburian* (27 July 1940).

Wight, Martin. "Western Values in International Relations" in Herbert Butterfield and Martin Wight, eds., *Diplomatic Investigations: Essays in the Theory of International Politics* (London: George Allen and Unwin, 1966).

Yost, David S. "Political Philosophy and the Theory of International Relations," *International Affairs* 70:2 (April 1994).

About the Contributors

Jean Bethke Elshtain is the Laura Spelman Rockefeller Professor of Social and Political Ethics at the University of Chicago. She is the author or editor of twenty books, most recently *Just War Against Terror: The Burden of American Power in a Violent World*, published by Basic Books.

Roger Epp is associate professor of Political Studies at Augustana University College (Canada). He has published numerous articles in international relations theory with a particular interest in the English school, Martin Wight, philosophical hermeneutics, ethics, and the place of aboriginal diplomatic practices in international society. His publications include article, "The English school on the frontiers of international society," in *Review of International Studies* (1998), "The 'Augustinian Moment' in International Politics," International Politics Research Papers, No. 10 (Aberystwyth: University of Wales, Department of International Politics, 1991); and "Martin Wight: International Relations as Realm of Persuasion," in *Post-Realism: The Rhetorical Turn in International Relations* (1996).

Leon Hooper, S.J. is a fellow at the Woodstock Theological Center, Georgetown University. He has authored *The Ethics of Discourse: The Social Philosophy of John Courtney Murray* (Washington, DC, Georgetown University Press, 1986), followed by two edited collections of primary Murray texts and a co-edited volume of secondary Murray studies, entitled *John Courtney Murray & The Growth of Tradition* (Kansas City: Sheed & Ward, 1996). Hooper is currently completing a book-length comparative study of Murray and

Dorothy Day, the co-founder of the Catholic Worker movement, on the theme of their common Catholic approaches to social goods and evils.

David McCreary grew up in Los Angeles where he attended public schools, college, seminary, and graduate school. He was ordained in the United Methodist Church in 1969 and has served churches in Nebraska, taught religion in college, and currently is the pastor of Chadron United Methodist Church near the Pine Ridge reservation. He is interested in cross-cultural ministries and takes work teams to Mexico annually. He holds a Ph.D. in philosophy of religion and theology, specializing in Methodist studies, and has studied with John B. Cobb, Jr., Wolfhart Pannenberg, and Charles Hartshorne. While studying in Claremont, California, he became personally acquainted with John Bennett.

Eric Patterson is Assistant Professor of Political Science at Vanguard University of Southern California where he teaches courses in American and International Politics. He holds degrees from Evangel University, the University College of Wales at Aberystwyth, and the University of California at Santa Barbara. Patterson is a past Rotary Ambassadorial Scholar and Calihan Religion and Liberty Fellow. He is the author of numerous conference papers, scholarly articles and book chapters on religion and politics in the United States and Latin America.

Roger Lincoln Shinn is Reinhold Niebuhr Professor Emeritus of Social Ethics at Union Theological Seminary in New York. He was an occasional visiting professor at the Jewish Theological Seminary of America and was for twenty-five years adjunct professor of religion and society at Columbia University. He is a former president of the American Theological Society and of the Society of Christian Ethics. He is author or editor of a score of books, including *Wars and Rumors of Wars* and *Forced Options: Social Decisions for the Twenty-First Century.*

Malcolm R. Thorp graduated in British history from the University of Wisconsin, Madison, in 1972. He has taught at Brigham Young University since 1969 and is currently a Professor of History. He has written extensively on British religious topics, and is especially interested in religious dissent in British society. He has co-edited two books and has written over thirty five articles on various topics. His interest in Butterfield led to a monograph, *Herbert Butterfield and the*

Reinterpretation of the Christian Historical Perspective (1998). He is currently engaged in writing a study on religious violence in England from 1810-1850.

Dr. Mark G. Toulouse is Professor of American Religious History at Brite Divinity School, Texas Christian University. He holds a Ph.D. from The University of Chicago and is the author of numerous articles and books, the latter including *The Transformation of John Foster Dulles: From Prophet of Realism to Priest of Nationalism* (1985); *Joined in Discipleship: The Shaping of Contemporary Disciples Identity* (1992 and 1997); *Walter Scott: A Nineteenth-Century Evangelical* (1999); and the co-edited *Makers of Christian Theology in America* (1997) and *Sources of Christian Theology in America* (1999). Dr. Toulouse is currently working on a book tentatively entitled *A Search for Wholeness: Christian Faith and Public Life in America, 1955-1995*.

Daniel Young (Ph.D. candidate, Temple University) is Assistant Professor of Political Science at Northwestern College (Iowa), where he teaches courses in international relations and in political theory. A graduate of Calvin College, he holds a master's degree in public and international affairs from the University of Pittsburgh. He is currently writing his doctoral thesis on Martin Wight, and has presented papers at the Northeastern Political Science Association. In addition, he has been a Civitas Fellow at the American Enterprise Institute. His scholarly interest is in the intersection of political theory and international relations.